Powell's Life & Work of William Pryor Letchw

OP/5.98 **NDJ** (H)

Social Science 103973

Publication No. 182: Patterson Smith Series in
Criminology, Law Enforcement & Social Problems

THE LIFE AND WORK

OF

William Pryor Letchworth

STUDENT AND MINISTER OF
PUBLIC BENEVOLENCE

BY

J. N. LARNED

Illustrated

MONTCLAIR, N.J.
PATTERSON SMITH
1974

First published 1912 by Houghton Mifflin Company
Reprinted 1974 by Patterson Smith Publishing Corporation
Montclair, New Jersey 07042

Library of Congress Cataloging in Publication Data

Larned, Josephus Nelson, 1836–1913.
    The life and work of William Pryor Letchworth, student and minister of public benevolence.

    (Patterson Smith series in criminology, law enforcement & social problems. Publication no. 182)
    Reprint of the 1912 ed.
    "List of writings": p.
    1. Letchworth, William Pryor, 1823–1910. I. Title.
HV28.L43L34   1974   361'.92'4 [B]   71-172592
ISBN 0-87585-182-7

This book is printed on
permanent/durable paper

CONTENTS

I. ANCESTRY. — EARLY YEARS. — BUSINESS LIFE 1

II. GLEN IRIS 42

III. PRESERVING THE MEMORIALS OF GENESEE VALLEY HISTORY 72

IV. CHILD-SAVING WORK: PREVENIENT . . 106

V. STUDIES OF PUBLIC PHILANTHROPY IN EUROPE 164

VI. CHILD-SAVING WORK: REFORMATIVE . 210

VII. WORK FOR THE INSANE 263

VIII. WORK FOR THE EPILEPTIC 327

IX. THE GIFT OF LETCHWORTH PARK TO THE STATE OF NEW YORK 364

X. LETCHWORTH VILLAGE. — LAST YEARS 405

XI. THE MAN 425

APPENDIX: LIST OF WRITINGS . . . 447

INDEX 461

ILLUSTRATIONS

WILLIAM PRYOR LETCHWORTH AT THE AGE OF SEVENTY. . . . . . . *Frontispiece*

JOSIAH LETCHWORTH, SR., FATHER OF WILLIAM PRYOR LETCHWORTH 6

THE PARENTAL HOME AT SHERWOOD, N. Y. . 18

WILLIAM PRYOR LETCHWORTH AS A YOUNG MAN 26

GLEN IRIS: VIEW FROM "INSPIRATION POINT" 42

THE HOME AT GLEN IRIS 58

THE OLD CANEADEA COUNCIL HOUSE . . . 76

STATUE OF MARY JEMISON 98

WILLIAM PRYOR LETCHWORTH WHILE PRESIDENT OF THE NEW YORK STATE BOARD OF CHARITIES 130

THE MIDDLE FALL, GLEN IRIS 164

THE LAWN, GLEN IRIS 210

"ROCK-BOUND BATTLEMENTS" 264

DEH-GA-YA-SAH 328

ILLUSTRATIONS

VIEW FROM PROSPECT FARM, LETCHWORTH PARK 368

MAP OF LETCHWORTH PARK 390

THE LOWER FALL OF THE GENESEE, LETCHWORTH PARK 406

THE LIFE AND WORK OF
William Pryor Letchworth

CHAPTER I

ANCESTRY — EARLY YEARS — BUSINESS LIFE

THE life to be set forth in this book was one of singular beauty in its personal exhibition, of noble motive and purpose in all its activities, of golden success in its whole achievement. It was the life of a man who spent a moderate part of it in pursuits of personal business, until they had given him the freedom and the means for effective service to his fellow men, rendered through a long remainder of laborious years, and who exercised in that service a rare capacity for what may be described as the statesmanship of philanthropy, which labors for the reformation of evil-working conditions in the world. The instructiveness of his labors and the inspiration of his example seem equally to have given an importance to his life which death did not end, and which claims an effort of biography to keep its influence from being lost. If the story is not found to have an interest of no common degree it will be because it is not rightly told.

In devoting the greater part of his mature life to benevolent work (performed as an unpaid official of the State of New York, and wholly at his own cost), Mr. Letchworth was obedient, it is plain, to hereditary promptings, from an ancestry which had been spiritually cultured for two centuries by the humane Christianity of the Society of Friends. The family was of ancient English stock,— so ancient that its origin, if the tracing were possible, would most likely be found in Saxon times. The name, Letchworth, is that of a parish and village in the hundred of Broadwater, county of Hertford, England, two miles from the town of Hitchin and northwestward from London about thirty-three miles. It seems obviously a Saxon name, and whether the parish received it from the family or the family from the parish is an undetermined question which calls for no discussion here.

Our present interest in this genealogy [1] goes

---

[1] A compilation in manuscript of the family history, by Mr. Henry R. Howland, is the main source of the information given here.

back to about the middle of the seventeenth century, soon after George Fox began the preaching in England which inspired the formation of the Society of Friends. At that time one Robert Letchworth, living in the village of Chesterton, near Cambridge, and about twenty-five miles from Letchworth village, is found to have joined the religious followers of George Fox, and to have borne his share of the penalties of imprisonment and fine which the Friends or Quakers of that generation had to suffer, for refusing to pay tithes to the established church, or to attend its services, or to make oath in courts of law. This Robert Letchworth is believed to have been the grandfather of another Robert, born late in the seventeenth century, from whom the descent of all who bear the name in America is authentically traced.

English Quaker ancestry

The last-named Robert Letchworth, a business man of London, served also in the ministry of the Friends for many years, and his third son, Thomas, became a very notable preacher of the sect. "Twelve Discourses," by Thomas Letchworth, "delivered chiefly at the meeting-house of the people called Quakers, in the Park, Southwark," were published in London in 1787, and republished at Salem, New Jersey, in 1794. Evidence that the preacher was a man of fine mind and culture is abundant in these discourses; and the same testimony is borne in an admirably written "Life and Character of Thomas Letchworth," by William Matthews, which was published at Bath and London in 1786. The reputation of Thomas Letchworth in America, as well as in England, was such as to induce Benjamin Franklin to republish, at Philadelphia, a small volume of blank verse from his pen, containing two pieces, entitled, respectively, "A Morning's Meditation, or a Descant on the Times," and "Miscellaneous Reflections, or an Evening's Meditation, addressed to the Youth." From this Thomas Letchworth the families who bear the name in England derive their descent.

On our western continent the family name was planted by John Letchworth, the second son of Robert, who emigrated to America in 1766. Leaving his wife and four children in England, he came alone, to test the conditions of life at Philadelphia before venturing to bring his family thither. In 1768 he had established himself in business as a builder so satisfactorily that wife and children were called to join him in the new home. The

<small>American ancestry</small>

reunion was unhappily brief; for the father, being summoned back to England on some errand of business, in 1772, fell sick while there and died. His widow, thus sorely bereft, remained at Philadelphia and reared her children, two sons and two daughters, under circumstances of much hardship, in the troubled years before and during the Revolutionary War. The elder son, John, grew to be a man of high standing and influence, prominent in all benevolent and religious work, signalized especially in heroic labors at Philadelphia during the awful visitation of yellow fever in 1793, for which, like Stephen Girard, he received a formal testimonial from the Governor of the State. As a preacher, among the Friends, he travelled far westward, into Kentucky and Tennessee, when travel in those regions was full of hardship and peril. Naturally, he was one of the Quakers who organized the first antislavery society in the United States.

The younger son of this transplanted family, William Letchworth, married and spent his life in Philadelphia, rearing a family of eight children, the eldest of whom, named Josiah, born in 1791, became the father of the subject of this biogra-

Josiah Letchworth, Sr.

phy. Josiah Letchworth, married in 1815 to Miss Ann Hance, began his wedded life at Burlington, New Jersey, but removed his young family thence, in 1819, to Brownville, on Black River, near Watertown, in northern New York. A second change of residence took them to Moravia, in Cayuga County, and a third to Sherwood, within thirteen miles of Auburn, where they dwelt most happily for twenty years. Most of the sons and daughters had then been called away from the parental home, and the father and mother were drawn by many attractions to Auburn, in 1852, for the spending of their last years.

The residence of Josiah Letchworth in Auburn was no longer than five years; but it sufficed to make him a citizen of note. He had not come to the city as a stranger, his life at Sherwood having brought him into much intercourse with the city; but nothing in that intercourse could account for the quickness with which he became affectionately known and esteemed by the public at large. He entered actively into social service work, along many lines; interested himself greatly in the schools; spoke much and earnestly for temperance and against slavery, and appears to have caused the fine spirit of benevo-

JOSIAH LETCHWORTH, SR.,
Father of William Pryor Letchworth

lence and justice in true Quakerism to be felt in the city as a potent force. When he died, in the spring of 1857, there was a profound sense of public loss in Auburn, which Senator Seward gave voice to some months later, on returning from Washington to his home. In opening an address to his fellow townsmen he referred to some words of impatience and rebuke that he had used on a former occasion, and said : —

When I descended from the platform a fellow citizen, venerable in years and beloved by us all, gently asked me whether I was not becoming disheartened and despondent. He added that there was no reason for dejection, and what I had seen was but the caprice of the day. "Go on and do your duty, and we, your neighbors, will come around you again right soon and sustain you throughout." Do you ask who it was that administered that just though mild rebuke? Who else could it be but Josiah Letchworth, a man whose patience was equal to his enthusiastic zeal in every good cause, and to his benevolence in every good work? His prediction is fulfilled, and I am here to speak with more boldness and confidence than ever before. But my faithful monitor no longer has a place in our assemblies. Josiah Letchworth, the founder of our charities, the defender of truth and justice, is no more. You deplore his loss as I do; for he was not more my friend than a public

Senator Seward's tribute

benefactor. I do injustice, however, equally to my own faith and to that which was the inspiration of his life, when I say that I miss his benevolent smile and the cordial pressure of his hand to-night. No, — he yet lives, and his shade is not far from us whenever we assemble in places where he was once familiar, to carry on a good work in which he was accustomed to labor.

A more significant tribute to the memory of Josiah Letchworth was paid by children of the schools, who raised a fund with which to procure the engraving of his portrait on steel by Mr. Buttre, a noted artist of the day. Prints from this excellent engraving went into many Auburn homes, and the portrait shown here is from one such print.

It goes without saying that the father who won the hearts of a community was loved and revered in his own household; and this was equally true of the mother, — a strong and admirable character, who ruled her children with a firmness that was ever kind and wise. Between the brothers and sisters, too, the ties of affection were more than common in strength and warmth. From an abundance of family correspondence, confided to the writer of this memoir, he receives no other impression so clear as that of the atmosphere of love, of piety in the large sense, of all simple rightness of feeling, in which the young were reared, and the influence of which they carried with them from the parental home.

Inasmuch as the brothers and sisters of William Pryor Letchworth held close relations to him always and came into his life in many ways, it is needful to introduce them at the beginning. He was one of eight children,—four daughters and four sons. The eldest was a daughter, Mary Ann, who became Mrs. Crozer, and who, when widowed, joined her life with that of her bachelor brother, William, presiding over his household and giving him, by her companionship, some of the happiest of his years. Another daughter, Eliza (Mrs. Hoxie), came second in the family. Then followed three sons, Edward Hance, William Pryor, and George Jediah, in that order of succession; after whom two daughters were born, namely, Hannah, who became the wife of William Howland, and Charlotte, who married Byron C. Smith. The youngest of the family received his father's name, Josiah. *Brothers and sisters*

William, as will be seen, was the fourth child and the second son. He was born on the 26th of May, 1823, while the family was still at Brownville; and probably it *Earliest recollections* was the home in that town which left a curiously fanciful remembrance in his mind, so amusing to him that he gave on one occasion this account of it: "The earliest recollections of my childhood are of a low stone house standing back from the street, with a green lawn in front of it, on which were a few trees with broad-spreading branches. Acros the gable end of the house which stood toward the street was a raised balcony with a balustrade intertwined with rosebushes. From my sleeping-room I could step out on this balcony. I love even now to recall what I saw in those early days, in the sunlit branches of the great trees opposite my window. One morning in particular I beheld an innumerable throng of little fairies, — knights and ladies in flowing scarfs and plumes and gay-colored dresses, — flitting to and fro in the golden beams of the early morning. I presume the picture was reflected on my imagination by stories that had been told me or pictures I had seen of fairy land. At all events, it was an impression as pleasing as it has been lasting."

Other references which he sometimes made, in talk or writing, to his earlier recollections, disclose a similar dreamy working of imagination; and this, no doubt, which created realms of fancy for the child, found its later chosen use in illuminating and warming the sympathies of the mature man, keeping him from the stiffened lines of a selfish life. Along with the dreamy fancifulness of his childish mind there seems to have gone naturally a degree of innocence and simplicity which childhood can rarely keep long enough to remember the loss. The present writer once heard Mr. Letchworth tell of the surprise with which he first learned that there were such things as untruth and deceit. The first conception of them that dawned on him came from the prank of a boy who ran into the yard in which he was playing to tell him that a big black bull was on the other side of the next building and that he had better run to the house. He doubted the ability of the bull to reach him, but did not for a moment suspect that there was no bull; and the discovery of that fact was a cruel revelation to him of the nature and the possibility of a lie. A still more cruel and perplexing revelation to him was made, he said, at about the same period, when a boy who was playing with him became angry and threw at him an open penknife, which struck him just over the eye, coming near to the destruction of his sight. As he remembered the feeling excited in him by this assault, there was no anger in it, but sheer bewilderment and surprise. Why should the boy want to hurt him? He could not in the least understand the motive in such an act. These little incidents are interestingly suggestive of the purity and wholesomeness of the family life in which William Letchworth was reared and of the training he received.

Very little of autobiographical material is to be found in anything left by Mr. Letchworth, **Parental** of letters or other writings. In the **training** bits of reminiscence that he did now and then commit to paper he was always carried back to his childhood. One such tells of a project he formed, apparently in his twelfth or thirteenth year, of running away from home.

By reading the lives of some noted men, and various stories of marvellous adventure [he wrote], I was impressed with the idea that, to be successful and achieve great things, it was necessary that one should run away from home while a boy. This conclusion, and the secret resolution I had formed to act on it, I confided to an employé of my father of whom I was very fond. He basely betrayed me, and my father soon found the opportunity for a private conversation with me. To my dismay, he said: " William, it is understood that thee intends to leave us. I am sorry to learn this, as we all think a great deal of thee. Through thy early childhood and down to the present time thee has been a great care to mother and myself, to say nothing of considerable expense, and we had been looking forward to the time when thee would have the good will and strength to make us some return for what we have tried to do for thee. But, since thee has decided to leave us, we will conform ourselves to thy wishes. In the carrying-out of thy plan there is one thing, however, that troubles me, and that is thy leaving in the night, and without the opportunity of our bidding thee good-bye. Mother has a pair of new stockings she has knit for thee, and thy brothers and sisters would like to make thee some little presents." This brought me to my senses. I felt shame and disgust with myself, and nothing more was said of the running-away plot.

Nothing could be told of the father of William Pryor Letchworth that would illustrate more significantly the wisdom with which the youth of the latter was trained, and the fine inheritance of mind and temper on which it was his good fortune to draw. He himself, in one of his reminiscent notes, has given us just a glimpse of the family government and of the home in which it was exercised.

I imagine [he says] that the ways adopted by my parents for bringing up their children did not differ materially from those of other people; although I believe they had stricter rules regarding their boys running in the street, and were more diligent than most parents in providing means of recreation and useful employment at home. My mother was quite practical in her views, and I am much indebted to the inculcation of her economic principles. She made much of the adage that "procrastination is the thief of time"; to which she would add: "Never put off till tomorrow, William, that which should be done to-day." Time, she said, was the most valuable thing in the world, as nothing could be done without it, and its loss was irreparable.

On winter evenings, during the season in which we attended the public school, we would gather round the large table in the cheerful dining-room, with our books, slates, and writing-lessons, and prepare ourselves for the next day's recitations at school. Spelling was difficult to me, but I was so desirous of perfecting myself in it that, in addition to the evening study, I would have my father call me at four o'clock on winter mornings and then pursue my studies alone. . . . My ambition to perfect myself in spelling was stimulated by the fact that there was a young miss whom I felt determined to excel. In those days we had what were called "spelling-matches," in which the pupils of different country schools came together on a winter evening, under a challenge, to determine which was the best speller by the process of "spelling down."

He proceeds to give an account of a spelling-match which finally was narrowed to a contest between the young miss above referred to and himself. Interest in the struggle had been heightened by people in the audience, who built up a small heap of silver coins on the teacher's desk, which should go as a prize to the winner of the match. William stood his ground till Cobb's spelling-book had been exhausted; but the resort then to Webster's, which he had never studied, accomplished his defeat. He felt chagrined, at first, but was reconciled to his discomfiture by the thought that his opponent would have felt worse if she had lost.

One of the few gleanings of autobiographical material from Mr. Letchworth's papers is a note, as follows, of the circumstances of his going from the family home into the outside world, to begin the career of business which he followed from about his fifteenth to his fiftieth year: — *Leaving home*

Father was doubtless convinced that, with my ambitious views, I would never be content at home, and, not long after the running-away plot had been disclosed, he made application to the head of an importing and manufacturing house [at Auburn] for a place for me. He soon received a reply, asking him to bring me to the city. A conversation followed between the head of the firm and my father, at the close of which my father said: "Well, William" (addressing the merchant by his given name), "I have endeavored thus far to make a man of my son, and will ask thee to finish the task." Before leaving, my father gave me a dollar, with the remark that I might need a little pocket-money. This was all that my father ever gave me, and with this I began life. A few years after I had become of age I was disposed to envy one of my former chums whose father gave him five thousand dollars to start business with; but his experience made me finally thankful that my father never was able to give me anything beyond the one dollar.

My salary with the firm [Hayden & Holmes, manufacturers and dealers in saddlery hardware] which engaged me was fixed at forty dollars a year, and living, and out of this I was to clothe myself and meet all my personal expenses. I set out with the determination that this sum, small as it was, should suffice for all my requirements. The result was that I saved during the year between two and three dollars, and placed the same on interest, with about one hundred dollars that my father had presented to me for accumulation while a boy at home.[1] The realization that I could practice

[1] This may seem contradictory to the statement above, that the dollar which his father gave him when he began work at Auburn was all that he ever received; but evidently his meaning in that statement was, that he had no help in money from the time that his own earnings began.

sufficient self-denial to live within my means gave me greater confidence in myself and strengthened my character. Living within one's means is as necessary to success as it is essential to one's peace of mind and happiness.

In later years Mr. Letchworth had great enjoyment in telling of his first home-going for an over-Sunday visit, after beginning his life at Auburn, and of the disappointing reception he had. Homesickness had made the first week seem almost unendurable, and he had counted surely on being liberated from the end of the week until Monday; but no suggestion to that effect came, and he mustered fortitude to go through seven days more. Saturday came again, with no hint of a thought in the mind of his employer that he could wish to visit his home; and he bore his unhappiness for another week. Then, in desperation, he found courage to ask for the coveted leave, and it was granted with readiness; but a hope which he had fondly cherished, that offers of the use of a horse for the journey to Sherwood would go with the permission, had no realization. There were thirteen miles to be walked, if he would have the joy of a day in the home circle, and he walked them, arriving at some time in the evening, supercharged with his own excitement of delight, and expecting to see an equal excitement when he showed his face. His feeling would have carried him into the beloved house with a rush; but he held himself back and knocked formally, like a neighbor making an evening call. His mother opened the door, recognized him with perfect serenity, and said: "Why, William, what has brought thee home so soon?" It was like a dash of cold water in the face,—the revelation that his family had not been longing as impatiently for him as he for them.

But time wrought a change, as between mother and son, in feeling on the subject of his visits to the parental roof; for we find his father, writing to him in April, 1841, quoting his mother as asking: "Why don't that boy come home?" and then saying: "I answer that, glad as I should be to see thee oftener, thou hast a duty to perform, and the performance of duties frequently requires the sacrifice of personal enjoyment and comfort. I am much more gratified to find thee faithful to thy trust than I should be to find thee more frequently at home, much as such visit would gratify me."

Thus William had his graduation from home and common schools, in or about his fifteenth

THE PARENTAL HOME AT SHERWOOD, N. Y.

year, and was matriculated in the university of practical affairs, to learn the ways of men and be trained for entrance into the activities of the world. Ambition had an early growth in him, as he more than once confessed. Apparently it was an ambition quite undefined in those early years. Nothing indicates that his aspirations were directed toward any particular goal, of political or literary or scientific renown, or of wealth. What he felt as ambition may have been just an upward-impelling eager spirit which would have the same potency in all situations, to make the most of them, get the best out of them, rise to the highest of their offered possibilities. All that is told of his youthful clerkship in the service of Hayden & Holmes goes to show that this spirit was as manifest in it as in the higher, final work of his life. He studied the making, buying, and selling of saddlery hardware as carefully, thoroughly, zealously as, forty years later, he studied the saving of homeless children, the care of epileptics, and the treatment of the insane. As a boy he accepted the assignment to him of a field of work in which his means of living were to be earned, and labored in it without stint; as a man, when his independence had been won, he chose for himself a

Clerkship at Auburn

mission of social service, and gave himself unsparingly to that. The fidelity to his undertaking was in each case the same.

It was in this period that he either formulated or borrowed and adopted the following "rules of conduct," a copy of which, dated 1842, has been preserved:—

Rise at 6 o'clock. Breakfast at 6.30. Dinner or lunch, 12.30. Supper at 6.30. Retire at 9.30. Attend divine service once every Sunday. Tell the truth under all circumstances, when necessary to speak. Never wound the feelings of others if it can be avoided. Strive to be always cheerful. Review the actions of the day every night, and apply to them the test of my conscience. In business affairs keep in mind that "procrastination is the thief of time," and that "time is money." Be temperate in all things. Strive to speak kindly, without giving offence, always with coolness and deliberation, having due regard for the views of others. Aim at a high standard of character. Attempt great things and expect great things. Aim to do all possible good in the world, and so live as to live hereafter and have a name without reproach.

Those who knew Mr. Letchworth in his maturity will believe that it was easy for him to be obedient to these rules, most of which must have found dictates in his nature and needed no judicial mandate of will.

BUSINESS LIFE

In the service of Hayden & Holmes, at their establishment in Auburn, the youth grew to young manhood, remaining six or seven years, living in the family of Mr. Holmes, as a friend, and becoming more and more invaluable to the firm. Their business was an extensive one for that period, employing a large part of the convicts in the prison workshops at Auburn, under contract with the State. Mr. Hayden, the senior partner in the firm, was the head of several other establishments in the same line of business, at different points in the country, including one at New York. That gentleman had kept an eye on young Letchworth, noting his intelligence, his fidelity, the complete understanding he had acquired of every detail of the business, and the good judgment with which his duties were performed, with the result that the Auburn clerk was called to a post of more importance at New York.

This advance to a higher school of business and to the opening of a larger experience of life came to Mr. Letchworth in the sum- *Service in* mer or fall of 1845,—the year after *New York* his crossing the threshold into manhood's estate. Of the three years of his life and work in New York not much can be told. He wrote frequently to his parents and sisters, and his letters were carefully kept, as all similar family records were preserved; but they contain almost nothing that touches the work he was doing or the circumstances of his life outside of his work. One letter which would seem to have been exceptional in this respect, is not found in the mass of correspondence that came into the present writer's hands; but its purport is intimated in his father's reply to it, January 18, 1847, when the latter wrote: "Thy letter, after giving a satisfactory statement of thy affairs, propounds in some measure this query: 'Have I come up to your expectations?' To this I can answer affirmatively, and it affords me heartfelt satisfaction, not only to behold the fruits of those principles and sentiments which it was my desire to cultivate, being assured they were most conducive to happiness, but to find my endeavors so well seconded; to see my children themselves cherishing those principles which, if they do not lead to wealth, secure enjoyment and tranquillity under the various changes of life."

In a letter which he wrote to his younger sisters, in May, 1848, there is a passage which indicates that, in New York as in Auburn, he had immersed himself so entirely in business as to have little time or mind for any other interest in life. "For years," he said, "I have devoted my whole thought, strength and energy to one thing, *business*, and have made myself master of that which I undertook to perform; but this has drawn all my attention from literature, knowledge and art. I hope that ere long it will be otherwise.... I mean now to cultivate most assiduously the social ties which I have neglected so long, fearing they may become so weakened as to have no influence on my soul." His elder sister, Mrs. Crozer, who then lived at Morrisville, Pennsylvania, had been noting with anxiety, for some time past, the intensity of his absorption in business, and had remonstrated with him on the subject, remarking, in a letter of two years earlier writing: "I am afraid thee will get to be an old man before thee has been a young one half long enough."

This good sister, who was his elder by several years, wrote often to him, with warmly affectionate interest in his welfare, giving him counsel that seems to have been always wisely timed and directed, and not over-much. Soon after his going to New York she said to him: "I hope thee will form some agreeable acquaintances; but mind and form the right kind. And do not have too many of them; for too much company is of no advantage to a young man. Thee is placed in a situation where thee will meet with many temptations, and thee cannot be too much on thy guard. Form good resolutions, and then be sure not to break them. Perhaps these few words of advice are unnecessary, but they are from thy loving sister, who feels thy interest as near to her as her own."

In a letter of June 11, 1848, to his sisters in the old home he reported his removal to a boarding-house in Brooklyn, and described an interesting sight which he had witnessed in crossing the river. The incident, which appears almost alone in his letter-writing from New York, has a quite historical interest of its own:

Yesterday [June 10, 1848, he wrote] I saw a beautiful sight,— one which I wish you could have participated in seeing. I got aboard of one of the ferry boats crossing the East River last evening at precisely five o'clock, which was the hour for the sailing of the American steam packet United States. As the City Hall bell struck five she was loosed from her moorings, and her ponderous wheels, once set in motion, soon swung her into the river. From her deck a cannon bellowed forth a farewell to New York; the star-spangled banner mounted her mast and unfolded itself to the breeze, while simultaneously, from every packet-ship and steamboat in the harbor, flags mounted aloft, displaying the emblems of many nations beside our own. From the wharves and shipping each side of the river, which were black with people, there arose a prolonged and deafening shout, with the waving of hats and handkerchiefs. She seemed proudly conscious of the attention shown her, and, turning her head southward when in the middle of the stream, she departed like a huge thing of life. You may think it singular that so much anxiety should be felt at the departure of a steamer from this port, when it is such a common occurrence; but this is the first American steamer that has as yet met with even tolerable success. It has made but one trip, and has done well.

He was now near the ending of his residence in New York. Before the year closed he had entered into new arrangements of business which carried him to Buffalo, and into a partnership with the Messrs. Pratt & Co., leading hardware merchants of that city. They had known him, at Auburn and at New York, through their dealings with the firm of Hayden & Holmes, and evidently they had formed a high opinion of his worth. Accordingly, having planned to increase the importance of the saddlery hardware department of their business, they made overtures to

<small>In business at Buffalo</small>

Mr. Letchworth which became definite in October, 1848, and which resulted quickly in the organization of a new firm, under the name of Pratt & Letchworth, distinct in business from that of Pratt & Co., but in which Mr. Letchworth was associated with the three members of the latter firm, namely, Samuel F. Pratt, Pascal P. Pratt, and Edward P. Beals. In a "Sketch of the Life of Samuel F. Pratt," written and privately printed by Mr. Letchworth after his elder partner's death, he states that the negotiations which brought him into this connection were conducted by Mr. Pascal P. Pratt, with his brother's concurrence, and he adds: "I think few partnerships ever existed with so uniformly pleasant relations. In reviewing the long intercourse between Samuel F. Pratt and myself, I cannot recall, in all the discussions growing out of the perplexities of business, one unkind word or even harsh tone."

In their letter-headings the purposes of the new firm were made known by this announcement: "Pratt & Letchworth, having purchased of Messrs. Pratt & Co. their entire stock of saddlery and carriage hardware, will now devote their whole attention to this branch of business. Having made extensive arrangements for manu-

WILLIAM PRYOR LETCHWORTH AS A YOUNG MAN

facturing japanned goods, hames, etc., and employed skilful and experienced workmen for the purpose of carrying on the silver- and brass-plating business in all its various branches, they are now prepared to make goods of a superior quality." The firm were further described as "importers and manufacturers of every variety of saddlery and carriage hardware and trunk trimmings."

Here, then, William Pryor Letchworth, at the age of twenty-five, had come to the opening of a quite perfect opportunity for making, to his own advantage as well as to the advantage of others, a full use of the business knowledge and experience he had been storing carefully for ten years. He had come to it from bright prospects in New York. In a letter written to him that year by Peter Hayden, the head of the firm he had served, it was remarked that " he had been treated more like a partner than a clerk." His position had been one which, in his father's judgment, "thousands might envy, and so much better than thousands could attain to," that "no trifling inducements should have led to a change." So the father wrote, not in criticism of the change, but in expressing his belief that it was wisely made. Ample proof of its wisdom soon appeared in the growing business of Pratt & Letchworth, as developed by its young manager in the course of the next few years. In its first year it encountered the general depression of all activities by the cholera visitation of 1849; yet William could write in November to a friend that "business has been very good, notwithstanding the cholera."

That year he was visited by his father and mother, and had the pleasure of showing them Niagara Falls, which neither had seen before. In that year, too, he was joined by his elder brother, Edward, who without becoming a member of the firm, was connected importantly thereafter with the business of Pratt & Letchworth throughout his life. His younger brother, George, who had followed him into the service of his former employers, at Auburn, now acquired an interest in their business, and presently became the junior member of that firm.

The first exhibit of itself that Buffalo made to its new citizen was in its winter and spring aspect, which, most certainly, is not the best it can show. In March, 1849, he wrote laughingly about the Buffalo breezes to his sister Charlotte: "I suppose thee has become entirely out of patience in looking for a letter from that truant brother of thine at 'the West.' Perhaps thee imagines that I have got so far west as to have gone beyond the influence of good society, and lost sight of the good custom of correspondence among friends. . . . I have made as yet but few acquaintances here in Buffalo, save in the way of business. . . . I have enjoyed excellent health since I came here, and I like the place very well, notwithstanding it is quite windy sometimes. Not long since I saw a man on a load of lumber passing our store. His load was of pine boards, an inch thick. A gust of wind happening just then scattered the boards all over the street and tumbled off the man. Ladies who walk out in windy weather run from one awning post to another in the intervals between gusts, and get along in this way very well when the wind is in their favor. A few days ago I saw a lady, on arriving at the corner of a street, thrown off her feet, and the wind carried her completely round the corner."

In June he was feeling differently, and wrote to a friend: "The longer I stay in Buffalo the better I like it. When I came here it was winter, and everything looked cold and bleak; but it is a pleasant spot in the summer time. The breeze from the lake keeps it cool and the atmosphere pure."

In another letter he speaks of attending the Friends' Meeting, at East Hamburg (about ten miles from Buffalo), there being none in the city, and says that he should have done so more frequently if it had not been a cholera year, and he wished to keep as quiet as possible.

For some years after he assumed the responsibilities that attended the establishing and upbuilding of such a business as that of Pratt & Letchworth became, the burden on him must have been heavy to bear. Even more than in his 'prentice years with Hayden & Holmes, his life appears to have been immersed in the affairs of the factory and the counting-room. Outside of what relates to these there is little record of what he thought or felt or said or did, for four or five years. Probably it was still the fact, as he wrote in March, 1849, that he had made few acquaintances in Buffalo " save in the way of business." For social relaxations he cannot have had much time. In a letter to his brother George, written on Christmas Day, 1852, there is a cry that seems wrung from him by the consciousness that he is overtasking his strength. He can never have

Strenuous years of business

been robust in physique, and, though no illness or disability is spoken of, he had been brought somewhat sharply, perhaps, to a realization that his health was insecure. " Oh, that I had an iron constitution, as some have," he exclaimed. " Of all things earthly that God could bestow upon me I could pray for nothing more fervently than for strong, rugged, robust health. If I was a parent or a husband I should be careful of my health; as it is I am reckless."

There is an unwonted exaggeration in this language; for it was not in Mr. Letchworth's nature to be reckless of anything that had claims on him as serious as the claims of health. In the course of the following year he must have been so shaping matters in his business as to relax its demands on him; for in the next December he announced to the family at Auburn his intention to spend some months of the winter in Florida, and he addressed a pleading invitation to his sister Charlotte to be his companion in the trip. Disappointing circumstances refused him that companionship, by detaining his sister at home, and he went southward alone, in February, 1854, remaining in warmer regions until late in the ensuing spring. Apparently the rest and the change of climate and of scenes were of good effect, and he came back to about two years more of unbroken business cares. Then, in 1856, his brother Josiah came into the business, and was prepared to undertake its general management while William, sailing from New York on the 10th of December, indulged himself in a year of travel abroad. In the midst of his tour he was stricken with grief by news of the death of his father, which occurred at Auburn, on the 14th of April, 1857. He returned home in the fall of that year, much enriched in knowledge and ideas, and bettered no doubt in body as well as in mind, though his respite from business had not been rest. In his sight-seeing he had been as industriously thorough as in everything else that he did; but an intelligent interest in that sort of educational experience can make it as curative as rest. In letters to the home circle he wrote an elaborate narrative of his travels, all of which has been perfectly preserved. It offers nothing, however, that would have significance in this story of his life.

From his vacation year Mr. Letchworth came back to resume the headship of the business of Pratt & Letchworth, but under circumstances which undoubtedly eased his labors and cares. In his brothers

Business labors lightened

he now had a staff of the greatest possible helpfulness to him, and throughout the establishment there was an organized efficiency of work. Somewhat later, when the firm bought property at Black Rock for the location of their manufacturing plant, a great development of that side of their business was begun. The manufacture of malleable iron was undertaken soon after, and that became one of the leading industrial enterprises of the city, in the establishment of which Mr. William P. Letchworth and his brother Josiah were actively and closely coöperative. But, generally speaking, from the time of the former's return, in the fall of 1857, there appear signs that he had more leisure to give to interests outside of the making and marketing of goods, and was enjoying a widened intercourse with people in Buffalo on other than business lines. Many of the important friendships of his after life seem traceable to this period, and there is really no doubt that the trend of his life underwent a notable turn within a few years that followed the vacation of 1857.

It was soon after his return that he began to entertain the thought of acquiring a pleasant country place, for summer rest and for the entertainment of friends. In the first instance that thought was directed toward certain attractive spots on the Niagara and on the shores of Lake Erie; but before his quest had gone far in those regions a friend drew his attention to the upper falls of the Genesee and the beautiful valley in which they are set. This suggestion induced him to choose the Erie Railway for the return trip of a visit which he made soon afterward to New York, and to make a stop at Portage, where that road crosses the Genesee. One look then taken from the high railway bridge into the glen below sealed his mind against a willing acceptance of any other spot for the country home he desired. He did not easily or quickly win possession of the coveted ground, but it was yielded to him at last, as will be told. "Glen Iris," rescued from vandalism, restored to all its natural beauty and animated with a life as ideally Arcadian as itself, claims a chapter apart.

Among the people with whom Mr. Letchworth had formed recent intimacies were two ladies of literary note, Mrs. H. E. G. Arey and Mrs. C. H. Gildersleeve, who were close friends. Mrs. Arey had been the editor of a local magazine, "The Home"; but some differences arose between the publisher and herself which caused

Social and literary relationships

her to withdraw from that connection, in 1857, and the two friends planned the founding of a new magazine. Mr. Letchworth interested himself in their project very warmly, to the extent, at least, of subscribing for a considerable number of copies, which he caused to be distributed far and near. Possibly he gave financial assistance more directly; but, however that may be, he was importantly a patron of the new periodical. Its first number was issued in January, 1859, bearing the title of "The Home Monthly." It had a good reception, and achieved as much success for several years as a literary periodical provincially located could expect. In its second year of publication Mr. Letchworth contributed to the magazine two serial tales entitled "Aston Hall" and "The Burial of a Broken Heart," veiling the authorship with the pseudonym of Saxa Hilda,—a *nom de plume* which he signed to occasional letters in the daily newspapers of the city during several years. His authorship of these writings was effectually concealed for a time; but the secret leaked gradually, with a resulting disappearance of Saxa Hilda from the world of print. Apparently Mr. Letchworth made no further essays in fiction,—though these were not discouraging, in the least. He was destined to do much and greatly valuable work with his pen; to win a wide reputation by his writings, extending to many lands; but the subjects of his writing would be sought in the most serious realities of life.

At some time in 1859 Mr. Letchworth was invited to membership in a club, called "The Nameless," which a few young men of congenial tastes had formed in Buffalo within the previous year. In most circumstances this would not have been an occurrence that called for biographical mention; but it proved to be of no small influence on the life recorded here, because of the important friendships to which it led. A few of those who formed the club had been brought together in the first instance by their common discovery, in 1857, that the pleasant library room of the Young Men's Christian Union (as the Y. M. C. A. was then named) in what was known as the Kremlin Hall Block, had been made a most attractive place of resort by the presence in it of a charming librarian, David Gray. Half a dozen of these discoverers acquired quickly the habit of spending all possible evenings in the company of Mr. Gray, clustered for talk in a corner of what might be called his *salon*. Out of those gatherings came the club which Mr. Letchworth joined in its second year. There he met at least two men to whom his heart went out with a warmth of affection that he gave, probably, to no others, apart from his own nearest kin. One was David Gray, whom he loved as the first of Davids was loved; the other was James Nicoll Johnston, to whom, after half a century of the closest friendship and constant association, he referred in his last will as "my warm friend and wise counsellor through many years." With William C. Bryant, George H. Selkirk, Jerome B. Stillson, and others of the Nameless circle, he grew into relations that differed from mere friendly acquaintanceship in a marked degree. The writer of this memoir was of that circle when Mr. Letchworth came into it, and knew him with intimacy until his death.

The little circle was soon undergoing painful breakages by the going of one and another, at the call of the country, to do battle in defence of its national union; and, if Mr. Letchworth could have been blessed with the "strong, rugged, robust health" for which he had prayed so earnestly a few years before, he would have been one to answer the call. He knew that his body would not endure the hardships of the soldier's duty, but he wished to join the army-hospital service and find there a field of usefulness to the cause. His physician and the army surgeon agreed, however, in deciding that even that undertaking of war-service was beyond his strength.

Glen Iris, which he had secured, was now affording him frequent escapes from the city, and the great enjoyment of planning and working for the restoration of its whole perfect natural beauty and charm. His business had assumed an organization and an order which lessened its demands on his personal action in it more and more. In 1863 his staff was greatly strengthened by the enlistment of a new aide, in the person of his friend, James N. Johnston, whose subsequent years of confidential employment in the house of Pratt & Letchworth gave the friendship its superlative seal. He gained another close friend and strong helper in the business when Mr. Henry R. Howland came into it, in 1869. Marriage recently had brought Mr. Howland into a nearness of relationship with Mr. Letchworth which his personal qualities drew closer, with consequent intimacies of association that were important to both.

While his own business was relaxing its hold

on him, other interests in Buffalo were having opportunity to recognize the capacity of Mr. Letchworth for important service to them, and his inborn disposition towards usefulness to his fellows in life. Important institutions were soliciting him to accept places of trust and leadership in the management of their affairs. By consecutive annual elections he was made and continued president of the Buffalo Fine Arts Academy from 1871 to 1874. The Academy was then entering the tenth year of its hard struggle for existence, throughout which he had been one of its staunch supports. Its situation was set forth at the annual meeting, March 9, 1871, when Mr. Letchworth took the chair as president, in an address by Mr. Joseph Warren, who said:—

President of the Fine Arts Academy

The Academy was formally instituted on the 11th of November, 1862. Among those most earnest in the enterprise were ex-President Fillmore, Oliver G. Steele, Henry W. Rogers, Sherman S. Jewett, Bronson C. Rumsey, A. P. Nichols, Rev. Dr. Chester, George S. Hazard, E. P. Dorr, William P. Letchworth, Henry A. Richmond, John Allen, William Dorsheimer, and L. G. Sellstedt. These gentlemen, reinforced from time to time by others, have held the laboring oar in this enterprise for the past nine years.

They have not met with the support and encouragement which the citizens of Buffalo owe to those who toil for the public good.... The financial situation is this: If the managers can secure about $2000 with which to pay outstanding debts, and a fund of $10,000 to be permanently invested, so that the interest may be applied to the payment of any deficit that may occur, or, if there be no deficit, to the purchase of paintings, the Academy can be maintained; otherwise the cloud of doubt will continue to darken its future. A book has been opened and $4500 have been subscribed, upon the condition that the $12,000 needed shall be raised.

It was at the crisis of its history, therefore, that Mr. Letchworth took the presidency of the Fine Arts Academy. One year later, at the next annual opening, on the 24th of February, 1872, he was able to announce that the $4500 of subscriptions to the permanent fund which Mr. Warren had reported twelve months before had been raised to $20,350, including $10,000 from Mr. Sherman S. Jewett, alone. Thus "the cloud of doubt" on the future existence of the Academy had been lifted; its dissolution was no longer in question, though the upbuilding of the institution as an agency of culture in the city would still be difficult and slow work.

To that work Mr. Letchworth gave the best of his energies and the best of his thought. In the four years of his administration as president, and subsequently as one of the trustees of its permanent fund, he has always been credited with an influence in the systematizing of the finances of the Academy that was lasting and wise. His influence was directed with equal wisdom toward the broadening of the educational mission of the Academy, — as when, in his address at the annual opening of 1872, he urged the great need in the city of a school of design, "where may be taught," he said, "not only painting and sculpture, but also a variety of lesser but kindred arts, which have their part of use as well as of beauty in our daily lives. Such a feature engrafted on this institution would fill in part a hiatus now existing between the point where our present educational system leaves off and that at which practical labor begins." Going further than the suggestion, he initiated the raising of a fund for beginning such instruction. The Art School, however, as a child of the Academy, did not come until a score and a half of years had run past; but Mr. Letchworth has no share of responsibility for that delay.

CHAPTER II

GLEN IRIS

IT was not long after Mr. Letchworth's return, in the fall of 1857, from his European tour, that he stopped at Portage Bridge, on the Erie Railway, to see the glen in which the Genesee River makes its upper and middle fall. Probably it was in the spring of 1858. From the bridge he saw how nature had produced here a perfect masterpiece of scenic composition, blending beauty with grandeur in transcendent accord, and how man had done what he could with his tools of destruction to wreck the noble piece of work. But he saw, too, that the vandalism of men had no power to do more than mar the surfaces of such a picture, and that nature would very lovingly renew them if she could be given the chance.

Climbing down from the bridge to the stretch of narrow "flat" which borders the river on its left bank between the upper and the middle fall, he strolled along the stream to a sawmill, which was finishing, in a

<small>Wreckers of the forest</small>

GLEN IRIS: VIEW FROM "INSPIRATION POINT"

feeble way, the havoc of the ancient forests that had clothed the hillsides of the glen. It was evident that few trees which would "pay" for the cutting remained, and Mr. Letchworth, on entering into conversation with the proprietor of the mill, soon found that its resources of business were nearly spent. Afterwards, from the recollection of old inhabitants, he learned that the "mill-power" at the middle fall had been bought as early as 1821, and that a sawmill was put in operation there at some time between that date and 1824. The first attempt to develop power was by excavating a raceway from the brink of the middle fall to a point some distance upstream, and the breaking-up of the rock was undertaken by dropping a ninety-six-pound iron ball from some considerable height. This crude attempt failing, the river was finally dammed, a little above the fall. Later a wooden bridge was thrown across. Both the dam and the bridge were in existence for some time after Mr. Letchworth became lord of the domain. The original sawmill was carried away by a flood, and was succeeded by a more ambitious lumbering plant. This included a set of gangsaws, a planing-mill and a sash and blind factory, all of which had been pursuing their attack on the neighborhood forests until just before Mr. Letchworth came on the scene. As he first saw the glen there was no planing-mill and no accompanying factory to aggravate the sawmill's offensiveness. They had been burned on the 23d of January, 1858.

From this first reconnoissance of the ground Mr. Letchworth returned to Buffalo with fragments of information concerning the mill property and adjacent pieces which led him to conclude that it would not be impossible for him to buy what he desired at no extravagant cost. Negotiations to that end were opened presently, but did not run with smoothness to an early consummation. The land necessary for taking in to one estate, on the west side of the river, the view that embraces the upper and middle falls, the plateau above the latter and the hillsides behind the plateau, was in a number of hands. Mr. Letchworth would purchase none of this if he could not purchase all. Some of the first offers proposed to him were rejected emphatically, and the negotiations appear to have been at a standstill for several months. Then he submitted to the several owners a proposal which he assured them was an absolutely final one, beyond which he

Purchase of the glen

would not go. They understood, evidently, that he meant what he said, and early in February, 1859, the conveyance he desired had been made to him.

In happy possession now of the long abused glen, with the right and the power to offer nature a free hand in it again, his first tasks were to make himself a habitation and to clear the wreckage and the rubbish of the lumbermen's work from the face of the scene. On the plateau which overlooks the middle fall, at precisely the place he would have chosen for his home, his earliest predecessor on the ground had built, in the first instance a small log house, and then a larger framed structure, of two stories, which he opened as a temperance tavern for the entertainment of picnic parties and other summer visitors, who came in considerable numbers from neighboring towns to see the falls. To increase the attractions of the place he built a large boat and launched it on the long pond which the mill-dam had created between the two falls. These popular attractions were of the past; the house was no longer a tavern when it came to Mr. Letchworth, and he set about converting it to his own use. He had no ambition to build a mansion in its place. His taste was superior to the bringing of obtrusive architecture into the noble landscape of his estate. With no definite planning for the future, perhaps, he began with some simple remodellings and new constructions in and about the building, which converted it presently into a pleasant and comfortable abode, contenting himself and delighting his guests. He may sometimes in the after years have had thoughts of building differently, but if so he never went beyond the thought. From time to time there were changes made, additions built, conveniences improved in the modest house, and thus it satisfied him to the end of his life.

His correspondence in 1859 shows that he spent a good deal of time that year on his new estate, supervising the work in progress there; and it indicates that he was in residence before many months, with a household sufficiently organized for some entertainment of guests. His mother had visited him, and he could write to her of what he was doing in a manner which implies her personal acquaintance with the place. Until November in this year his letters to his mother were dated simply from Portage; one written on the 2d of October is captioned so. But the next letter, of Novem-

Work of restoration

ber 6, is under the new heading, "Glen Iris, Portage," and may be taken to mark, approximately, the time when the Glen received its name. Seemingly it had had none in the past. Only the river and its falls were named; and they were but part of what that cup of the hills contained. The glen in its wholeness required a geographical designation, and the suggestions for it were plentiful, no doubt; but the aptest of them all was recommended to the eye, on every sunlit day, by the rainbow-painted mists which rose out of the gorge of the falls to perfect the whole verdure and glory of the scene. Glen Iris is the name for which the place would seem to have been made.

Development of the beauty of the Glen was an undertaking of careful workmanship in Mr. Letchworth's hands. He was hasty in nothing; he would not be meddlesome with nature; there was study in all that he did, and patience to wait on slow processes of vegetable growth for effects which surpass the artifices of man. Yet the change he wrought upon the scene came amazingly fast. His earliest visitors appear to have felt the enchantments of the place as profoundly as any can feel them now, despite the scars and the relics of rude usage which long time and much labor were needed to remove. The writer of this is able to compare impressions of Glen Iris that are fifty years apart; and it is only by a reckoning of perfections added and flaws subtracted that he can realize in his thought of it a greater beauty than when he saw it first.

From what fashioning, some reader may ask, does this bit of the earth derive so rare a beauty and charm? — and the question is not answered easily. The best attempt can be made, perhaps, by offering to imagination, first, the bare outlines of a topographical sketch of this part of the valley of the Genesee, and overlaying on that a picture of the same as nature had vestured it and as a poet described it some thirty and more years ago.

Topographic features of Glen Iris

The topographic features can easily be set forth. Their axis is the Genesee River, which traverses the western part of the State of New York from south to north, emptying its waters into Lake Ontario, near the city of Rochester, through which it flows. There is beauty and great fertility in the Genesee Valley throughout; but its picturesqueness is developed most remarkably within one short section, hardly three miles in length, where the river is dropped nearly three hundred feet, in three falls, with intervening rapids and pretty cascades. The first or Upper Fall is near a village which received the name of Portageville in early days, when there was some carrying trade on the river and some necessary land portage of goods between the navigable waters above and below the three falls. The drop of the river in this Upper Fall is seventy-one feet. Almost overhanging it, at a height of two hundred and thirty-four feet above the level from which it drops, the Erie Railway is carried over the Genesee by a great bridge, eight hundred feet long. This affords a measure of the chasm through which the river is brought to its first fall.

Below this fall the river is still confined narrowly between perpendicular walls, but no longer to the same height. The crest of wall is lowered by more than the lowering of the river bed after its fall, and the higher tiers of the previous rock-enclosure to the stream are pushed back for some distance and transformed into sloping hills, especially on the western side. Thus that which is a gorge above this fall is rimmed below it into the grace and beauty of a glen — Glen Iris; and on a broad plateau that overlooks the river, from a height which is but pleasing and not terrifying, and which has wooded hills behind, stands the modest manor-house of the Glen. It overlooks the river just far enough below the second or Middle Fall to secure the most perfect view of that fine cataract, which makes a plunge of one hundred and seven feet.

A few hundred feet below the Middle Fall [borrowing further details of the topography from an accurate description in one of the reports of the American Scenic and Historic Preservation Society] the walls of the canyon are sheer precipices three hundred and fifty feet high — twenty feet higher than the palisades of the Hudson River opposite New York City — and on top of the rock walls the land on the right and left banks rises still higher, seventy-five and one hundred and fifty feet respectively. About seventy-nine hundred feet from the Middle Fall are the Lower Falls, an irregular set of cascades, unevenly worn back, and seventy feet high. The three Portage Falls with their intermediate cascades represent a total descent of about two hundred and ninety feet. Thence the river makes a great semicircle to the left, sweeping by the High Banks and continuing through the chasm for about fourteen miles to Mount Morris, where it emerges into a broad alluvial valley, from one to two miles wide.

Into this framework of fact the reader may be able to set a word-picture of Glen Iris sketched by the late David Gray, in an article written for *Scribner's Monthly Magazine*, July, 1877, when he was editor of the Buffalo *Courier*. He was writing of what was to him, undoubtedly, the dearest spot on earth. He pictures it as seen first by a traveller on the Erie Railway, at the crossing of the high bridge, "when the summer morning has come over the hills and filled the valley."

<small>A poet's description</small>

Innumerable lights and shades of the varied verdure, the warm tints of the rocks and the flashing of the fallen waters enliven a picture to which its sunken remoteness superadds an almost visionary charm. The two or three cottage roofs that peer from thick nests of foliage far down beside the river suggest a life blissfully held apart from the world and its ways. Over all an atmosphere of thinnest mist, smitten to whiteness by the sunlight, wavers and shines like a translucent sea. The valley, indeed, is a region of lapsing streams and delicate rising mists, and never a gleam of sunshine visits it but it deserves its name of Glen Iris.

From the west end of the bridge the descent into the Glen is made by the aid of flights of rustic steps and a steep path through thick woods of beech, maple, and hemlock, leading to the margin of the stream. Halfway down, and crossed by a footbridge, a little brook, christened by the valley folk De-ge-wa-nus, — an Indian name of note along the Genesee, — dashes headlong from the mysterious green darkness of the upper forest, and commits suicide at the cliff of the river's bank. On the way, too, fine views are afforded of the Upper Fall of the Genesee, which has hewn its way backward through the rock almost to the foundations of the great bridge. As we emerge from the wood the river grows quiet again among its stones, and the valley widens into tranquil pasture lands. . . .

Ascending the slope toward the farther end of the valley, we come in sight of the second or Middle Fall, a full, rounded shoulder and flounced skirt of rock, over which the water is flung in a single broad shawl of snow-white lace, more exquisite of pattern than ever artist of Brussels or Valenciennes dared to dream. On a green tableland almost directly above this fall is the dwelling of the valley's good genius — a rustic paradise embowered in foliage of tree and vine, and islanded in wavy spaces of softest lawn. Here art has aided nature to plant a true "garden of tranquil delights." Each group of trees becomes the cunning frame of an enchanting picture or beautiful vignette. The hills, sentinelled at their summits by lofty pines, are walls which shut the world out, while across the upper and sole visible approach to the Glen, the bridge stretches like a vast portal reared by Titans. It is the Happy Valley of fable realized, and the lulling sound of the near cataract gives fitting voice to its perfect seclusion and repose. . . .

GLEN IRIS

This carries Mr. Gray's description to the foot of Glen Iris, as the name is correctly used. Going on, with the river, down the deep and winding canyon into which it rushes, below Glen Iris and the Middle Fall, he wrote further: —

Following its onward course, the tourist makes his way cautiously along the dizzy brink of the westerly wall of the gulf. Higher and higher, as he progresses, towers the perpendicular rampart on which he treads, until soon it is from a sheer height of about four hundred feet that he leans, shuddering, to descry the river in its rocky inferno, and hearken to its voice softened by distance to a rustling whisper. About a mile from the Middle Fall the gulf partially relaxes its hold on the brawling prisoner, and the visitor may make his way down a steep and thickly wooded bank to what are called the Lower Falls of the Genesee. Here, in the midst of a wilderness still virgin and primeval, the waters shoot furiously down a narrow rock-hewn flume, their descent being nearly a hundred feet, and the width of the torrent at some points scarcely more than the compass of a good running jump. From the sombre chasm in which the cataract terminates, the canyon once more draws the river and repeats on a still more magnificent scale the scenery at which I have hinted above. A walk of four or five miles down the river from the Lower Fall, and along the westerly battlement of the canyon, brings us to a sudden opening and retrocession of the rocky walls, and here, a fertile expanse of bottom land extending from the river to the hills, are the Gardow Flats, the ancient home of "the White Woman,"—of whom much will be told hereafter.

Something of a defined idea of Glen Iris may be taken from these descriptions, and something further from the accompanying photographic illustrations, to carry in the mind while reading of the life and work that were centred principally in this scene. The supremely beautiful view which takes in the Middle and Upper Falls, looking up stream from a point some distance below the Glen Iris residence, was made the subject of a painting, seventy years ago, by Thomas Cole, one of the most admired of American landscape painters. The painting was purchased for presentation to William H. Seward, then (1841) Governor of the State of New York, and now hangs in the home of his son, at Auburn, New York.

All that he had expected from his purchase of the Glen was assuredly realized to Mr. Letchworth, and very soon, in his happy home-making for himself and his generous opening of its delightful hospitalities to his friends. Singly and in companies he called them often and in numbers to share with him the fine refreshments of mind and body that were in its gift. For several years, beginning in 1860, his associates of "The Nameless Club" were summoned to celebrate the Fourth of July at the Glen; and out of those congenial gatherings came some of the earliest and most perfect of the many poems which Glen Iris, first and last, has inspired. Possibly it would be an extravagance of eulogy to say that no other spot in America has been celebrated equally to it in the fervor and the quality of the verse it has called out; yet searching criticism might uphold that suggestion, on the evidence of a collected volume of Glen Iris verse which was printed under the title of "Voices of the Glen," in 1876, and of which a new edition, with added poems, has been issued since Mr. Letchworth's death by the administrator of his estate, but under the auspices of the American Scenic and Historic Preservation Society. The preparation of this new edition was one of Mr. Letchworth's last tasks, and the order to the Knickerbocker Press for the printing of it was given only five days before he died.

Poetical "Voices of the Glen"

Inasmuch as nothing said in cool prose can

communicate nearly so much of the spirit and influence of the place as is wrought into some of these lyric strains, it will be fitting to cite a few of them here. In the original concert of the "Voices" the keynote of their choral singing was given by James Nicoll Johnston, and he shall lead them here, in —

A MEMORY

Bright summer dream of white cascade,
  Of lake, and wood, and river!
The vision from the eye may fade, —
  The heart keeps it forever.
    There beauty dwells
    In rarest dells, —
There every leaf rejoices;
    By cliff and steep,
    By crag and deep,
You hear their pleasant voices.

From forest flower and meadow bloom,
  The soft wind, passing over,
Brings the wild roses' fresh perfume,
  The sweet breath of the clover;
    And odors rare
    Pulse through the air,
In waves of pleasure flowing, —
    We dream away
    The passing day,
Regardless of its going.

GLEN IRIS

On leafy boughs the sunlight glows,
    The skies are blue above us,
The happy laugh that comes and goes
    Is from the friends that love us.
        O! bliss combined
        Of sense and mind,
    Rare boon to mortals given!
        Before our eyes
        Is Paradise,
    Above the blue is heaven.

Take, Memory, to thy choicest shrine,
    And guard as sacred treasure,
The hours of ecstasy divine,
    The days of untold pleasure.
        Though many a scene
        May come between
    In way of future duty,
        We still shall deem
        Our summer dream
    As peerless in its beauty.

This from David Gray: —

TO GLEN IRIS

[*Impromptu*]

To thee, sweetest valley! Glen Iris, to thee!
More fair than the vision of poet may be,
And beyond what the artist may dream, when his eyes
Are dim with the hues of the loveliest skies;

To thee and thy forest, whose foliage forever
Is fresh with the mists of thy light-flashing river;
Thy flowers that are swayed in the softest of airs;
Thy birds in the greenest and deepest of lairs;
Thy lights and thy shadows, thy sweet river's fall
That sings into slumber or reverie, all;
To thee, though our lips cannot utter a word,
Our spirits are singing in rapture unheard;
For 'tis part of thy magic — thy beauty-wrought spell —
What thou whisperest to us we never can tell.

Sweet Glen of the Rainbow, to thee there are given,
As fresh as the day when they sprang into birth,
All the joys and the graces we love most of earth,
And the sunlight flings o'er thee the glories of heaven.
So the Nameless now drink from thy pleasure-brimmed chalice,
And pledge thee the rainbow-ideal of valleys —
A Beulah, where thrice happy mortals that see thee
Forget all their care, for thy waters are Lethe,
And we shout and rejoice that thou art what thou art —
The beautiful home of a beautiful heart.

This from Henry R. Howland: —

> We sat on the lawn, 'neath the shade of the trees,
>   And read of Ulysses, far-sailing;
> Of the rare lotus lands, mid those isles of the seas,
>   Whose slumberous joys were ne'er failing;
> Yet surely the odors that breathed o'er them there,
>   Their dream-laden pleasures bestowing,
> Scarce could bring to the heart such a surcease of care
>   As our Glen, with enchantment o'erflowing;

THE HOME AT GLEN IRIS

GLEN IRIS

For soft-murmuring waters, and odors of balm,
  Delights of the eye without ceasing,
Lull our senses to rest with their magical calm,
  Their pure, gentle spell ne'er releasing;
And sweeter than songs sung by sirens of old,
  Or sea-fairies' music delighting,
Are the voices that reach us from river and wold
  To new blissful pleasures inviting;
Yet we listen and hear in their quiet refrain
The song of the sea-fairies sung o'er again —
  "Who can light on so happy a shore
    All the world o'er, all the world o'er?"

This from Miss Annie R. Annan (Mrs. William H. Glenny): —

O, WHERE DO YOU COME FROM, SUNSHINE SWEET?

O, where do you come from, sunshine sweet?
  For dark is the street, —
Blessing my eyes with a swift rare gleam,
Whose light and shadow all mingled seem
Of the green woods and the white of spray, —
  Yet the day is gray!

And whence do you come, O haunting rhyme?
  Unmeet for the time;
With your "Sweetest eyes" and "The Old Canoe,"
Till the good old faith again seems true —
Life is not prose, though to duties wed;
  Nor the poets dead.

>   I am the ghost of the sunshine born
>   At the Glen one morn;
>   And I, the echo of song and rhyme
>   That, dying not with the dying time,
>   Gives life the rhythm and color of May —
>   Makes the day less gray.

And these stanzas, culled from a "'Nameless' Anniversary Poem," by Miss Amanda T. Jones: —

> For when the days were in their rosiest bloom
>   We shook away the dust of city marts;
>   And with a happy sense of lightened hearts,
> Let fall awhile our heavy weights of gloom.
>   Right princely was our welcome to the wood,
>   The green-roofed paths, the valley and the flood,
> And to the generous board and tasteful room!
> . . . .
> We trod the dim cool windings of the trail
>   That through the forest led to sacred nooks,
>   Where lightly laughed the ever-raptured brooks,
> And the mitchella repens blossomed, pale
>   From love of shade and rich excess of dew;
>   Where pulsed the bubbling spring, and downward threw,
> From tiny heights, its moss-entangled veil.
> . . . .
> O home of peace! O cedar-bowered land —
>   Glistening Glen Iris, beautiful as heaven!
>   O cloven hills, by flood or earthquake riven!
> O riotous stream, impetuous and grand!

GLEN IRIS

> There while we dwelt, gay laugh and mimic feud
> Our youth revived, our childhood half renewed,
> And knit, forever one, our songful band.

Mr. Gray, in his description of the Glen, speaks of the railway bridge as stretching "like a vast portal" across "the upper and sole visible approach" to it. This has reference to the original timber-built bridge, which was a wonderfully effective adjunct of the scenery, filling, as it did, the whole opening between the walls of the river by the lattice-like structure of its timber trestles, and seeming to be just a great gate, hung with no other design than to shut out the external world. The present light structure of steel has nothing of that effect. *The railway bridge*

The old bridge, a famous piece of engineering work in its day, and said to have contained the entire product of two hundred and forty-six acres of pine timber, was opened to use, with a good deal of ceremony, in August, 1852. It was destroyed by fire in the first week of May, 1875. As can easily be imagined, the burning of this mighty mass of pine wood, in such a setting, offered a spectacle that may never have had its like, and which few were privileged to see. Fortunately, Mr. Letchworth was one of the few, and he wrote an account of it for the Buffalo *Courier*. The fire was discovered by a watchman at the bridge, about one o'clock in the morning. It was not until three hours later that Mr. Letchworth became aware of it; but it had then just seized the whole great frame.

> I was aroused from sleep [he wrote] at ten minutes to four o'clock, and in a few minutes was standing on the lawn at Glen Iris, from which point every portion of the bridge was visible, as well as the Upper Falls, the river, and the Middle Falls. The spectacle at precisely four o'clock was fearfully grand; every timber in the bridge seemed then to be ignited, and an open network of fire was stretched across the upper end of the valley. Above the bridge and touching its upper line a black curtain hung down from the sky, its lower edge belted with a murky fringe of fire. The hoarse growl of the flames and the crackling of the timbers sounded like a hurricane approaching through the forest. At this time the Upper Falls seemed dancing in a silver light. The water in the river was glistening with the bright glare thrown on it, and the whole valley of Glen Iris was illuminated with tragic splendor. . . . At fifteen minutes past four the superstructure of the west end of the bridge sank downward, and the depression rolled throughout its length to the east end like the sinking of an ocean wave. The whole upper structure, including the heavy T-rails, went down with

a crashing sound. . . . Lighter portions of the framework still remained. . . . Blazing timber still continued to fall uninterruptedly, and the rocks, becoming heated, exploded in loud and almost continuous bursts of sound. . . . Burning fragments of the bridge fell all about the upper end of the valley, covering the hill-sides. . . . Probably the pine groves and every building in the Glen Iris Valley would have been destroyed had the leaves of the woods and the shingles of the buildings been dry, — but they had been dampened by a recent rain.

The beauties of Glen Iris were not the only gifts that nature had endowed it with, and which the timely interposition of Mr. Letchworth saved from pillage and waste. Naturalists, whose eyes went searching through the country for the good earthmother's *caches* of treasure, found many things to reward them in this glen, even while it was suffering the abuse of the axemen and the sawyers of the devouring mill. After it came under careful protection it was a place which they loved to explore. Judge Clinton, devotee of botany, came often from Buffalo, to prowl through its woods and fields and fill his "drum" with rare or choice specimens of the native flora of New York. Principal E. E. Fish, of the Buffalo Pub-

Birds and wild plants of the Glen

lic School No. 10, lover and student of birds and plants, was similarly attracted to the Glen. In 1887 the latter contributed to one of the daily newspapers of Buffalo a series of admirable papers on "Birds and Flowers," one of which told of a visit to Portage that spring and of what was found there. "By selecting Portage as the field to be explored," he said, "one was sure to renew the acquaintance of many of the rarer and more interesting birds." The recital of his findings, especially in "the upper Letchworth woods," fills the greater part of two columns of interesting chat, in the course of which he remarks: "Those acquainted with this region know how rich and varied are the flora and fauna. Later will come azaleas, pyrolas, sweet-scented crab, several species of wintergreen, including the beautiful flowering one with purple fringe, Mitchella, Clintonias, orchids, lady's slipper, fringed gentian, and many others. The rare and interesting birds are equally numerous. Within the radius of a hundred yards I have found the nests of six of the different species of thrushes."

Recently (in 1907), since the gift of the Glen Iris property to the State of New York, the head gardener of the New York Botanical Garden, Mr. George V. Nash, was delegated to visit the ground and designate a number of the most interesting species of trees for labelling with their botanical and popular names. In his report, as quoted by the American Scenic and Historic Preservation Society in its thirteenth annual report, he says:—

Native trees

The object of my visit to this park was to name and have properly labelled the trees in the vicinity of the roads and paths which Mr. Letchworth has constructed and is constructing through this tract, that the public may have easy access to all of its beauties. One is at once struck here by the purity of the vegetation. By this I mean the almost entire absence of plants not native to the tract. Even in the immediate neighborhood of the house, where the open lawns would permit of such treatment, but few extraneous species are to be found. . . . It is plain on all sides that every attempt has been made to keep things as nature made them. The arboreal vegetation is well represented, and in one region, down near the lower fall, inaccessible to the lumberman, on account of the precipitous drop on one side and the raging waters of the river on the other, are some large trees, perhaps representing the original growth. I had a most enjoyable time for two days going over this tract. Of course in that limited period it was not possible to make an exhaustive study of the trees, my operations being confined to the vicinity of paths. But here a large proportion of the species must be represented. . . . It would be an interesting work to prepare a list of all the plants growing wild within the confines of this park.

In the forestry of his Glen Iris estate, during the half-century and more of his personal care of it, Mr Letchworth, according to his own estimate, planted more than ten thousand trees.

To the scientific interest attaching to the trees in the Glen, Mr. Letchworth added a personal interest, by introducing, in different parts of the grounds, many "memorial trees," planted by relatives, friends and visitors whose names he wished to associate with the place. Among these are a Kentucky coffee tree, planted by Judge George W. Clinton, son of Governor De Witt Clinton, — one of the warmest of the friends of Mr. Letchworth and of the lovers of the Glen; a white oak planted by the late President Martin B. Anderson, of Rochester University, — a specially intimate associate of Mr. Letchworth on the State Board of Charities; an elm by his honored friend James O. Putnam, of Buffalo; a tulip tree by F. B. Sanborn, the eminent social

Memorial trees

worker of Massachusetts; a sweet gum tree by Mr. S. C. Locke, of the Charity Organization Society of London, England; pine trees planted by Sir William George Johnson and Captain Charles Johnson, two grandsons of Sir William Johnson, the Loyalist leader in New York State preceding the War of the Revolution. One group of trees growing near the old Indian Council House is connected in interest with the holding of the Last Indian Council on the Genesee, of which some account will be given in the next chapter. They were planted on the day of that ceremony, and spring from roots that were brought from the graveyard where Red Jacket and Mary Jemison, the captive white woman of the Senecas, were buried. The planting of one of these was performed by Mrs. Kate Osborn, a descendant of Captain Brant, assisted by Millard Fillmore, ex-President of the United States; another was placed in the earth by John Jacket, a grandson of Red Jacket; a third by Thomas Jemison, grandson of Mary Jemison. Other trees memorialize brothers, sisters, and other relatives of Mr. Letchworth, or close friends, such as James N. Johnston, David Gray, Henry R. Howland, and others; while some are in memory of his colleagues of the State Board of Charities. A differently interesting tree on the estate is of a new variety of hawthorn, to which Professor Charles S. Sargent gave the name *Crataegus Letchworthiana*, in honor of the master of Glen Iris.

Practically, Mr. Letchworth continued to be a Buffalonian to the end of his life, maintaining unimpaired relations with the city and all of its best interests; but he identified himself, nevertheless, very fully and closely with the communities of the neighborhood in which he had now planted his home. He took pains to make acquaintance with his new neighbors; he established understandings with the local authorities of county and town, and became coöperative with them, in highway and other improvements, securing an influence that was soon working good effects in the country round.

One of the first of the neighborhood interests that drew his attention was that of the schools. As early as the 11th of February, 1860, we find him in correspondence with the principal of the Portageville and Castile Union School, arranging for a provision of prizes, in books and silver medals, to

Mr. Letchworth and the schools

be awarded to the pupils most proficient in penmanship, arithmetic, spelling, composition, reading, declamation, grammar, geography, history, philosophy, chemistry and algebra. Subsequently he established money prizes of twenty and fifteen dollars in the Genesee Wesleyan Seminary, to be awarded yearly for "general scholarship." In 1861, on the 2d of June, he entertained the school-children of Portageville and Pike at a flag-raising on his lawn. He visited the schools at intervals, as his father had done, and sought in many ways to be helpful in stimulating their work. Miss Caroline Bishop, who became, for many years, his secretary and executive assistant at Glen Iris, was a schoolgirl at this time, attending at a district schoolhouse which "stood on a small plateau on the bank of the river" at some distance northward from the Glen Iris residence. In a paper written for the Wyoming Historical Pioneer Association, Miss Bishop has told of Mr. Letchworth's "frequent visits" to that school, and of the many useful lessons he taught.

Among others [she says] I distinctly recall a lesson on the use of the word "awful," suggested by hearing from the lips of one of the pupils the expression "awful cold"; and a lesson which he gave us in geography, by drawing on the blackboard a map of Wyoming County with its sixteen townships represented and the Genesee River forming a portion of the boundary on the eastern side. With the questions and explanations that followed we soon began to realize that Wyoming County was one of the geographical divisions of the earth, and that our playground and our fathers' farms formed a part of the subject which before had seemed far off and difficult to understand. He provided for our enjoyment and instruction books of melodies designed especially for children, and placed in the school room for our benefit a new cabinet organ of Prince & Co.'s manufacture. When the old school house became too dilapidated for use in winter he prepared for us a comfortable and attractive room in a building which stood near the entrance to the Glen Iris grounds. He invited us to his home and prepared entertainments for us, and stimulated our ambition, as well as that of the pupils of the Castile and Portageville schools, by prizes which he repeatedly offered for good conduct, proficiency in spelling and reading, and the greatest progress made during a specified time in penmanship and mathematics.

Miss Bishop adds : —

His interest in the welfare of young persons was not confined to children in the schools. In one of the bank pass books is a considerable list of items — each five dollars — paid to newsboys and boys in orphan asylums who had started a bank account.

As he showed in the devotion of his later life to work for them, children were, to him, the most precious possessions of the world, and the objects of the most sacred responsibility. From his first acquisition of Glen Iris, as will be shown later, he was planning to make it a gift to children in the future,—a bit of Paradise in which large companies of them, for many generations, might have a rearing, a health and a happiness of life which their parental homes could not afford to them. It was not with self-indulgent designs that Glen Iris was so eagerly sought, so perseveringly acquired, so laboriously made what it came to be in his hands.

CHAPTER III

PRESERVING THE MEMORIALS OF GENESEE VALLEY HISTORY

THE valley of the Genesee, especially in the middle region which embraces Glen Iris, has a remarkably interesting early history, from the time of the white man's first acquaintance with it until he took it from the red man and made it his own. It was the seat of the Seneca Nation, the westernmost of the tribes of the Iroquois Confederacy; and the Senecas were active allies of the British and the Tories in the Revolutionary War. Events connected with that war, especially with Sullivan's expedition against the Senecas, in 1779, and subsequently with the buying of the Seneca lands and the removal of the tribe from the region, put the stamp of historic interest on many places in the neighborhood of Mr. Letchworth's home. They engaged his attention, and led him to an interest in Indian history which he does not seem to have felt before. He was troubled on finding that relics and mementos of the aboriginal possessors of the valley, still existing, were treated with neglect and were fast disappearing. As soon as he became free, in some degree, from immediately pressing demands on him, he made it part of his public duty to repair this neglect, to the extent that he could do so, by action of his own and by coöperation with others of like mind. In these undertakings he had much encouragement and stimulation from some of his closer friends, especially William C. Bryant, Henry R. Howland and O. H. Marshall, who shared his interest in Indian history.

The most interesting historical relic in the Genesee Valley was the ancient Council House of the Seneca Nation, which stood about eighteen miles from Glen Iris, in the village of Caneadea. For many years after the Senecas left the Genesee Country this building, of hewn logs, which had been their parliament house, — their capitol, — supplied a habitation to the white farmer who tilled the surrounding land. It had long been out of use, however, and was falling into decay, when Mr. Letchworth, in the fall of 1871, acquired title to it and had it removed, for preservation, to his own grounds. It was an antiquity when the first white settlers came into the

The ancient Seneca Council House

valley, and tradition had preserved little more of its history than the fact that it had long been the rendezvous of the nation, for councils, for the planning and preparation of warlike expeditions and for festive celebrations of victory. According to some opinions it saw the starting and the return of the Seneca war-party which had to do with what is known as the massacre of Wyoming. From a little volume published many years ago in western New York, recounting the life and adventures of Major Moses Van Campen, who won renown in the Revolutionary War, the following incident connected with this council house was derived by Mr. Gray, in the article already referred to : —

In the spring of 1782, Van Campen, then a young officer in the Continental army, was captured on the upper waters of the Susquehanna by a party of Iroquois in command of a British lieutenant. Narrowly escaping the usual death of prisoners by torture, he and several of his soldiers were led by forced marches through the forest to Caneadea. Their arrival was the occasion of a savage jubilee, and the amiable villagers straightway demanded for themselves the customary privilege of causing the captives, in Iroquois fashion, to run the gauntlet. The course selected was about forty rods in length, and the council house, as was usual on such occasions, was designated as the goal and place of refuge of the runners. Close behind them and on each side of their path crowded the population of the village, young and old, and of both sexes, armed with cudgels and long whips, the warriors alone remaining dignified spectators of the scene. The signal was given, and the indomitable Van Campen darted off first, as nimble as a deer. The armed mob closed quickly upon him, and his case would have been desperate but for a bold *coup* to which he had resort. Directly in his track stood two stout young squaws, waiting their chance to strike the captive. Squarely at them, as if shot from a catapult, he threw himself, and with such effect that both were pitched headlong, and described several somersaults on their way to the ground. The absurd spectacle was too much, alike for Indian dignity and ferocity, and, amidst yells of uncontrollable laughter on the part of the crowd, the captives made their way easily to the council house.

Another mention in the scant chronicles of the frontier contributes still further to render Caneadea classic. It was the place where Mary Jemison, "the White Woman of the Genesee," a name famous in the early annals of western New York, halted for a day to rest in her weary pilgrimage to the Genesee Country.

Something of the interesting story of this woman will appear later in the present chapter. In Mr. Letchworth's rescue of the ancient

Council House of the Senecas from destruction, by removing it from Caneadea to Glen Iris, it hardly needs to be said that the removal was effected with "almost religious care,"—using the words of Mr. Gray. At Glen Iris "the timbers, duly marked, were reërected in precisely their ancient order, and the edifice, carefully and exactly restored to its original condition, may easily survive another century." It is of the customary form of the "long house" of the Iroquois—about fifty feet in length by twenty in width. "The walls of the Glen Iris edifice, formed of pine logs, smoothly hewn and neatly dove-tailed at the corners, are carried up to the height of twelve or thirteen feet, without windows, the only openings in the original building having been two doors, opening to west and east respectively, and two smoke vents near the centre of the roof. The roof-covering is of split 'shakes' [large split shingles] secured by transverse poles, which, again, are fastened at each end by twisted withes."

Having restored to its historic dignity this primitive parliament-house of an extinct nation, **The last Indian council** Mr. Letchworth was fortunately able to attach a new distinction to it and a final memory, by bringing about, on the 1st

THE OLD CANEADEA COUNCIL HOUSE

of October, 1872, a remarkable assembly of representative Senecas and Mohawks, descendants from famous chiefs and notable personages in Indian history, to light once more the council fire in the ancient hall, and sit round it in grave exchange of speech, as in the ancient days. These two nations of the Iroquois Confederacy had been estranged from one another since the War of 1812, when the Mohawks, settled in Canada, were in arms for the British, and were met in battle by the Senecas, who fought on the American side. The enmity then kindled had never quite been extinguished, and it was not without some difficulty that their leading people were now brought together, to give a reconciliatory significance to this "Last Indian Council on the Genesee."

The Indians who came were nineteen in number, of men, and they were accompanied by several women, who took no part, of course, in the proceedings of the day. The Mohawk Nation sent a single male representative, Colonel Simcoe Kerr; but he, grandson of the famous Joseph Brant, and great-grandson of Sir William Johnson, was not only the highest of Mohawk chiefs, but looked up to by all of Indian blood in Canada as their foremost man. His sister,

Mrs. Osborn, came with Colonel Kerr. Among the Senecas present were grandsons of Red Jacket and Cornplanter,—the two chiefs of greatest renown in such part of Seneca history as connects with that of the whites,—and two grandsons of "the white woman," Mary Jemison. One of these latter, Thomas Jemison, bore her name, while the other, James Shongo, had that of "Colonel Shongo," who is thought to have been a leading actor in the tragedy of Wyoming. Other notables of the assembled Council were Nicholas H. Parker, a grandnephew of Red Jacket and brother of General Ely S. Parker, who served on the staff of General Grant in the Civil War; William Blacksnake, whose grandfather, known as "Governor Blacksnake," lived on the Alleghany Reservation to be considerably more than a century old, and William and Jesse Tallchief, whose grandfather, Tallchief, had his home at Murray Hill, near Mount Morris, and was highly esteemed.

The account which follows, of incidents and speeches at the Council, is quoted from an interesting paper contributed to the publications of the Buffalo Historical Society (volume VI) by Mr. Henry R. Howland, who was present, as one of the guests of Mr. Letchworth, and who wrote from notes made at the time: —

Some of the invited guests had come on the previous day, and when the morning train arrived from Buffalo the old King George cannon on the upper plateau thundered its welcome, as once it was wont to wake the echoes from the fortress of Quebec, and all climbed the hill to the spot where the ancient Council House stood with open doors to receive them. They were the lookers on who found their places at one end of the council hall, where rustic seats awaited them, save that in a suitable and more dignified chair was seated the former President of the Republic, Hon. Millard Fillmore, whose gracious and kindly presence — that of a snowy-haired gentleman of the old school — honored the occasion.

The holders of the council were "robed and ready." Upon the clay floor in the centre of the building burned the bright council fire, and as the blue smoke curled upward it found its way through the opening in the roof to mingle with the haze of the October day. Upon low benches around the fire sat the red-skinned children of the Ho-dé-no-sáu-nee [People of the Long House] who had gathered from the Cattaraugus and the Allegheny and from the Grand River in Canada as well; for on that day, for the first time in more than seventy years, the Mohawks sat in council with the Seneças. They were for the most part clad in such costumes as their fathers wore in the olden days, and many of the buckskin garments, bright sashes and great necklaces of silver or bone and beads, were heirlooms of the past, as were the ancient tomahawk pipes which were gravely smoked, while their owners sat in rapt and decorous attention as one after another their orators addressed them. No sight could be more picturesque. . . . Colonel Kerr . . . wore the chieftain's dress in which he had been presented to Queen Victoria: a suit of soft, dark, smoke-tanned buckskin with deep fringes, a rich sash, and a cap of doeskin with long, straight plumes from an eagle's wing. He carried Brant's tomahawk in his belt. . . .

For a short time these children of time-honored sachems and chiefs sat and smoked in dignified silence, as became so grave an occasion, and when the proper moment had arrived, as prescribed by the decorum of Indian observance, one of their number arose and, following the ceremonial method of the ancient custom, announced in formal words and in the Seneca tongue that the council fire had been lighted, and that the ears of those who were convened in council were now opened to listen to what might be said to them. Resuming his seat, there was a moment of quiet waiting, as if in expectation, and then the opening speech was made by Nicholson H. Parker, Ga-yeh-twa-geh. . . . Mr. Parker was a tall, well-built man, with a fine clear face not unlike that of his distinguished brother. Around his sleeves above the elbows and at the wrists were wide bands of beaded embroidery, and, besides a long-fringed woven belt of bright colors, he wore an ample shoulder scarf that was also richly embroidered. His tomahawk pipe was one that had belonged to Red Jacket. Mr. Parker was a well educated man, had served as United States interpreter with his people, and was a recognized leader among them.

All of the speeches made in the council that day, until it approached its close, were in the Seneca language, which is without labials, very guttural, and yet with a music of its own, capable of much inflection and by no means monotonous. Its sentences seemed short and their utterance slow and measured, with many evidences of the earnest feeling aroused by the unwonted occasion and its associations with the past, and, as each speaker in turn touched some responsive chord in the breasts of his hearers, they responded with that deep guttural ejaculation of approval which cannot be written in any syllable of English phrasing. Many of the orators spoke at great length, and it is unfortunate that the full texts could not be preserved. Such portions as we have of three or four of the principal speeches were taken down after the council from the lips of the speakers themselves; they are, however, but brief epitomes of their full orations.

The reported part of Nicholson Parker's speech shows it to have been full of dignity and eloquent feeling, most appropriate to the occasion and the place. He ended it by saying: —

Brothers, we are holding council, perhaps for the last time, in Jenisheu [the native form of the name Genesee, signifying " The Beautiful Valley "]. This beautiful territory was once our own. The bones of our fathers are strewn thickly under its sod. But all this land has gone from their grasp forever. The fate and the sorrows of my people should force a sigh from the stoutest heart.

Brothers, we came here to perform a ceremony, but I cannot make it such. My heart says that this is not a play or a pageant. It is a solemn reality to me, and not a mockery of days that are past and can never return. Neh-hoh — this is all.

Thomas Jemison, or Sho-son-do-want, spoke with the same gravity, but in a somewhat less saddened tone.

I am an old man [he said], and well remember when our people lived in this valley. I was born in a wigwam on the banks of this river. I well remember my grandmother, " The White Woman," of whom you have all heard. I remember when our people were rich in lands and respected by the whites. Our fathers knew not the value of these lands, and parted with them for a trifle. The craft of the white man prevailed over their ignorance and simplicity. We have lost a rich inheritance; but it is vain to regret the past. Let us make the most of what little is left to us.

Nevertheless his thoughts went back to the days of Iroquois power, and carried him into some briefly retrospective remarks, which he closed by saying : —

Brothers, these are painful thoughts. It is painful to think that in the course of two generations there will not be an Iroquois of unmixed blood within the bounds of our State; that our race is doomed, and that our language and history will soon perish from the thoughts of men. But it is the will of the Great Spirit, and doubtless it is well.

Most picturesque of all who lingered around that dying council fire [says Mr. Howland] was the figure of old Solomon O'Bail, "Ho-way-no-ah," the grandson of that wisest of Seneca chiefs, John O'Bail, "Gayant-hwah-geh," better known as Cornplanter. His strong, rugged face, deeply seamed with the furrows of advancing age, was typical of his race and of his ancestry, and was expressive of a remarkable character. His dress was of smoke-tanned buckskin with side fringes, and all a-down his leggings were fastened little hawk-bells, which tinkled as he walked. Shoulder-sash and belt were embroidered with oldtime beadwork, and around his arm above the elbows were broad bands or armlets of silver. From his ears hung large silver pendants and, strangest of all his decorations, deftly wrought long ago by some aboriginal silversmith, was a large silver nose-piece that almost hid his upper lip. His headdress was an heirloom made of wild-turkey feathers fastened to the cap with such cunning skill that they turned and twinkled with every movement of his body.

He had been an attentive listener to all who had spoken, and as the memories of the past were awakened, the significance of the occasion filled his heart and the expression of his honest face showed that he was deeply moved. Especially significant to him was the presence at this council fire of the Mohawk chief, Colonel Kerr, and the burden of his soul was that the broken friendship of the League should be once more restored. His speech was the most dramatic incident of the day. It ended with these words: —

"In the last war with England the Mohawks met us as foes on the warpath. For seventy-five years their place has been vacant at our council fires. They left us when we were strong, a nation of warriors, and they left us in anger. Brothers, we are now poor and weak. There are none who fear us or court our influence. We are reduced to a handful, and have scarce a place to spread our blankets in the vast territory owned by our fathers. But in our poverty and desolation our long-estranged brothers, the Mohawks, have come back to us. The vacant seats are filled again, although the council fire of our nation is little more than a heap of ashes. Let us stir its dying embers, that by their light we may see the faces of our brothers once more.

"Brothers, my heart is gladdened by seeing a grandson of that great chief Thay-en-dan-ega-ga-onh [Captain Brant] at our council fire. His grandfather often met our fathers in council when the Six Nations were one people and were happy and strong. In grateful remembrance of that nation and that great warrior, and in token of buried enmity, I will extend my hand to our Mohawk brother. May he feel that he is our brother and that we are brethren."

The Indian character is reticent and hides the outward evidence of deep feeling as unmanly; but as the aged man spoke the tears rolled down his furrowed cheeks, and as he turned and held out his beseeching, friendly hand to the haughty Mohawk, strong ejaculations of approval broke from the lips of all his dusky brethren. With visible emotion Colonel Kerr arose and warmly grasped the outstretched palm. "My brother," said he, "I am glad to take your hand, once more held out, in the clasp of friendship; the Senecas and the Mohawks now are both my people." "My brother," said O'Bail, "may the remembrance of this day never fade from our minds or from the hearts of our descendants."

As speaker after speaker had addressed the council, the hours slipped swiftly by, and only the embers of the fire still glowed, when, at a pause towards the close, there came a surprise for all who were present, as one of the palefaced guests quietly arose and, stepping to the circle of redskinned orators, spoke to them in their own tongue. It was the tall figure of Orlando Allen of Buffalo, then in his seventieth year, who addressed the Council. Mr. Allen, who came to Buffalo when a boy, had had much to do with the Senecas of the neighboring reservation in his early years, and acquired then a command of their language which he had not wholly lost. Using it now in a few words of greeting and introduction he turned to English speech, and gave interesting reminiscences of the Senecas of the last generation whom he had known.

When Mr. Allen had ended his interesting address, President Fillmore, with a few kindly words, presented, on behalf of Mr. Letchworth, a specially prepared silver medal to each of those who had taken part in the council. . . . This ceremony ended, Nicholson Parker, who made the opening speech, arose, and in a few words, gravely and softly spoken in his native tongue, formally closed the council. Then turning to the white guests, whom he addressed as his younger brothers, he spoke the farewell words — ending thus: "The Hó-de-no-sáu-nee, the People of the Long House, are scattered hither and yon; their league no longer exists, and you who are sitting here to-day have seen the last of the confederated Iroquois. We have raked the ashes over our fire and have closed the last council of our people in the valley of our fathers." As he ended, his voice faltered with an emotion which was shared by all present. He had spoken the last words for his people, fraught with a tender pathos that touched the hearts of those who heard him with a feeling of that human brotherhood in which, " whatever may be our color or our gifts," we are all alike kin.

For a few moments there was a becoming silence, and then David Gray — name beloved of all who knew him — the poet-editor of the " Buffalo Courier," rose and read

THE LAST INDIAN COUNCIL ON THE GENESEE

    The fire sinks low; the drifting smoke
        Dies softly in the autumn haze,
    And silent are the tongues that spoke
        The speech of other days.
    Gone, too, the dusky ghosts whose feet
        But now yon listening thicket stirred;
    Unscared within its covert meet
        The squirrel and the bird.

    The story of the past is told;
        But thou, O Valley, sweet and lone, —
    Glen of the rainbow, — thou shalt hold
        Its romance as thine own!
    Thoughts of thine ancient forest prime
        Shall sometimes tinge thy summer dreams,
    And shape to low poetic rhyme
        The music of thy streams.

When Indian Summer flings her cloak
   Of brooding azure on the woods,
The pathos of a vanished folk
   Shall haunt thy solitudes.
The blue smoke of their fires, once more,
   Far o'er the hills shall seem to rise,
And sunset's golden clouds restore
   The red man's paradise.

Strange sounds of a forgotten tongue
   Shall cling to many a crag and cave,
In wash of fallen waters sung,
   Or murmur of the wave.
And, oft, in midmost hush of night,
   Still o'er the deep-mouthed cataract's roar,
Shall ring the war-cry, from the height,
   That woke the wilds of yore.

Sweet Vale, more peaceful bend thy skies,
   Thy airs be fraught with rarer balm!
A people's busy tumult lies
   Hushed in thy sylvan calm.
Deep be thy peace! while fancy frames
   Soft idyls of thy dwellers fled; —
They loved thee, called thee gentle names,
   In the long summers dead.

Quenched is the fire; the drifting smoke
   Has vanished in the autumn haze.
Gone, too, O Vale, the simple folk
   Who loved thee in old days.

> But, for their sakes, — their lives serene,
>   Their loves, perchance as sweet as ours, —
> Oh, be thy woods for aye more green,
>   And fairer bloom thy flowers.

It was the fitting close to a memorable day.

To these concluding words of Mr. Howland, is it going beyond the truth to add that Mr. Gray had sung the requiem of the Senecas in the most exquisite verse that the fate of the red men has ever called forth?

Some hours after the closing of the ceremonies of the council, Mr. Letchworth, yielding to an earnest request of his Indian guests, was formally adopted and initiated by them into the Seneca Nation, and given the name "Hai-wa-ye-is-tah," which was interpreted as signifying "The Man who always does Right" — or "the Right Thing."

As will have been noted in the preceding account, the descendants of Mary Jemison, "the white woman," had their place of distinction among the chiefs; and she was, indeed, a notable character in the history of the Seneca Nation. The story of her life with the Indians, first as a

Mary Jemison, "the White Woman"

captive, from childhood, and then as a freely willing member of their community, interested Mr. Letchworth greatly. He conceived a high estimate of her character, and had pleasure in giving permanence to memorials of her remarkable association with the Seneca dwellers on the Genesee. She was a daughter of immigrants, probably from Ireland, though her knowledge of their nativity was uncertain, and was born at sea during their voyage, in 1742 or 1743. Her father took a farm on the western border of Pennsylvania, and, according to her remembrance of the parental home, the family prospered and were happy for several years. Then came sudden destruction to this hopeful household, almost at the first stroke of the cruel French and Indian War, in 1755. A band of six Indians and four Frenchmen came upon the family on a pleasant day of that spring, and seized all but the two older sons, who escaped. For two days the captives were together, dragged in a hurried march through the wilderness; but on the second night, when they camped, Mary and a little boy from another family were taken apart from the rest, and she never saw any of her kin again. She learned afterwards that her father, mother, a sister, and two brothers were killed that night.

Mary was taken to the French Fort Du Quesne, where Pittsburg was founded a little later, and there her captors, who were Indians of the Shawnee tribe, gave her to two squaws of the Seneca Nation, who lived in a Seneca village farther down the Ohio River. These women were mourning the death of a brother, lately slain, and they solaced their grief for him by adopting this child, to be their sister. They treated her with fond kindness, and made her life as happy as they could. So, too, as her own account represents, did the husband, a Delaware Indian, to whom they gave her some years later and with whom she lived until she had borne two children, to one of whom she gave her father's name, Thomas Jemison, and his descendants are still carrying down that name. She described her first Indian husband as having been a noble man, who won her love. She parted from him presently, however, to visit her Indian sisters, who had gone northward from the Ohio two years before, to join their mother and other relatives at the main settlement of the Seneca people, at Gen-nis-he-yo, "the beautiful valley" of the river which we, keeping the Indian name imperfectly, call the Genesee. With two Indian brothers she made the long journey of some hundreds of miles on foot, carrying her youngest child on her back, in the Indian way; and she arrived at Gen-nis-he-yo in good health. Her husband was to have followed her in the next spring after their parting; but he did not come, and after some months she learned that he had died. Two or three years later she married again. Her second husband, named Hiokatoo, must have been more than twice her age, but she lived with him until 1811, when he died at the reputed age of 103. He was said to be a merciless savage warrior, whose cruelties shocked her; but he treated her with kindness and she spoke well of him to her friends.

Excepting at the time of General Sullivan's expedition against the Senecas, in 1779, when the Genesee Valley was devastated by his army, Mary Jemison appears to have lived in what had become a state of comfort to her, and was so fairly contented that she refused opportunities, when they came, to exchange it for a life with people of her own race. The red men were now her people; she identified herself with them, and they held her in profound respect. At their great "Big Tree Council," in 1797, they granted to her by deed a magnificent tract of the choicest land in the Genesee Valley, containing nearly eighteen thousand acres, measuring, east and west, more than six miles in length, with a width of more than four and three fourths miles, having the Genesee River running through it. It was a tract of her own choosing, and included the ground on which she had lived since the Sullivan invasion of the valley. It was known in her day and is still known as the Gardeau Tract or Reservation. In 1823 she was induced to sell most of this superb estate to white purchasers, who guaranteed to her and her successors forever a yearly payment of three hundred dollars. A little later, when most of the Senecas had sold their lands in the valley and left it, to settle on other reservations,—Buffalo Creek, Tonawanda or Cattaraugus,—Mary Jemison grew lonely in the midst of white neighbors, and she not only sold her remaining lands, but gave up her annuity for some moderate payment of money in hand. With the proceeds she came to Buffalo and established a home for herself and for a married daughter, with the latter's husband, George Shongo, and five grandchildren. In some transaction with a white man whom she trusted, her little capital was soon lost, and she was dependent thereafter on her son-in-law and daughter for support. She died in September, 1833, aged ninety or ninety-one years.

The facts of Mary Jemison's extraordinary life were obtained from her and first published in 1824, by James E. Seaver, of Batavia, New York. In an introduction to the narrative, Mr. Seaver remarked that her first association "with moral, social, civilized man, from the time of her childhood," may be dated at 1797, when the Indian lands on the Genesee were sold and white settlers began to come into them. "Still," he adds, "she had retained her native language with great purity, and had treasured up and constantly kept in her own breast all those moral and social virtues by the precepts of which civilized society professes to be guided. . . . In all her actions [she] discovered so much natural goodness of heart that her admirers increased in proportion to the extension of her acquaintance." Mrs. Asher Wright, whose long missionary labors, with her husband, among the Indians of western New York are well known, saw Mary Jemison in the last year of the latter's life, and gathered much information about her, from which she drew this conclusion: "From all that I have learned of her, from those who were, for years, contemporary with her, she possessed great fortitude and self-control; was cautious and prudent in all her conduct; had a kind and tender heart; was hospitable and generous and faithful in all her duties as a wife and mother."

The original edition of Mary Jemison's autobiography, as put into writing by Mr. Seaver, is now one of the rarest of American books. A number of reprints and abridgments were published, in this country and in England, prior to 1877, when Mr. Letchworth acquired ownership of the plates of one of these, which had been edited, in 1856, by the eminent student of Indian History, Mr. Lewis H. Morgan, of Rochester. Mr. Letchworth then published an edition, with appendices of important new matter, contributed by William C. Bryant and Mrs. Asher Wright, and he republished the same in 1898, and again in 1910.

The removal of the ancient Seneca Council House from the farm at Caneadea, where it was exposed to destruction, to a prominent site in Glen Iris, was but the beginning of proceedings by Mr. Letchworth to save and to bring together, in that same place, what could be saved

Mary Jemison memorials at Glen Iris

of the fast disappearing relics of the Senecas, in the time of their lordship on and around the Genesee. Presently, a log house or cabin that had been built by Mary Jemison while she lived on the Gardeau Tract, for one of her married daughters, was brought over and placed near the Council House, at the entrance of an enclosure which holds both. Then, on the 7th of March, 1874, the remains of Mary Jemison were disinterred from the Indian Mission burial ground at Buffalo and deposited in a new grave, between the two buildings just named. Some displacement of these remains from their original grave was impending, as a consequence of the opening of a street through the burial ground at Buffalo, and the most fitting of places to receive them was that which Mr. Letchworth gave.[1] At the head of the grave he erected a tasteful monument, having on one side the inscription which the original gravestone had borne, and on the other side a second one reciting the facts

[1] Recently the remainder of the old Indian burial ground, not taken for a street, has been purchased by Mr. and Mrs. John D. Larkin, and given to the city for the purposes of a small public park. A brief record of its history, inscribed on a bronze tablet, is about to be fixed durably to a boulder placed on the ground.

of the removal. The original gravestone, much mutilated, is preserved in the adjacent cabin.

But Mr. Letchworth was contemplating a still higher honor to pay to the memory of Mary Jemison. As early as September, 1876, he wrote to a Dr. Munson, of Independence, Ohio, saying: "I am contemplating causing to be made a statue in bronze of 'The White Woman,' Mary Jemison. . . . I address you, having been informed that you have a retentive memory of her," and he asked Dr. Munson to give information as to her figure, features, dress, etc., for the guidance of the sculptor who might undertake the work. A third of a century passed, however, before this intention was fulfilled. But Mr. Letchworth rarely failed, to do what his mind had once decreed, and there was no failure in this. In the last year of his life, on the 19th of September, 1910, ten weeks before his death, the long contemplated bronze statue of Mary Jemison, erected on a pedestal near her grave, was dedicated with appropriate ceremony, under the auspices of the American Scenic and Historic Preservation Society. It is a much admired, beautiful work of art, by the sculptor Henry K. Bush-Brown, representing its subject as a young woman, in her Indian garb, as she must have appeared when she arrived at Gennis-he-yo, carrying her infant child, in the Indian mode, on her back.

The unveiling of the statue was attended by many of the officers of the American Scenic and Historic Preservation Society, including its president, Mr. George Frederick Kunz, of New York; its secretary, Mr. Edward Hagaman Hall, of New York; the chairman of its Letchworth Park Committee, the Honorable Charles M. Dow, of Jamestown, New York, and two of its trustees, Professor Liberty H. Bailey and Mr. Charles Delameter Vail. Addresses were made by each of these. Professor Arthur C. Parker, of the New York State Museum, who is a descendant of General Ely S. Parker, conducted the unveiling of the statue. The American flag which draped it was withdrawn by Miss Carlenia Bennett, assisted by Mrs. Thomas Kennedy, both of these ladies tracing descent from Mary Jemison.

On the morning following the unveiling an Indian dedicatory ceremony took place, which Professor Parker described in a subsequent letter to Mr. Letchworth, as follows:—

The ancient rule is that only the closest of friends and nearest of kin shall be at the graveside. Repre-

STATUE OF MARY JEMISON

senting you and your family were Miss Howland and Miss Bishop; representing the people of Mary Jemison's natal soil [Ireland] and her parents was Mr. J. N. Johnston; and representing the Indian family and her adopted nation were Mrs. Thomas Kennedy (*née* Sarah Jemison), called in Seneca Ga-wen-no-is, or Outpouring Voice, Miss Carlenia Bennett, Ga-o-yo-was, Sweeper of the Sky, and Arthur C. Parker, Ga-wa-so-wa-neh, a descendant of Handsome Lake and General Ely S. Parker.

The maiden was handed two ears of squaw corn by Mrs. Kennedy and bidden to cast four handfuls of the grain on the grave, from the foot to the head. Mrs. Kennedy then made a short address in which she said: "This is the corn which so often you cultivated. Many times you husked it in harvest and on the following spring sowed it again, and it grew. It is a symbol that as it dies only to spring up anew, likewise we shall live again. The birds eat it from the ground where we place it and fly again to the skies. This is like the body that tarries on the earth to eat of its fruits, but flies upward when the Great Wisdom knows it is time."

At Mrs. Kennedy's request Mr. Parker laid the grave fire, and, lighting it from four points, threw upon it the incense ordained for such purposes, the tobacco herb, which the Senecas know as O-yen-kwa-o-weh. The leaf from which it was cast was thrown to the flames, and an evergreen bough placed over the flames of the grave fire. The ears of corn were then handed by Mrs. Kennedy to Miss Bishop, with the instruction that they should be preserved as a memorial of the event. To the Indian all these things are symbolic and things to be obeyed.

As the party left the graveside, Indian file, each one gave one glance over his shoulder, to see that the thin blue stream of smoke still lifted to the skies, and with this last glance went away.

The securing of the Seneca Council House was substantially the beginning of an extensive collection of objects connected with Indian history and archæology. With effective assistance from Mr. Henry R. Howland, Mrs. Asher Wright, and other friends, Mr. Letchworth acquired, during the next thirty or more years, a very large and scientifically valuable store of archæological relics, illustrating the primitive arts of the North American Indians, together with objects interesting as memorials of the aboriginal history of the Genesee Valley and Western New York. For the housing of most of these a practically fireproof building, sheathed with iron and roofed with slate, was erected in 1898, within the Council House grounds. In this they were scientifically arranged, with much care, by Mr. Howland,

The Genesee Valley Museum

and the collection received the appropriate name of the Genesee Valley Museum. A "Guide" to the Museum, prepared by Mr. Howland and printed in 1907, states that it "contains about five thousand exhibits of stone implements, weapons, articles of dress, ornaments, ancient articles of copper, brass and iron, found upon the sites of old Indian villages, and other interesting specimens related to Indian life and customs, many of which have been deposited here for safe-keeping."

A prominent exhibit in the Museum, of more antiquity than the most prehistoric of the Indian relics, is furnished by the remains of a mastodon, unearthed in the summer of 1876 by men who were ditching a farm near Pike, not far from Glen Iris. These were bought by Mr. Letchworth, who had them mounted, at Rochester, by Professor Ward.

Among historical memorials in the Museum, the most interesting, perhaps, are a portrait of Major Moses Van Campen (painted during his life) and a tomahawk with which the Major, having fallen into the hands of a war-party of ten savages, in 1780, slew five of them in their sleep and made his escape. Captured a second time, he ran the gauntlet, at the Caneadea Council House, with success, as related already in this chapter, and again escaped death.

Another similar incident of the Revolutionary War, on the Seneca border, and having the same Council House scene, is commemorated, outside of the Museum, by a tree planted on its hundredth anniversary, August, 1879. The planting was by a son of Captain Horatio Jones, who, being no more than a boy, in a company of rangers, and taken prisoner by the Indians, was compelled to run the gauntlet at Caneadea, coming through it without hurt; whereupon he was adopted into Chief Cornplanter's tribe.

The famous "Big Tree" of the Genesee — the great oak which gave its name to the "Big Tree Treaty" of 1797, whereby the Senecas ceded to Robert Morris most of their lands west of the Genesee — is represented here by a liberal section of its huge trunk. This was given to Mr. Letchworth by the heirs of General James S. Wadsworth, of Geneseo, on whose estate it stood, near the river's edge, until a spring freshet in 1857 undermined it and caused its fall.

As one of the founders and supporters of the Buffalo Historical Society, organized in 1862, Mr. Letchworth was always identified actively and earnestly with the society's work. He was its president in 1878–79, and his address on retiring from the office was devoted in the main to a report of what had been and was being done by William C. Bryant, O. H. Marshall, himself, and others, to bring about a removal of the remains of Red Jacket, and other chiefs of the Senecas, to the Forest Lawn Cemetery of Buffalo, from the burial ground of the Cattaraugus Reservation, where the identification of them seemed likely to be lost. The councillors of the nation had assented to this removal, and it was accomplished not long afterward, under the auspices of the Historical Society. Ultimately a fine statue of Red Jacket was erected on the plot of ground which holds these remains.

Apart from their history, Mr. Letchworth showed always a warm interest in the Indian peoples themselves, and made careful use of his opportunities to promote their welfare. In that part of his career which has not yet been touched in this biography, when he came officially into the service of the public, as a commissioner of the New York State Board of Charities, he gave close attention to the Thomas Orphan Asylum, on the Cattaraugus Reservation, and was in constant correspondence with Mrs. Asher Wright, who continued the missionary work of her deceased husband on the reservation. Mrs. Wright's letters to him show how much she depended on his advice, his influence, and his contributions of money, to sustain the efforts she made to relieve distress and to introduce employments among the women and the young.

In the last year of his life Mr. Letchworth received (February, 1910) a gratifying recognition of the importance of what he had done for the promotion and illustration of Iroquois history. This came in the award to him of what bears the name of the " Cornplanter Medal," founded by Professor Frederick Starr, of Chicago University, in 1904. Funds for instituting the medal were obtained by the sale of pen-and-ink drawings of Indian games and dances, made by Jesse Cornplanter, a twelve-year-old Seneca lad of pure blood. The award, for Iroquois research, was confided to the Cayuga County Historical Society, of Auburn, New York. The medal is of silver, struck from dies cut by Tiffany & Co., of New York. The awards are made every two years. That to Mr. Letchworth was the fourth.

The historical associations of what is now Letchworth Park are not wholly confined to these memorials of the distant past and of a disappearing race; for it holds within its area a bit of ground that became sacred in the memory of many who fought for the Union half a century ago, and is cherished no less in the remembrance of their neighbors and friends. It was the site of the rendezvous camp of a notable regiment in the Union Army, formed originally as the 130th New York Volunteer Infantry, but mounted when it went to the front, in 1862, and known thereafter as the First New York Dragoons. This regiment, made up of volunteers from Wyoming, Livingston, and Allegany counties, went through hard experiences in the field. The camp in which it was assembled and organized for service was pitched on the eastern side of the river, not far from opposite to Mr. Letchworth's house, and within the bounds of his final estate. The survivors of the regiment, since their return, have been holding annual reunions on this ground, and have erected upon it a monument to commemorate the use it had in 1862. It is, assuredly, not the least in interest among the features of the park.

A memorial of the War of Rebellion

CHAPTER IV

CHILD-SAVING WORK: PREVENIENT

EARLY in 1873 Mr. Letchworth withdrew from all connection with the firm of Pratt & Letchworth, having deliberately resolved to devote his remaining years to philanthropic work. He was in his prime, at fifty years of age; the business which he dropped was highly prosperous and profitable; he had accumulated no great fortune in it, but there were safe promises of large wealth in what he gave up. To secure needed rest, or a pleasure-seeking freedom of life, many men in like circumstances may do as he did; but to quit the labors of the counting-room in mid-life, and at the crest of prosperity, renouncing their substantial rewards in order to take up an increased burden of labor, for no other reward than the satisfaction of doing good to one's fellow men, is surely a rare act.

It does not appear that any definite place or plan of labor in the field he wished to enter was in Mr. Letchworth's mind when he retired from the business that had occupied him for twenty-five years; but the place which seemed made for him was awaiting his acceptance of it, and he was called to it almost at once. In April, 1873, on the suggestion of his name by the Honorable James O. Putnam to Governor Dix, he was asked to become one of the commissioners of the New York State Board of Charities, filling a vacancy in the representation of the Eighth Judicial District (western New York), and he readily accepted the post. At about the same time he was offered the Republican nomination for Congress in the district of his country residence, where the nomination ensured election; but that proffer he declined. Neither tastes nor ambitions drew him toward public service in the political field.

Entering service in the New York State Board of Charities

The Board of State Commissioners of Public Charities — commonly referred to as the State Board of Charities — was in its seventh year of existence when Mr. Letchworth became a member. Prior to its creation, in 1867, there had been no state supervision over public charities in New York, though the need of some exercise of supervisory authority had been made apparent frequently, by the disclosure of uncorrected wrongs and evil conditions in charitable institutions of every kind. The Honorable John V. L. Pruyn, of Albany, had been for some years a leader in efforts to secure the needed legislation, and when, at last, authority was obtained for the constitution of the Board, he accepted the presidency of it, which he held until his death, in November, 1877. The other members of the Board in 1873, when Mr. Letchworth entered it, were Nathan Bishop, Howard Potter, Benjamin B. Sherman, of New York City (representing the three judicial districts of that city); James A. Degrauw, of Brooklyn; Harvey G. Eastman, of Poughkeepsie; Edward W. Foster, of Potsdam; Samuel F. Miller, of Franklin; John C. Devereux, of Utica; Martin B. Anderson, of Rochester; to whom were added, *ex officio*, five state officers, namely, the Lieutenant-Governor, the Secretary of State, the Comptroller, the Attorney-General, and the State Commissioner of Lunacy. The secretary of the Board was Dr. Charles S. Hoyt, who had been, as a member of the legislature, its earnest advocate, taking a leading part in the passage of the creative act.

Legislation in 1873, on the eve of the entrance of Commissioner Letchworth into his duties, had enlarged the jurisdiction and the powers of the Board in precisely the direction that he would prefer to have given to his work, so far as he would specialize it at all. The Board was now authorized to extend its inquiries concerning dependent children to private as well as to public institutions. The organic act of 1867 authorized the commissioners, or any of them, to visit and inspect annually, or as much oftener as they might deem proper, all charitable and correctional institutions receiving state aid. It gave authority to the commissioners to inquire and examine into the condition of all such institutions, as to their management, care of inmates, and other matters bearing on their usefulness and right influence; with power to administer oaths and to summon witnesses by compulsory process if necessary.

Enlarged jurisdiction of the Board

Of dependent children, the jurisdiction of the State Board of Charities, in 1873, extended over nearly 16,000, shown in the next annual report of the Board as follows:—

In county poorhouses,[1]	644
In city almshouses,	371
In orphan asylums and homes for the friendless,	7,739
In hospitals,	1,034
In reformatory institutions,	3,551
In institutions for foundlings and homeless infants,	1,824
In institutions for the blind,	9
In institutions for the deaf and dumb,	407
In institutions for idiots,	89
	15,668

Males, 9059.
Females, 6609.

The rearing of children in county poorhouses and city almshouses was the most serious of the evil conditions that had been engaging the attention of the Board since its work began. Public interest in the matter had been undergoing a slow awakening for several years, and a gradual movement of reformation was in progress; but it needed a push of individual energy, with a resolute will behind it, to break the impediments down.

Children in poorhouses

[1] For some reason, probably to be found in the statutes under which they were established originally, the county institutions of this character in New York are designated as "poorhouses," while those maintained by cities are called "almshouses."

Mr. Letchworth supplied that need. He seems to have resolved at once to make this, in a special way, his first field of work. No doubt he gave his colleagues to understand his readiness for what was certain to be an arduous task, and they took responsive action, as stated in the report of the Board for 1874 :—

At the meeting held in June last Commissioner Letchworth [elected Vice President of the Board at that meeting] was requested to give the subject [of the removal of children from poorhouses and almshouses] special attention, and was authorized to confer, personally and by letter, with superintendents of the poor and other officers, and also to institute such inquiries and examinations into the matter as he might deem desirable and proper.

As set forth in a later report of the Board, the conditions it had found at the outset of its undertakings in this direction were as follows : —

In the first examination of the poorhouses of the state, by the Board, in 1868, there were found in these institutions, not including New York and King's counties, 1222 children under sixteen years of age, or 17.41 per cent of all the inmates. The almshouses of New York City contained at the same time 630 children, and that of King's County 379, making a total of 1009, or 15.48 per cent of the inmates of these institutions. These last-mentioned almshouses had separate buildings for the children, but, as they were brought into constant association with adult pauper inmates, their situation was little or no better than that of the children in the county poorhouses. It thus appears that the number of pauper children in the state at that time was 2231, equivalent to 16.49 per cent of all the paupers. The examination and subsequent inquiries by the Board fully demonstrated that poorhouses were not fit places in which to rear children, and that all attempts for their improvement under such circumstances would be almost vain.

Commissioner Letchworth had not waited for the formal commission that was given to him by his Board in June, 1874, before taking up the special child-saving task which he chose to make his own. He saw in his own county a state of things which summoned him to the work as soon as official authority had come into his hands. A brief account of this beginning of his official service was written once by himself.

Mr. Letchworth's first child-saving work

The first work on which I entered after my appointment as a commissioner [he said], was that of correcting abuses in the Erie County Poorhouse, as affecting the care of the dependent children and the insane, and reforming the county system in reference to these two classes. There were at that time seventy-two children in the poorhouse from two years of age upwards. These were of all grades of mental, physical, and moral condition. Their associations and the influences surrounding them were degrading, and there was an entire absence of systematic moral and religious instruction. A school, or the semblance of one, under the charge of a daughter of one of the supervisors, was maintained; but the freedom of the place, the absence of necessary rules, and the listlessness of the pupils, made the attempt to benefit them by this means abortive. I saw no other way to effect a complete reform than by the removal of the children.

Through the influence of the press, so far as it was favorable to my views, I endeavored to create an intelligent public opinion on the subject. Personal appeals were made to members of the Board of Supervisors and to influential persons interested in charitable work. Conferences between managers and officers of the orphan asylums and the Superintendent of the Poor and myself were held, at which I had the opportunity to set forth my views. The public conscience was at length awakened, and I was formally invited to come before the Board of Supervisors and address them on the subject, which I did in an earnest appeal. With the Superintendent of the Poor, who had become interested, I examined all of the institutions in the county where children were cared for, in order that we might bear testimony as to the kind of care the children in them were receiving; also to ascertain whether they would receive what might be regarded as their quotas, in case all children were removed from the poorhouse. A director of one institution said she would send out her matron and direct her to select six children whom they would receive. She was told that that would not answer; that this movement meant the removal of all. The kettle must be cleaned and scraped to the bottom.

At my request Dr. H. P. Wilber, the humane and intelligent Superintendent of the Asylum for Feebleminded Children, at Syracuse, came to Buffalo twice to examine children with reference to receiving them there. He concluded to take seven, who were not intellectually suited to orphan-asylum care. Among them was a crippled boy, so deformed that he could not walk. His legs were curled under his body, and he was obliged to sit through the day on the floor. His only mode of locomotion was by placing his hands on the floor at right angles with his wrists and arms and lifting himself along. He was not a bright boy, but fairly intelligent. His case was a sad one, as his future seemed pointed to a life in the poorhouse. Some two years later, when I was visiting the institution at Syracuse, as I stood in one of the classrooms, a lad about twelve years old, with a bright, smiling face, came to me from across the room, saying, "How do you do, Mr. Letchworth," and advanced to shake hands with me. Dr. Wilber said: "You do not remember this boy. This is ——, the crippled lad from the Erie County Poorhouse, who used to walk with his hands." I learned that the efforts of Dr. Wilber, assisted by physicians in Syracuse, had enabled the boy to walk erect. In exercises at the blackboard which I saw him take part in he did not differ materially in appearance from the boys around him. As I looked on his bright, happy face and watched his natural movements I could not but breathe a silent blessing on good Dr. Wilber. All the other boys taken from the poorhouse with the cripple were promising pupils, considering their mental condition.

With the approval of the county supervisors and the coöperation of the boards of managers of the various orphan asylums, all the children were finally removed from the poorhouse and the system of rearing children there was effectually broken up.

In a paper on the "Placing-Out System in Dealing with Dependent Children," written some years ago by Mrs. Robert McPherson (matron of the Buffalo Orphan Asylum at the time of this rescue of children from the poorhouse, and, later, the invaluable agent of the Board of Supervisors for placing homeless children in families), the great deliverance in Erie County is spoken of as having been accomplished, in the main, if not entirely, on one definitely named day. Said Mrs. McPherson: —

One of the most gratifying and pleasing sights I have ever witnessed was the exit of the dependent children of Erie County, on that memorable morning in February, 1874, when they were removed from their pauper home to happier surroundings. As I looked on those interesting children, seated in the carriages that had been provided for their transfer to the various asylums in the city of Buffalo, a prayer trembled on my lips that their future might be one of industry, honesty, and independence. In my general child-saving labor I have been privileged to follow the history of many of those children, and as I see them now, — self-reliant, self-sustaining men and women, — I realize how much they owe to that friend of children, the Honorable William P. Letchworth, by whose unwearied efforts and personal solicitations for their admission to institutions they were released from the bondage of chronic pauperism long before the mandatory law, compelling the removal of children from the poorhouses of New York State, was passed.

Seemingly Erie County was the first in the state to purge its poorhouse of the pauperizing and corrupting mixture of children with adults. Elsewhere the reformation movement was slow in response to the strenuous pressure upon it which the new State Commissioner of Charities was bringing to bear. Eight months after the Erie County deliverance he wrote to Secretary

Hoyt (October 5, 1874) that he had received reports of action on the removal of children by boards of supervisors in only three other counties, namely, Jefferson, Madison, and Yates. Throughout that year he had been laboring as no other official in the state is likely to have been laboring at the time. His correspondence discloses the intensity and ardor of feeling that went into his work; his special report to the Board, at the end of the year, shows how big a task of inquiry and investigation he had performed, and what a mass of information he had gathered up. He was executing a mission that engaged his whole heart. He strove to torment all consciences with his own burning sense of the deadly wrong done to homeless children by housing and classing them with pauperized adults. He could not bear the thought of allowing a single child to be so ruined when it might be saved.

Writing to Dr. Hoyt, the secretary of the Board, in August, he said: "I am working incessantly; almost, I might say, night and day, on the children question. . . . I hope you will plead earnestly wherever you go for the removal of the children from the poorhouses. If by your intercession a single child is saved from perdition, how vast are the results and how remunerating the labor. I rely greatly on you in carrying on this work, knowing your influence with county officials."

In June he had secured the privilege of addressing a state convention of the superintendents of the poor, at Rochester, and drew it into an earnest discussion of the subject, resulting in the adoption of a resolution that "the superintendents of the poor of the State of New York carry out as far as practicable the recommendations of Commissioner Letchworth." Newspaper discussion was thus started, and presently Mr. Letchworth was enabled to gather up an impressive body of opinion from leading journals, together with resolutions from boards of supervisors in different counties, and with expressions from some former governors, and others, condemning the retention of children in poorhouses; and this he published in an effective pamphlet, to which a wide distribution was given — all at his personal expense.

Instances of personal expenditure in promotion of public causes, like this of the pamphlet printing, were incessant throughout Mr. Letchworth's official career. For example, in December of the year we are now reverting to, we find

CHILD-SAVING: PREVENIENT

him asking and receiving permission to print at his own expense a paper by his colleague, President Anderson, of Rochester University, on "Alien Paupers," which should have, as he thought, a public circulation.

The special report submitted by Commissioner Letchworth at the close of the year 1874 showed the number of children remaining in the poorhouses of the state at the several dates of inquiry, in that year, to be 615, of whom 362 were boys and 253 were girls. The infants under two years of age numbered 143. Of the remainder, 348 were between two and ten years of age; 124 were from ten to fifteen in years. The fathers of 329 and the mothers of 115 were known to be intemperate; 32 were known to be descendants of pauper grandfathers; 47 of pauper grandmothers; 105 of pauper fathers; 441 of pauper mothers; 249 had brothers and 223 had sisters who were or had been paupers; 204 were of illegitimate birth; 190 were born in the poorhouse.

First official investigation and report

Thoughtfully discussing the exhibit of dreadful facts, Mr. Letchworth laid an impressive stress on the deadliness of the effect on character in childhood which must be produced by such pauperizing examples and influences as a poorhouse surrounds them with. "A study into the history of pauperism," he wrote, "shows that this condition is rarely reached except through a gradual 'letting-down' process, sometimes descending through two or more generations before culminating." Hence the vital importance of breaking up that degenerative process at the point of its passage from one generation to another, by removing children "from poorhouse life and its stigma," "to place them, immediately upon their sinking to the line of public dependence and before being stigmatized as paupers, among such surroundings and under such remedial influences as shall be likely to reclaim them."

Of the labor which his report represented and the difficulties encountered in it he gave some indication, saying that it had occupied his entire time, with that of an assistant,—employed by himself, which fact he did not state. He adds: "A widely extended field has been travelled over. I have found the records relating to this and kindred subjects very incomplete, and sometimes difficult to reach. . . . Previous to the convening of the boards of supervisors, the records of the proceedings of the boards of such counties as had taken action in reference to the care and maintenance of their pauper children elsewhere than in the poorhouse were carefully examined, so far as they were accessible, for a period extending back from fifteen to twenty years. The difficulty of reaching the reports of the several boards made the work of compiling this material protracted and laborious. Printed proceedings of the boards of supervisors were in many cases not found on file in the county clerk's offices of the several counties, and, when found, were seldom properly indexed."

Thus far in the undertaking to bring about a removal of dependent children from association with adult paupers there had been nothing but persuasion and some pressure of public opinion to bring to bear on the local authorities concerned. Now Commissioner Letchworth invoked the aid of mandatory law. Calling attention to the fact that, by statute, it had already been made "obligatory upon county officials to transfer every deaf-mute child of a certain age, becoming a dependent, to asylums for instruction," and that virtually the same had been done in the case of other defectives, he asked " whether a statute extending the benefits of this principle to other dependent children would not be desirable, —

Securing mandatory legislation

requiring county officials to place in families or fitting asylums all children over two years of age, excepting unteachable idiots and others unfitted for family care, who become dependent, and prohibiting their being hereafter committed to poorhouses."

On this suggestion the State Board of Charities, at the meeting to which the report containing it was submitted, acted promptly, and recommended in its general report to the legislature that "the commitment of children of intelligence over two years of age to county poorhouses be hereafter prohibited by statute, and that the proper authorities be required to remove all such children now in those institutions and provide for them otherwise, within a reasonable, specified time." The legislature responded with equal promptitude, passing a mandatory act which declared that on and after January 1, 1876, no child over three and under sixteen years of age, of proper intelligence and suited for family care should be committed or sent to any county poorhouse of the state, and that all children of this class then in the county poorhouses should, within the time named, be removed from such poorhouses and provided for in families, asylums, or other appropriate institutions. The law enjoined the boards of supervisors of the several counties to take such action in the matter as might be necessary to carry out its provisions.

With this backing of positive law and the hearty coöperation of his colleagues in the State Board of Charities, Commissioner Letchworth, in his special mission of child-saving from pauperism, had only to contend thereafter with difficulties in some counties that arose from a present deficiency of institutions to which the pauper children could be removed. He had satisfied himself that, generally throughout the state, the required transfers could be made without overtaxing the capacity of existing asylums, etc., provided that proper exertions were made systematically at the asylums to place their children in families — which ought to be the constant aim. This now gave him a new special duty — to inspire earnestness and energy in the work of securing good family homes for the homeless children of the state, to the end that no public asylum for such children, of good promise in body and mind, should be conducted otherwise than as an agency for their early introduction to family life in reputable private homes.

[sidenote: Homes for homeless children]

In a paper read by Mr. Letchworth before the State Charities Aid Association, after the passage of the Act of 1875, called "the Children's Act," he said:—

It was thought at the time of the passage of the Act of 1875 (chapter 173), for the better care of pauper and destitute children, which required that they should be removed from poorhouses prior to the 1st of January, 1876, that accommodation existed in the state for all children of this class in families and orphanages. This proved to be the case. The children were either placed in families by the officials, or orphanages were availed of for their disposal. In many of the latter a more vigorous placing-out policy was adopted, and thus the emergency of providing for the great number of liberated children was promptly met. . . . I look upon the orphan asylum — call it by what name you please, orphanage, home of the friendless, or aught else, so that it be conducted on the principle of a temporary home — as being the most expeditious and efficacious means of restoring the child to family life. . . . The children once within the institution, it would appear then to be in keeping with sound policy to encourage the placing of them in families as quickly as they are prepared to enter. The case of every child upon entering an orphanage should be carefully considered with reference to its fitness for the family, and all habits and practices that might in any way lead to dissatisfaction and perhaps subsequent expulsion from a good family should be well understood and eradicated, if possible, by special training, before attempting to place it out.

Longer experience convinced him that a state supervision of the "placing-out" of orphaned children in private homes was necessary to prevent serious results from carelessness in that important undertaking. In a paper on "Dependent Children and Family Homes," read at the National Conference of Charities and Corrections, in Toronto, 1897, he said : —

<small>Final opinions</small>

In my observations, extending through twenty-three years of official inspection as a State Commissioner of Charities in New York, I found the wrongs which dependent children suffered from being placed in unsuitable homes, through indifference before placing them and inattention and neglect afterwards, to be very great. Legislators and philanthropists, however, are devoting their attention to correcting this evil. In the last session of the New York Legislature a bill was introduced under the auspices of the State Board of Charities providing that the work of placing out dependent children and of supervising them afterwards should be governed by rules established by the State Board of Charities. The legislature added a clause to the effect that all dependent children should be placed with foster parents of the same religious faith as the child.

As this could not always be practicable it was opposed, and the Governor disapproved the bill. In further remarks on the subject, Mr. Letchworth summarized the provisions of law in several states, and urged that, in every state, "a system should be provided regulating the manner in which homeless children shall be placed in families, and providing a method of supervision over them afterwards which is not obtrusive or offensive to foster parents."

One of the last official writings of Commissioner Letchworth, before his resignation from the State Board of Charities, gives some interesting details of the experience which had led him to the conclusions set forth above. It is a report to the Board "On the Erie County System of Placing Dependent Children in Families," dated November 14, 1896. It explains that "the plan of placing dependent children in family homes by a county agent was put in operation in Erie County in 1878"; that a salaried county agent was appointed, "authorized to remove children that were county charges from the asylums and to place them in families, either by adoption, by indenture through papers executed by the superintendent of the poor, or by verbal agreement." "Mrs. Robert McPherson was the first agent appointed. She had had large previous experience in placing out children, and she did her work carefully and conscientiously. In 1881 it became evident that it was impracticable for one person to do all the work, and provision was made for the appointment of an additional agent to place out Roman Catholic children." In the next year Mrs. McPherson retired from the work.

In the early part of 1896 certain cases were brought to the attention of Mr. Letchworth which led him to institute an investigation of the workings of this county agency, and his report recites with considerable detail the resulting disclosures, on which he remarks:—

It is impossible to suppress the conviction that great mistakes, if not wrongs, have been committed, when it is seen that careful search for some of the addresses given failed to reveal the homes where children were reported to have been placed; that information was obtained to the effect that a house in which a child had been placed by one of the agents had been raided by the police; that Mrs. ———, who took a child, kept a house of assignation; that a foster father was an ex-pugilist and a foster mother "slung beer"; and that certain families who took children were receiving public relief. . . . From the examination I have made of the Erie County methods of placing out children, and from instances of grave abuse that have come to my knowledge affecting dependent children placed out by various public officers, agents and agencies in other counties, I have come to the conclusion that the system of placing out children in this state should be radically reformed; and I respectfully recommend that this important subject receive the deliberate consideration of the State Board of Charities and of the legislature, in order that a proper system may be adopted throughout the state, which shall secure good homes to the dependent children placed out, and embrace official supervision and ample protection over them, after they have left the guardianship of asylums and officers of the poor.

Mr. Letchworth's long experience brought him finally to the further conviction that institutions provided for the care of homeless children should be brought into closer relations to the state and more closely supervised. This is indicated in an undated memorandum, found among his papers after his death. "I regard the child-saving work," he says in this, "as the most effectual means of upbuilding society, of reducing the volume of pauperism and crime, and of lessening the burdens of taxation"; and he argues that this work should be partly at public and partly at private cost, proceeding to say: " I am therefore led to believe, after a study of the different systems of caring for homeless children in different countries, that the institutions we call orphan asylums, children's homes, and juvenile reformatories, should receive a *per capita* allowance for each child under their care; that this allowance should be determined by the legislature, but should not be so large as fully to support the child, or to carry on the work of the institution, but leave a reasonable margin to be supplied from private means, in order to maintain an active and benevolent interest in the work conducted by these private corporations. These institutions I would have placed under the supervision of the Department of State,—a purely disinterested body, free from political or religious bias, —and organized after the manner of some of our state boards of charities."

The memorandum goes on to suggest that the institutions thus privately created and conducted, but partly supported by the state, should be licensed by a State Board, and be subject to yearly examination, on which the yearly renewal of their licenses should be made to depend. "In licensing the institution the question of religious instruction, whether Roman Catholic, Protestant, or Hebrew, should be left to the choice and discretion of the board of management. It should be provided, however, that the secular education of the inmates should be in accordance with the rules and regulations of the State Department of Public Instruction."

The remarkable effectiveness of Mr. Letchworth's work as a commissioner of the State Board of Charities was now recognized by all who gave attention to the governmental dealing with want and misdoing. They saw that a new force had come into that field of official service, and they welcomed it with acclaim. For example, the very eminent sociologist, Dr. Elisha Harris, then Corresponding Secretary of the Prison Association of New York, afterward Secretary of the State Board of Health, wrote to Mr. Letchworth in March, 1875: "Your study of the rights of children and of our duty to them and the state is worth a lifetime of toil. You have thrown such a true light on the almshouse children that the doors of good homes and the

[sidenote: The valuing of his work]

WILLIAM PRYOR LETCHWORTH WHILE PRESIDENT OF
THE NEW YORK STATE BOARD OF CHARITIES

hearts of thoughtful citizens and good women will open and bless them." Six months later we find Dr. Harris writing again : "It is by such persistent effort as yours for the friendless children that causes of crime and vice are to be repressed. It is not in the power of language to convey my thanks for your service in this matter."

With still more warmth did Miss Louise Lee Schuyler, President of the State Charities Aid Society, express her feeling in a letter to Mr. Letchworth written on the last day of that important year 1875. "I cannot," she said, "let this day go by without telling you how deeply I sympathize in your happiness at the thought of the hundreds of little ones whom you have, with the help of God, been instrumental in rescuing from lives of suffering and crime. All day I have thought of the little children I have seen — oh! so uncared for in those horrible poorhouses ; and to know that *to-day* they are away and happy (the last Randall's Island children left to-day) makes me very happy. *They must never go back*. And if those of us who are grateful for having been allowed to help you in the smallest way in your great work feel this, how grateful you must be that God has allowed you to do such blessed work. I know how devoted you have been to it, how self-sacrificing and faithful. Surely you have the reward of those who 'go about doing good,'—the deep joy and peace of those who are doing their Master's bidding. Your New Year will indeed be a happy one."

The year 1875 was one of the busiest for Commissioner Letchworth in his special en-deavor to arrest the pauperizing of children; but that undertaking did not absorb his whole thought. In his visitation of the county poorhouses he saw an amount of able-bodied and idle pauperism in them that was profoundly offensive to his sense of reason and right. He brought the subject before the annual state convention of superintendents of the poor, in June of that year. "My idea of a poorhouse," he said to them, "and when I say poorhouse I use the term as synonymous with almshouse, is that it should be a retreat for invalids, or those incapacitated to earn a livelihood. In other words, that a poorhouse should be a hospital, and that there should be barely enough healthy inmates, or of those in partial health, to care for the invalids.... Beyond this, I hold that able-bodied paupers have no place

Employment for paupers

in a poorhouse. Strictly speaking, the term 'able-bodied pauper' is contradictory. The statute, as you are aware, as found in Wade's Code relating to the poor, section 20, page 10, does not accord to healthy, able-bodied persons this kind of public charity. The precise language used is,—'that every poor person who is blind, lame, old, sick, impotent, or decrepit, or in any other way disabled or enfeebled so as to be unable by his work to maintain himself, shall be maintained by the county or town in which he may be.' If, notwithstanding, such as are able-bodied must be sent to poorhouses, I think they should be committed for a stated period, in order that, when put to work by the keeper, he may know how long he can rely upon their labor, and how much time he can profitably expend in giving instruction." He then proceeded to discuss in a very practical way the kinds of employment that could be given to such able-bodied inmates of the poorhouses. Firstly, needed labor for a considerable number could be applied to the " bringing of the poorhouse farm into the highest condition of productiveness, and its outbuildings into the best of order." Secondly, they could be employed on the roads of the poorhouse neighborhood, spending this pauper labor on them until they are made "as substantial as the old Roman roads." Thirdly, basket-making and the culture of the willow for its material offer an easily opened field for the employment of this kind of labor. And there are other openings to be found, if they are sought. His propositions were approved and endorsed by the convention, and nobody having anything to do with poorhouse management could by any possibility gainsay them; but it is probable that "able-bodied paupers" can still be found in our poorhouses, while the roads of their neighborhood are not yet "as substantial as the old Roman roads."

The main task of Mr. Letchworth in 1875 was to learn for himself and to report to his board and to the public the existing resources of the state orphan asylums and other institutions provided for the care of dependent children, and the conditions in each under which such care was being given. So thoroughly was this extensive survey carried out that the special report of it, presented by Commissioner Letchworth at the end of the year, fills 510 pages of the general report of the State Board of Charities for 1875.

Along with the preparation of that report there

went, moreover, an important continuation of the poorhouse investigation of 1874; and this, too, was reported within the year. It related to the children's department of the almshouse establishments of New York City, of which Mr. Letchworth's investigation had not been finished in time for inclusion in the report of the previous year. It does not seem to have been intended by the legislature that the Act of 1875, requiring the removal of children from poorhouses, should apply to the almshouses of New York City, which are under the control of a board of commissioners; but the courts gave a construction to the law which extended it to those institutions. "Then was presented," as Mr. Letchworth said afterwards, in writing of events at this time, "the curious spectacle of a change in the opinions of the metropolitan press; for while it had fully realized and condemned the system of poorhouse care for children in the rural districts, its continuance was thought necessary in the large city almshouses. Accordingly an appeal was made to the legislature to exempt New York City from the operation of the law." Probably nothing but Commissioner Letchworth's investigation could have prevented such legislative

Investigating child-pauperism in New York City

action. It gave the authority of knowledge to his remonstrances, even before the publication of his official report of facts disclosed.

The establishments maintained by the county and city of New York for the care of pauper children, located on Randall's Island, comprised an infant or foundling hospital, an idiot asylum, a nursery hospital, and "The Nursery." The report of Commissioner Letchworth related mainly to the two institutions last named, in which were 545 boys and 224 girls. "During the past year," he wrote, "I have made several visitations to these establishments, accompanied on one occasion by Commissioner Roosevelt. These visits were made with a competent stenographer. The buildings and inmates were carefully inspected and a minute inquiry made into the methods of administration."

The Randall's Island "Nursery"

In this part of his investigations he was assisted by his close friend, Mr. James N. Johnston, whose "rare tact, discrimination, and perseverance" he spoke of some years later, when referring to the work of this period, as having been invaluable to him. Mr. Johnston, he said, had undertaken what he did "for the love of the work, and for the good expected to result from it, rather than for any pecuniary consideration." How difficult and trying the task was on which Mr. Johnston spent a month of keen inquisition at Randall's Island is revealed in his letters to Mr. Letchworth written during that month of December, 1874. "There is no superintendent, keeper, or matron," he wrote in one, "who knows the history of any of the children or cares a fig about it. The sources of information, then, are the children themselves and the books. The facts elicited from the class of children, at their tender ages, are very unreliable. . . . The books give only the so-called age, the date of admission and discharge, and who brought the child to the Almshouse Nursery." Of the training received by these children he wrote: "Generally, the children in the school are not very far behind in their studies, for the class they represent; but they are far behind in the training that children should have to make them citizens of the Republic. The school, as you know, is under the Board of Education, and quite a corps of teachers is employed. . . . The women and employees about the place (I do not refer to the teachers) are, to say the least, hardly of the class to train young minds to noble thoughts."

Among the facts set forth by Commissioner Letchworth in his report were the following: "In the dense buildings of the Nursery and Nursery Hospitals, grouped quite closely together, there were at the time of the examination of this Board 773 girls and boys under sixteen years of age. Brought into more or less intimate association with these tender natures, were 23 females who had, either through misfortune or some controlling weakness of character, sunk into the rank of the dependent class. There were also 51 females who had drifted downward and had sunk into the rank of the criminal class, many of them, as has been shown, having been committed again and again for drunkenness and disorderly conduct, for street brawls and other offences which had rendered them amenable to penal servitude. There were also, going and coming on various duties, 40 male adults belonging to the pauper and criminal classes, making, in all, 114 persons who were at the time either actually paupers or criminals, or had been committed at some time as such, ... brought more or less into contact with the children. Even with the strictest rules forbidding it, the association of the children with these persons must, from the nature of the case, be inevitable; but, so far as our observations went, the rules did not even appear to forbid it." In this connection Mr. Letchworth quoted from a paper read at a recent congress of state boards of charities, written by the well-known English leader in charity work, Miss Mary Carpenter, who had visited the Randall's Island "Nursery," while in this country, and who wrote of it: "Seldom have I witnessed a more soul-sickening spectacle than the degraded women and incapable men having the charge of these children."

The most damning fact disclosed in Mr. Letchworth's report was that stated in the following paragraph: "Over this large community [of the Randall's Island institutions — pauper and criminal — as a whole], with a considerable extent of harbor shore, one nightwatch holds guard. The abuses which may result during the night hours to the helpless and unprotected may easily be imagined. On being questioned the watchman said: 'I walk around the hospital and go through every building except the girls' department. The workhouse women are not locked up at night. They go up at seven o'clock in the evening. There is nothing to prevent their going out and getting around the grounds, unless I am around. When I came here first I was disturbed by the boats coming to assist the women away.' It will be borne in mind that here is an island with miles of shore, abundance of ambush, subject to abuse within and without, and one night watchman over the nursery."

The report submitted abundant reasons for the conclusion to which it led, "that the whole Randall's Island Nursery system should be set aside agreeably to the statute, and that the children should be placed in asylums suited to their various needs, under the charge of those devoted to the interests of the young, or into good families where they may be trained and educated to useful and respectable citizenship." "The King's County nursery system was bad enough," continued the report, "but this is infinitely worse. That was not abolished by force of legal enactment alone, but by the exercise of an enlightened public sentiment."

Enlightened public sentiment, however, could not move Tammany to give up so important a part of the profitable machinery of its politics, nor would it surrender to a legal enactment without contesting it to the last. It was a weakened "Ring" at this time, not yet recovered

CHILD-SAVING: PREVENIENT

from the great overthrow of 1871; but it was busily and hopefully laboring to reconstruct the vicious fabric of its power, into which went just such material as the Randall's Island institutions supplied. Naturally, therefore, the sympathetic politicians of the legislature were being besought again to release New York County from the operation of the law, and Mr. Letchworth had grave fears that the Tammany demand would prevail. Writing to Mr. Johnston on the 8th of December, 1875, he said: "I do not feel safe from some reactionary steps by the legislature in the Randall's Island matter. There is certainly reason for grave apprehension; but I shall do all that I think it is becoming for me to do, in view of the position I hold, and trust to God's providence for results. . . . As to the treatment of the subject, I see but one way to handle it. If taken hold of at all it must be done fearlessly. 'God's truth' must be told."

In this spirit he gave battle to the politicians, leading and inspiring all the forces that could be rallied against them, for the rescuing of the pauperized children of Randall's Island from the evil influences they wished to maintain. In private letters he did not hesitate to say that the conditions at Randall's Island were the worst in the state and the most needing to be reformed under the new law. To the conductors of the New York *World* and the New York *Sun*, which had joined the cry for an exemption of New York County from the requirements of the law, he appealed for a suspension of judgment on the question until the report of his investigations could be laid before them. For some weeks he spared no effort to arouse influences that would overcome those working at Albany from the political rings of New York; and his efforts were not in vain. He succeeded, as he succeeded almost always, in defeating opposition from ignorant sources or sinister motives to measures and undertakings which he believed, on well-studied grounds, to be for the public good.

This was the second demonstration that Commissioner Letchworth, in his official service, had given of the very potent and peculiar executive force he possessed. One of the mildest, most gently mannered of men, — Quaker-bred, and realizing in his whole character the ideals of that culture of the quiet spirit, — he was capable, nevertheless, at need, of an iron determination

An exhibit of strong qualities

in what he undertook to do, and a persistence which never tired, never yielded to discouragement, and rarely suffered defeat. His first exhibit of those qualities was called out soon after he took his seat in the State Board of Charities. The Board was then becoming an object of attacks, inspired evidently by the manipulators of party politics, who had discovered that it might be made a useful instrument in their hands. The enlarged powers conferred on it in 1873 appear to have equipped it to their liking, as a piece of machinery for political work, and they lost no time in starting measures for bringing it under their control. An account of what occurred was written subsequently by Mr. Letchworth, as follows : —

As I was coming down Main Street, in Buffalo, one morning in the early part of 1874, I met Mr. Joseph Warren, editor of the Buffalo " Courier," who had just left the train after a night's ride from Albany. He informed me that action had been taken in the Senate the day before to abolish the State Board of Charities. I asked him upon what grounds. He could not tell me, but supposed it was in consequence of some irregularities. I told him that this was not possible, in view of the personnel of the Board and lack of opportunity on the part of the commissioners for deriving any personal advantage from their office. He had given little attention to the matter, but, as he then recalled what he had heard, there was some whispered scandal connected with the movement.

I went immediately to Albany and, seeking the president of the Board [Mr. John V. L. Pruyn], asked him the meaning of the attack. He could only divine that it was a political movement to bring the Board eventually under partisan control, as were the state prisons, over which there was but one superintendent. The movement had such backing that Mr. Pruyn thought nothing could be done. He had heard from several members of the Board, who expressed themselves as excessively chagrined and mortified, and declared their intention to resign. I told the president that I had not sought this office; that I had endeavored to discharge my duties faithfully during the short time I had held it; that I regarded this action as a reflection on my integrity, and that I should not rest quietly under it, but should demand an official investigation. He sympathized with the members of the Board in their chagrin, but did not feel like entering into an angry controversy over the action taken. He said, however, that he would sanction every effort I might make to protect the Board. With this assurance from the president I entered upon the campaign.

Senator Ganson, of Buffalo, a man of high character and a leader of one of the political parties, and

CHILD-SAVING: PREVENIENT

Senator King, leader of the opposite political party and chairman of the Senate finance committee, — a man of benevolent impulses, — espoused the cause of the Board on the floor of the Senate and were supported by others. The Board was finally vindicated and the charges were withdrawn, leaving it stronger than when the attack was made.

This issue having been set aside, I asked the chairman of the finance committee to insert in the appropriation bill an item of $3000 for the use of the Board in making an inquiry into the causes of pauperism and crime, — something it had been authorized to do by the previous legislature, but for which no appropriation had been made, and nothing had been done. The chairman of the committee, who was a friend of the Board, advised me not to ask for this grant, in view of the recent attack on the Board, and, though consenting to do this if I insisted, wished me to understand that he would not be responsible for the consequences. The appropriation was inserted, however, at my request, in the supply bill, and was approved by the committee.

As soon as the safety of the appropriation was well assured I took a train for New York and consulted with Dr. Elisha Harris, secretary of the Prison Association of New York (who had given much attention to the causes of degeneracy), with reference to the formulation of a schedule to be used in the examinations of inmates of the poorhouses and almshouses of the state. Having had some experience as a merchant in former years, it seemed to me desirable at this juncture — using the mercantile phrase — to take an account of stock, and that the Board could render a great public service by making such an inquiry. Dr. Harris very kindly prepared a schedule which, as subsequently modified by Dr. Hoyt, secretary of the State Board of Charities, to make it more conveniently applicable to the examination of the inmates of the poorhouses and almshouses of the state, was finally approved by the Board and used by Dr. Hoyt in the inquiry authorized by the legislature.

Thus the Quaker member of the Board, no more than fairly seated in it, was the one to spring to its defence and find cudgels for beating off the attack. Not only that, but the encounter roused him to push forward and snatch a positive trophy of victory from the discomfited assailants of the Board, in the form of an increased appropriation for its work. It was a striking revelation that he gave then of the reinforcement of energy, courage, earnestness, and sound practical judgment which his appointment had brought into the important body that supervises the public charities of the state. Without self-assertion or assumption on his part, there was a natural and necessary leadership in

CHILD-SAVING: PREVENIENT

what he did, which had recognition very soon in his election (June, 1874) to the vice-presidency of the Board, and to the presidency in 1877.

To return now to Commissioner Letchworth's investigation, in 1875, of the "orphan asylums, reformatories, and other institutions of the state having the care and custody of children," it appears, from a list found among his papers, that he visited that year one hundred and fifty-four institutions of that nature, great and small, in the State of New York, and that eight, only, existed which he had not been able to visit. It is certain that his official inspections were never perfunctorily performed, and it fairly fatigues one to think of the travel and labor which this investigation required, crowded as it was with other work into a single year. When preparing the elaborate report of it, in November, 1875, he wrote to the Secretary of the Board: "I am working very hard on my report, . . . to the extent of my strength, and if it is not completed in time it will be through no lack of effort on my part. I have set aside everything else, and am working on it not only every hour, but every minute except what I take for sleep. I

Survey of orphanages and reformatories

have also got Randall's Island nearly done. I have come out pretty strongly on this abomination, and Mr. Pruyn and yourself may think I need toning down; but I am inclined to think the people will sustain us in an outspoken position."

As set forth in the report, his chief aim in the inspection of orphan asylums, reformatories, etc., was "to obtain and present the views of as large a number as possible of those whose long experience in the care and reformation of children renders their opinions on the subject valuable; also, in the notes taken, to incorporate largely the language of those identified with asylums and reformatories, in order to illustrate better their workings. . . . The attempt has been made to outline with some care the system of at least one of each of the different classes of institutions, in the hope that the report, taken as a whole, might give a tolerably correct idea of the manner in which this great work of benevolence is carried on throughout the state. . . . In almost every instance minute inquiries have been made, the premises carefully inspected, and, with the assistance of a competent stenographer, full notes taken upon every department." The Commissioner's visits, he states,

CHILD-SAVING: PREVENIENT 149

in every case excepting one, were made unexpectedly to asylum officials.

The notes on institutions visited are preceded by an interesting presentation of opinions and suggestions, derived from the observations he had made, touching almost everything that has an important bearing on the location, construction, equipment, sanitation, economic management, and educational aims of these paternal establishments of the state. The report closes with the remark that "a general survey of the benevolent work carried on throughout the state, in asylums, reformatories, aid societies, industrial schools and other institutions for the care of children, gives one a higher conception of our humanity and its unselfish capabilities."

A certain number of copies of the three reports made by Mr. Letchworth of his investigations in 1874 and 1875 were subsequently bound together in a volume entitled "Homes of Homeless Children." In this volume the report on orphan asylums, reformatories, and other institutions for the care of dependent children in the State of New York, was followed by the general report on children in poorhouses and almshouses in the state, and the supplementary report on the pauper children of Randall's Island. In an introductory note it was stated that 1730 children had been removed from the almshouses of New York and King's counties alone, and that "the degrading system was forever set aside."

Summary of child-saving results

The removals, however, of healthy and intelligent children from association with adult paupers was not yet completely carried out. The mandatory law of 1875 had required such removal of all above three years of age. An act of 1878 went farther, requiring *all children over two years of age* to be removed from poorhouses, "without regard to their mental and physical condition"; on which the State Board of Charities, in its report for that year, remarked: "This law has not, as yet, been generally put in force, except in the case of the healthy and intelligent children. The poorhouses contain considerable numbers of unteachable, idiotic, epileptic, and [otherwise] diseased children, for many of whom no adequate public provision exists. In order fully to carry out the wise and humane intentions of the Act of 1878, some additional provision by the state for these classes will need to be made." Three years later, in its report for 1881, the

Board made the following statement of facts: "During the past year the Board, by its members and officers, made an examination and inquiry into the condition of the children between two and sixteen years old, in the various county poorhouses of the state. . . . The examinations show that there were seventy-one such children in the county poorhouses, forty-seven of whom were males and twenty-four females. Of these, thirty were idiots, mostly unteachable, nine epileptics, one paralytic, three crippled, ten otherwise diseased, and eighteen healthy and intelligent." These, of the last-named class, were said to be "mostly depraved and vicious children, some of whom had been in orphan asylums and returned as incorrigible." They were found in ten counties. In twenty-eight counties no children older than two years were found.

The reform for which Mr. Letchworth had labored so strenuously had been carried then, we may conclude, as nearly to completeness as the public provision for a better treatment of defective children than the poorhouses could give them would permit. Twelve years later (1893), in a "History of Child-Saving Work in the State of New York," prepared, upon request, for the Twentieth National Conference of Charities and Correction, held at Chicago during the Columbian Exposition, he could speak of it as a completed reform. "The reform," he said, "has been complete and effectual, and there are now virtually no healthy, intelligent children over two years of age subject to the soul-destroying influences of the county poorhouses or city almshouses of the state."

Substantially, so far as concerned his own state, the child-saving labors of Mr. Letchworth in this particular field were finished by the year 1876. The finest tribute paid to the great importance and effectiveness of the social service rendered in those labors came many years afterwards from an intelligent head of the finance department of the City of New York, where they had been most obstinately and violently opposed. Comptroller Edward M. Grout, in an official report on "Private Charitable Institutions in the City of New York," made in 1904, referred to this part of Mr. Letchworth's work as follows:—

Official tribute from New York City

In the early seventies charity workers, impressed with the iniquity of the almshouse system, determined to effect a change. A crusade against almshouses—

CHILD-SAVING: PREVENIENT

for it may properly be called that — found its leader in the Honorable William P. Letchworth, of Portage, New York, one of the indefatigable workers in the State Board of Charities. It is fair to call him the father of the movement to take children out of the degrading conventions in poorhouses and almshouses. In 1874 he began a systematic visitation of all charitable institutions, both public and private. He visited the orphan asylums, reformatories and institutions of all sorts and conditions. His investigation was broad and complete, for he went throughout the state with his stenographer and witnesses, noting facts and taking testimony. His energy and patience were exhaustless. He made elaborate reports, plans, diagrams and charts. These he presented to the State Board, and then to the legislature. Gathered together, these different reports made a volume of over six hundred closely printed pages. The result of it all was such an indictment of almshouses and of public institutions for children that the conclusions were irresistible.

After extended quotations from Mr. Letchworth's reports the comptroller goes on to say: —

The result of Mr. Letchworth's work was tremendous and overwhelming. The legislature asked, — "What can be done with these children, and where can they be placed?" Fresh from his examination of every institution in the State, Mr. Letchworth replied that the private institutions were the natural and logical way out. . . . As the year went by the opinions of Mr. Letchworth, urged also by the State Board and others, prevailed, and it was determined to follow the plan suggested. There appeared to be no other satisfactory solution to the problem. The city determined, definitely, either to turn all its dependent children over to the charitable institutions or return them to their parents and guardians, allowing them to make such choice among the institutions as their religious inclinations might dictate. . . . The last of the children were transferred from Randall's Island December 31, 1875; and in the report of the Commissioners for that year, presented to the mayor early in 1876, the whole matter was summed up in these words: " The Nursery on Randall's Island, by act of the legislature, was abolished with the close of the year, and it is prohibited by law to receive children over three years of age. The children have been removed and were distributed, some to the Protectory and others to different institutions of this city." Five and a half printed lines, the result of over six hundred printed pages of effort! And such effort!

This, then, is how and why and when the city of New York began to do so large a part of its charitable work through private institutions. It was a matter of investigation, resulting in a state law, and was a deliberate choice. It is true that many children were supported in private institutions, through various acts

CHILD-SAVING: PREVENIENT

of the legislature, prior to this date; but those cases were exceptional and individual. It was this law and these resulting acts which constituted what can be called a "system," and is often referred to as "the New York System," as against systems of charitable endeavor bearing the names of other states. New York City chose to care for its children in private institutions because it had tried public institutions for three quarters of a century, and was worse off at the end than in the beginning. Because the difference between the two systems was the difference between sight and blindness, disease and health, crime and morality, life and death. . . .

The conditions of child life in private institutions after they were taken from the almshouses and county houses, through the law of 1875, were revolutionized. It would be folly to say that the highest ideals were immediately realized; that would be expecting too much of human nature. Institutions increased in number. Their work was partly specialized or classified. Reformatories were few. Dependent children's institutions many. Everything, however, was greatly improved.

This emphatic official testimony from the metropolitan city affords conclusive evidence that the fight to rescue children from pauper-keeping establishments in the State of New York was fought and won by Commissioner

Letchworth, as the general commanding the reformatory forces in the state; and that it was won practically within the first three years of his service in the field.

But, while this finished his exertions on that particular child-saving line in New York, it carried him on the same line into other fields of struggle, to the same end. He was called to become a missionary in other states of the appeal against child-pauperism, and performed heavy labors in that mission for a number of years. In March, 1875, he addressed an argument on the subject to a convention of superintendents of the poor in Michigan. In September of the same year, at the Second National Conference of Charities and Corrections, held at Detroit, he read a paper received from the noted English philanthropist, Miss Mary Carpenter, entitled: "What shall be done for the Neglected and Criminal Children of the United States?" Miss Carpenter had recently visited America, and she keenly criticized conditions that she observed in some of the poorhouses and other institutions having the custody of children. Mr. Letchworth led the discussion of her paper, and made use of the opportunity to relate what New York had

[marginal note: Missionary work in other states]

been doing towards a reformation of the conditions in question. He also introduced resolutions recommending that the state boards of charities in various states use their influence to bring about legislation requiring the removal of children from poorhouses, reformatories, and all association with adult paupers and criminals, and that they be placed in families and appropriate institutions; recommending further that a systematic visitation of such children when placed in families be provided for, and that periodical reports of their condition, physically, morally and intellectually, be made to some supervising official. The resolutions, after discussion, were adopted unanimously.

In June, 1876, finding himself unable to attend the meeting of the International Prison Association, he wrote to the president of the association, Dr. E. C. Wines, expressing his regret, and saying: —

The branch of prison reform in which I feel the deepest interest is that of the prevention system. My own study of the subject has fastened the conviction in my mind that we must "dry up the fountain," and that the labor of philanthropy must be zealously directed to this purpose.... While the custom of rearing children under the evil influences of poorhouse life has received the condemnation of the legislature of this state, it is still prevalent in some others, and under more aggravated conditions than existed here. . . . Should you deem it proper so to do, I wish you would ask the consideration of the Congress to the following resolution : —

"Resolved, That this Congress recommends that the various organizations having for their object the reformation of prisoners use their efforts to bring about, wherever practicable, such legislation as shall cause dependent children to be removed from county poorhouses, city almshouses, common jails, and from all association with adult paupers and with criminals, and placed in families, asylums, or other appropriate institutions."

An earnest "Appeal on behalf of the pauper children in the poorhouses of Michigan" was addressed by Mr. Letchworth, in March, 1876, to the secretary of the Michigan Board of State Charities, for reading at the annual convention of superintendents of the poor, before which he had been invited to speak.

In 1877 he was called to discuss the subject of "Dependent Children" before a convention of the Directors of the Poor and Board of Public Charities of the State of Pennsylvania, held at Lock Haven. He had learned that conditions in the Pennsylvania poorhouses were very much as they had been in New York before the rescue of children from them, and he spoke on the subject very plainly, relating the experience and action in his own state, showing how easily the important change could be made. He besought his hearers, collectively and individually, to exert every possible influence on public opinion in favor of a removal of the young from poorhouse stigmas and contaminations. The result of his appeal was the adoption of a resolution by the convention recommending that dependent children "be provided for in orphan homes or asylums, now in operation, or in others which may be established, to be supported by private contributions, and by aid, encouragement, and coöperation from the state and from the counties, boroughs, and cities in which they are located, and to be subject to the supervision of the Department of Public Instruction and the Board of Public Charities."

Two years later, in September, 1879, he was asked to come again to the help of the supporters of this reform in Pennsylvania. The invitation came from the Organized Charity Society of Philadelphia, and, being unable to attend their meeting in person, he wrote a letter, which was published in pamphlet form. The argument and appeal in this for separating dependent children entirely from pauper and criminal associations was presented with great earnestness and force. "I feel," he said, in closing his letter, "that I can speak advisedly of the almshouse system as it affects children, for I have taken pains to visit, aside from great numbers in my own state, some of those in Massachusetts, Kansas, Nebraska, Minnesota, Rhode Island, Connecticut, Maine, New Hampshire, Vermont, Ohio, Indiana, and Missouri, and I find that an almshouse, poorhouse, or infirmary, as they are indifferently called, whether in the prairies of the West, on the hills of New England, or in the valleys of New York, is filled with baneful influences that depress and debase childhood." Here we have an intimation of the range of country over which he had now pursued his studies of the subject and the propagandist work he had undertaken. By correspondence, by addresses, by personal visits to institutions, he had contributed more or less to the arousing of public attention in all parts of the country to one of the most serious evils of the day.

In the next year, being invited to a state

CHILD-SAVING: PREVENIENT

convention of county poor officers in Ohio, and unable to attend, he wrote an extended "Appeal" to the convention on behalf of the pauper children of that state.

Even from Massachusetts, and as late as 1897, a call came to him for the help of his influence in securing the passage of an act to accomplish the separation of dependent children, adult paupers, lunatics, and criminals in the charitable and correctional institutions of that state, and he responded to it in a letter to the Honorable Samuel J. Barrows, which was made public, with commendatory comments by the Boston Press.

From July, 1880, until the following January, Mr. Letchworth was in Europe, not for rest or for pleasure, but on a mission of inquiry and observation, the most strenuous that his enlistment in social service had yet moved him to undertake. His special purpose was to see how other countries dealt with delinquent children and how they treated their insane, and thus to learn what they might have to teach with helpfulness to the solving of the two problems in public benevolence which now claimed the most of his thought.

Mission of observation abroad

Two years before this undertaking of studies abroad, he had written to a brother, who asked his advice on some matter concerning a hospital: "This subject of charity is a very broad one,—too broad, I imagine, for any one mind to cover it completely. Since taking up its study I have confined myself, firstly, to dependent and delinquent children, and secondly, to the care of the chronic insane. I cannot boast of having gone much further." Consequently he did not give the advice asked for. It is evident that he had made this choice, of subjects and objects on which he would concentrate his study and his work, soon after he entered the field of philanthropic public service; and he was strict in adhering to that concentration. As we have seen, he had trained himself from boyhood to define his undertakings and hold himself to them with resolution. This was the secret of his success.

Having substantially accomplished what he could for the dependent children of his state, the energies of his mind were directed now to the remaining two of his three chosen aims. There was far more of problem in these than in the subjects of his previous work, and he sought light on them from all that experience, practice, or theory, in Europe as well as in America, could afford. Hence his mission of inquiry abroad. What he learned in his tour and what use he made of the knowledge he acquired will be the subject of future chapters.

CHAPTER V

STUDIES OF PUBLIC PHILANTHROPY IN EUROPE

LANDING at Queenstown on the 8th of July, 1880, Mr. Letchworth spent two weeks in Ireland, visiting lunatic asylums, poorhouses, juvenile reformatories and orphanages, at Cork, Belfast, Letterkenny, and Dublin. He received a favorable impression as to the humanity and intelligence of the treatment of the insane at each of the four institutions for that purpose which he went through, and their construction, equipment, and methods are carefully described in the book which he published subsequently, on "The Insane in Foreign Countries." The Richmond District Lunatic Asylum, at Dublin, commanded his attention especially, and he characterized it, after having extended his survey to the whole United Kingdom, as ranking, in its management, "among the foremost institutions of its kind in either Ireland or Great Britain." Its superintendent, Dr. Joseph Lalor, was called "the father of the school system as applied to asylums." Dr.

<small>Irish insane asylums</small>

THE MIDDLE FALL, GLEN IRIS

Lalor's treatment of mental disorder was founded on the "efficacy of employment and training." "The main objects kept in view here," wrote Mr. Letchworth, "are to provide varied occupations for as many as are able to work; to apply a system of education that will divert and strengthen the mind; and to promote by every conceivable means the happiness and welfare of the inmates."

While in Dublin he visited a number of reformatory institutions, both Catholic and Protestant, and found much in them to interest him. St. Kevin's Reformatory, two miles from the city, conducted by the Oblate Fathers of Mary Immaculate, who gave training to two hundred and eighty boys, he found occupying, as its original building, one of the barracks erected by the military in 1798. Most of the additional buildings, including a chapel, had been constructed by the boys, who were instructed in many trades, and cultivated a farm, with a large garden, the latter, especially, showing excellent work. On entering the institution every boy was given a certain standing of honor, which he lost if he did anything wrong, and the restoration of which he must earn.

Irish reformatory institutions

The Rehoboth Place Reformatory (Protestant), a small institution, attempted no confinement of its thirty-seven boys. They were surrounded by no walls. If they chose to run away they could do so; but then they were almost surely caught and sent to the City Male Prison, which was a much less attractive place. No whipping was done in the Reformatory; no boy had been struck a blow within the past three years. Sometimes, when punishment became necessary, they were confined in a cell, with a half allowance of bread and water. Another Protestant Reformatory and Institute, for girls (Cork Street), did resort to corporal punishment at times, though lightly, and to cellular confinement; but "the most effectual effort is to keep the girls employed" was Mr. Letchworth's note. They were all knitting when he visited the place.

After leaving the island Mr. Letchworth wrote home: "I had a very interesting experience in Ireland and learned much; some things that will be of advantage to our state pecuniarily, if adopted, and others that will relieve suffering humanity." Passing from Ireland into Scotland, he became at once interested in some peculiar features of

Scottish treatment of the insane

the Scottish system of dealing with insanity, — especially the "boarding-out" of pauper patients in the families of small farmers, which is claimed to be for their good as well as economical in cost. About one fifth of the Scottish insane were found to be provided for in this way. For the large remainder a good provision of asylums was made, under district boards and a General Board of Commissioners of Lunacy which supervised the whole. Mr. Letchworth sought out a considerable number of the country cottages in which these mentally disordered boarders were being entertained, and what he saw of their situation is described in his work on "The Insane in Foreign Countries"; but he intimates neither approval nor disapproval of the system in this account of it. Subsequently he studied the workings of the same practice in Norway and Belgium, and it receives a cautious discussion in the admirable summary of conclusions which appears in the final chapter of his book.

At Glasgow, Edinburgh, Dundee, and elsewhere in Scotland, he visited a considerable number of asylums for the insane; and also a number of institutions in which children are the subjects of public care. Three only of the Scottish asylums, namely, Woodilee, Mid-Lothian and Peebles District, and Morningside, are reported on in his published work. The Woodilee Asylum, at Lenzie, near Glasgow, was examined by him "with peculiar interest, for the reason that it has the reputation, beyond any other of its kind in Great Britain, of making practical application of the most advanced theories respecting non-restraint and personal freedom." "It was stated," he writes, "that there were no strait-jackets nor restraining dresses — nothing involving mechanical restraint — within the institution. If violent, a patient is walked about until he calms down; and if very violent he is placed in charge of two or more special attendants. . . . Without attempting to decide to what extent the radical principles put in practice here are worthy of general adoption, it was evident that there was a remarkable degree of contentment and cheerful activity." The Morningside or Royal Edinburgh Asylum interested him greatly, and became the subject of a quite extended description. "In few other asylums visited," he wrote, "did the inmates approach so near the appearance of sane people in home life. . . . Walled enclosures or airing-courts have been abolished. . . . Looking over the spacious and highly improved grounds, the eye failed to detect any sign of irksome restriction in the form of interior walls or other barriers. . . . One of the first things Dr. Clouston did after his appointment in 1873 was to remove the iron gratings from the windows. . . . The training of the attendants is manifestly of a high order, developing patience and even tenderness."

Among the Scottish reformatory institutions that were visited by Mr. Letchworth, one at Glasgow—the Duke Street Reformatory for boys — was delightfully startling in its contrast to the prison-like "houses of refuge" of the State of New York. A fine open yard in front and an equally open playground at the back prepared the visitor to be told: "We have got along thus far without walls. There is something stronger than walls." But it was added: "We want to get into the country; for here we have not only to keep the boys in, but to keep pernicious influences out." Lately a field in the country had been engaged for football, and the boys were to be taken to it on Saturdays. The number of these boys was one hundred and sixty-five, and only seventeen of them had been sent to the reformatory for slight offences. They were released as soon as they were thought to be

Scottish reformatories for children

ready for self-control; places of employment were always sought for them, and, said the governor of the institution, "As long as they need our guidance, it is our duty and our pleasure to give it to them."

From Scotland Mr. Letchworth crossed to Sweden and Norway, finding much to interest him in some of their reformative institutions, but less that was instructive or suggestive in the care of the insane. At Gothenburg he inspected an institution for the reformation of young men who had fallen into evil courses, and who were committed to it for definite periods. They numbered at the time of his visit two hundred and sixty-one, and six were then being held in solitary confinement. The whole treatment appears to have been considerably prison-like, and the prisoners were known by number instead of by name. They were employed, however, at various common trades.

Scandinavian institutions

Another institution in the same place is described briefly in his notebook as follows: "At Gothenburg is a large and long two-story building, with wings, well furnished, and with a delightful garden in the rear, provided for respectable aged persons and supported by tax upon the city. The worthless and disreputable are provided for elsewhere."

At Christiania our inquirer found a reformatory for boys which commended itself in many features to his judgment of what such an institution should be. It was seated on a large tract of land, stocked with sixty-five cows, eighteen pairs of oxen, ten horses, the use and care of which gave healthy employment to a quite large part of its hundred and thirteen boys. Besides this farm work there was brickmaking, blacksmithing, wagon-making, and tailoring to keep them busy and to prepare them for earning their living. For all overwork they were allowed wages, and these earnings were deposited in a savings bank to their credit. They were hemmed in by no walls, and corporal punishment was rarely inflicted upon them.

From Stockholm the traveller wrote to friends at home: "My stay was a profitable and pleasant experience." In this city he visited a female prison, whose three hundred and fifty convicts included one hundred and fifty under sentence for infanticide; a school of domestic arts, which gave a three years' course of instruction in all branches of housework to girls of sixteen, and then sent them to places in families; an immense poorhouse, having twelve hundred tenants, including ninety insane, and employing them generally at all kinds of work; a home for idiots, a hospital, an asylum for the insane (the Conradsberg) on the outskirts of the city; but this latter, which exhibited certain "hard and forbidding aspects," contributed little to his discussion of "The Insane in Foreign Countries."

Going next to Copenhagen, he visited a boys' reformatory which pleased him much in many features. A private institution, receiving some public aid, it gave its care to only sixty-six, and employed them wholly in farm work. In winter they got their schooling, and were not exercised in any mechanic trades. In the farming season their studies were dropped, except on stormy days. Some were hired to neighboring farmers, and the institution took their wages. The place had neither window gratings nor walls. The boys seemed to feel towards it, quite generally, as towards a home, and many, after leaving, came back to visit it. No less than twenty-eight had done so on the previous Christmas.

Also, while at Copenhagen, he went through the St. Hans Hospital for the Insane, which is situated not far from the city, and it is favorably described in his book on the European treatment of the insane. The St. Hans Hospital had one special advantage, in the opportunity for beach-bathing, which the patients enjoy, and which seemed to be of excellent effect. "There have been abundant occasions," said the superintendent, Dr. Steenberg, "when I could date the beginning of convalescence, or at least of essential improvement both in mind and body, from the day when the patient began strand-bathing."

From Denmark Mr. Letchworth entered Germany, and paused first at Hamburg, to give close attention to the celebrated reformative industrial school named the Rauhe Haus, founded by Immanuel Wichern in 1833. Its first house had been formerly an inn, and Immanuel, with his mother, began there his work. Then a garden cottage was occupied; and so the extension appears to have gone on, not by enlargement of buildings, but by a multiplication of them, adding cottage to cottage, until about two hundred boys and forty "brothers," who are their guardians and teachers, were housed at the time of Mr. Letchworth's visit. Thus the "cottage system," which is being accepted as the best

In Germany — Rauhe Haus

habitation arrangement for nearly all institutional collections of people, grew up in a natural way, and if the Rauhe Haus did not afford the first object-teaching of this fact, the illustrative lesson it gave was early and impressive. It was a lesson which Mr. Letchworth, if he had not conclusively learned it already, appears to have been fully prepared to accept, with conviction, from that time.

Each cottage of the institution was the home of a "family," consisting, usually, of twelve boys and two or three "brothers," the former occupying the lower floor, the latter the upper floor, each having its sitting-room. Kitchen and flower-gardens were attached to each cottage. The cooking for all was done at one place. Work in several trades was being carried on, as well as the care of cows, horses, and poultry. The institution was intended, in the main, to provide for the reclamation of neglected children, but it had taken in about twenty of the criminal class, and did not set them apart. It did make a class, however, of children whose parents could pay for better furnishings and food than the others received. In all cases parents paid if they could, and what they could; otherwise the institution was supported by voluntary contributions. From its beginning it had dealt with about fifteen hundred boys.

In a neighboring village a school for girls was conducted on the same system, but on a small scale, its inmates numbering only twenty-five. This was under the care of a married "brother" and his wife.

Another institution at Hamburg to which Mr. Letchworth gave careful attention was the Friedrichsberg Asylum for the Insane. Two features of the Friedrichsberg Asylum impressed him unfavorably. One was the attempted "classification of the patients into social grades," in combination with a more rational classification of them according to their mental and physical state. "The aim," as he explained, "is not only to observe with care the social distinctions and requirements, but also to provide each of the several classes and their numerous divisions with separate accommodations and conveniences — down even to a separate tea-kitchen. But so complex is this method of classification that it is admittedly a source of much embarrassment to the administration." The other questionable characteristic of the institution is suggested in the remark that "the buildings are in the midst of beautiful grounds;

but the spectacle of patients restricted to small yards produces an unfavorable impression on the mind of the visitor. As one walks about the grounds and sees the patients through iron screenwork or wooden palings, the idea of a park menagerie is disagreeably suggested. It was asserted by the management that there was no 'forcing,' and that no mechanical restraint whatever was resorted to."

In Germany Mr. Letchworth gave careful inspection to numerous institutions in the several departments of public philanthropy which claimed his special study, but only one of the German institutions for the insane impressed him sufficiently to be the subject of much description or comment in his subsequent book. That one, however, the provincial Insane Asylum of Alt-Scherbitz, in the Prussian Province of Saxony, near Leipzig, appears to have come nearer to the realizing of his final ideals of what the treatment of demented humanity should be than any other that he ever saw, abroad or at home. He found the provision of care for the insane to be regulated by no general laws in the German Empire, but varying in the different states. He found, too, that only about one third of the in-

German treatment of the insane

sane in Germany were given asylum treatment, the remainder being considered suitable for family care; and that the asylums were small compared with those of England, the United States, and some other countries. Even that of Alt-Scherbitz, which impressed him so much, had no impressive magnitude, providing only for six hundred patients; but it was one of two institutions to which he gave distinct chapters in his account of the care of the insane in foreign countries; the other being the Belgian " Colony of Gheel."

The Alt-Scherbitz Asylum, when visited by Mr. Letchworth in 1880, had been in existence but four years. At its opening, in 1876, when it was founded by Professor John Maurice Koeppe, it received forty patients in the old farmhouse of the Alt-Scherbitz manor, and further buildings for it were then begun. These buildings included one for administrative purposes, two reception stations, two observation stations, two detention houses, and a hospital for the bodily sick, all "unpretentious brick structures, with outer porches," entirely separated from one another, and surrounded by seven hundred acres of the asylum estate. Lying within that estate is the

[margin: Alt-Scherbitz Asylum]

small hamlet of Alt-Scherbitz, and within the hamlet were ten cottages or villas belonging to the asylum and occupied by some of its quiet patients.

The reception stations (one for men and one for women), as described by Mr. Letchworth, "are clinical passageways for all newly received patients, who are detained here as long as they need continual care and treatment." The observation stations, one for each sex, "are for patients who, though not of the acute class, need special observation because they are not sufficiently capable of self-control nor reliable enough for reception in the colonial stations." The two detention houses "are for such male and female patients as it is necessary to restrict because of their being restless or dangerous, or from the suspicion of their having a desire to escape." The villas or cottages are of three classes, differently furnished according to the rate of payment made for the patients who occupy them. Of these Mr. Letchworth wrote: "It was a pleasant summer day when I was there, and the patients were passing in and out without interference, all, however, being under watchful supervision." Of "the institution cottages in the adjacent hamlet of Alt-Scherbitz," which appear to have had single occupants, he says: "At one of these the patient had gone out and locked his door, and the physician would not enter the dwelling without his permission."

Relative to the freedom given to patients generally in the institution, he quoted the superintendent, Dr. Paetz, as saying: "Every sort of restraint by force is strictly interdicted, as being against the fundamental principles of the asylum. The patients enjoy the largest imaginable freedom, the asylum representing the non-restraint system in the widest sense. Restraint is easy to dispense with if one earnestly wishes to dispense with it." Mr. Letchworth adds to this the remark that "the number of nurses or attendants averages about one to ten patients. They live with the patients and lodge in the same dormitories." Agricultural work and various trades for the men, with household occupations for the women, keep most of them well employed. In closing his account of the place, which pleased him greatly, he says : "The whole system of care and treatment seems adapted to insure highly satisfactory results; and yet a stranger passing along the highway and catching glimpses of the asylum buildings through the trees and shrubbery would hardly suspect, from their unpretentious character and their arrangement upon the estate, that the place was a public hospital and asylum for insane people."

An older institution for the insane, at Halle, Prussia, engaged Mr. Letchworth's attention but slightly. He was busy, however, for some days at Berlin, Duisburg, Kaiserwirth, Düsseldorf, and Boppard, visiting other institutions, mostly of the reformative class. Several of these latter he found to be copies, more or less faithful, of the Rauhe Haus, at Hamburg. The Evangelical Foundation of St. John, at Berlin, had been founded, in fact, by Dr. Wichern, of the Rauhe Haus, in 1858, and patterned very closely after the Hamburg original. The subjects of its care were the wayward youth, of both sexes, who had not become amenable to law, but were dangerously on the way to crime and vice. These, its pupils, were under the oversight of "brothers," who were trained for the function, in a *Brüderhaus* (brethren's house, or missionary house) within the premises, pursuing a course which occupied from three to five years. Pupils and "brothers" lived together, as at the Rauhe Haus, in families, occupying family houses, and the general eco-

Reproductions of Rauhe Haus

nomy, discipline, and employment was about the same.

Düsselthal Reformatory, near Düsseldorf-on-the-Rhine, an older and much larger institution, exhibited the "family" organization of its pupils, but differently carried out. Some but not all of the families were housed separately, and the "brothers" were wanting. The head of the institution and his wife were known as the "house-father" and the "house-mother," and between them and the pupils there appears to have been no intermediate authority. Düsselthal, having one hundred boys and seventy girls under its care, was one of three branches of a foundation which extended the same organization to a second at Overdieck, where forty boys were under training, and a third at Toppenbroeck, which received forty boys and twenty girls.

At a remarkable institution in Kaiserwirth, the Deaconesses' Institute, which included a kindergarten, an orphan house, a training-school for teachers, a *Feierabendhaus* (which means a house of rest, in the closing years of life, for those who have labored hard), and an insane asylum, Mr. Letchworth was surprised to find a new building for the insane being equipped with all the old-time constructions for shutting them behind grated windows and surrounding walls. He remarks in the notebook of his visit to the place that the reverend head of the institution "apparently had never heard of the no-restraint system," and "showed all these arrangements, for keeping the poor patients like wild beasts in cells and apartments of strict security, with perfect self-satisfaction."

The Prussian Government supports two reformatories for boys—Protestant and Catholic, respectively—for the Rhenish Province and the Province of Hesse-Nassau. One of these, at Boppard-on-the-Rhine, Mr. Letchworth visited, expecting, it seems, to find it organized, as it was said to be, on the family plan. But he failed to recognize in it the essential characteristics of that system. The eighty-four boys of the institution were grouped ostensibly in four families and the twenty girls in one; but the boys slept in the same dormitory, and were all together at play, in work, and at school. Their family life was only in the four rooms where they ate their meals together and sat when not otherwise engaged. Flogging and confinement in dark rooms were among the punishments permitted.

Proceeding from Germany into Switzerland, Mr. Letchworth's first visit there was to an admirably conducted City Orphan House, at Bâle, from which he brought many notes. At Burgholzli, near Zurich, he examined the workings of an extensive asylum for the insane, and could not approve some of its methods, or feel persuaded that the influences acting on the patients were what they ought to be. He questioned especially a device of treatment for refractory patients, by keeping them immersed, sometimes for hours, in hot-water baths, under locked covers to the tubs, their heads protruding through holes in these covers.

In Switzerland

He learned at Zurich that, generally, in the Swiss cantons, juvenile lawbreakers above twelve years of age were sent with other criminals to the common prison of the canton; but that houses of correction for such young delinquents were in contemplation. Meantime private benevolence had founded a considerable number of what were called "savings institutions," for the guarding of neglected children and the reclamation of the wayward. Kasper Appenzeller, a Zurich merchant, gave examples of this which caused his name to be connected with them, and they are known as "Appenzeller Institutions." The children taken were bound to remain four years, during which time they were industrially trained, and on leaving they received three hundred francs each.

Juvenile refuges or reformatories of this nature were visited by Mr. Letchworth in or near Zurich, Lucerne, and Berne; but at Berne he found also reformatories for boys and for girls established and supported by the cantonal government, and he visited both. Boys older than twelve years were committed to the place by a judge; younger ones were sent by the poor-board. For girls there were two institutions, one receiving the actually depraved, the other taking those who were innocent, but morally imperilled. The boys were employed only at farming. At about fifteen years of age they went out of the reformatory, to be apprenticed by the director, who still controlled them, and in case of need helped them, until they were able to support themselves. During this brief stay in Switzerland Mr. Letchworth visited many other institutions — prisons, orphanages, schools for the deaf, dumb, blind, and idiotic, and schools for the poor.

Coming now into France, the most interesting subjects of study that he found were the Mettray Reformatory, near Tours, dealing, as he remarked, with the "same class of boys as are in the New York House of Refuge," and the insane asylum at Clermont-en-Oise. Of course he visited, at Paris, La Salpêtriere and Bicêtre, where the paupers of the French capital are collected, females in the one, men in the other, young and old, sane, insane, and idiotic together. La Salpêtrière, in its population of more than six thousand, included nearly six hundred of unsound mind; but it had "little to engage the attention of the inquirer after modern methods." Nor, on going through the Asylum of Sainte-Anne, near Paris, was Mr. Letchworth able quite to agree in opinion with many French specialists in the treatment of mental diseases, who, he says, considered it to be a model institution. He was better pleased with the asylum at Charenton, in the suburbs of Paris; but the most that he learned in France concerning treatment of insanity was found evidently at Clermont-en-Oise.

This institution, he remarks, in describing it, "has long attracted attention by reason of its successful plan of colonizing the insane"; the central asylum, where about one thousand patients were accommodated, sending out certain selections from them to two auxiliary establishments in its neighborhood, called the colony of Fitz-James and the colony of Villers, where more freedom in their treatment could be afforded. These colonies were placed on more than a thousand acres of farming lands, which lands were cultivated by the patients, under a system very carefully organized. "If [he explained] a working patient betrays symptoms of violence, or becomes from any cause unmanageable, he is immediately transferred to the central asylum; and, on the other hand, whenever a patient in the central asylum becomes quiet and tractable he is removed to the colony and its industrial system. There is thus a steady and highly beneficial intercourse between the two divisions.... The examination of the Clermont colonies afforded me much satisfaction." But, says the writer, in conclusion, "the satisfaction derived from the inspection of the colonies of Fitz-James and Villers did not extend to the central institution with its one thousand inmates. Possibly owing to the large numbers brought under one management and the bur-

Clermont colonies of the insane

dens incident to the conducting of its extended business affairs, the central asylum at Clermont did not, as it appeared to the writer, reach a proper standard for a hospital for the treatment of the acute insane."

In the "Agricultural Colony for the Reformation of Boys" at Mettray, near Tours, Mr. Letchworth could study another institution which represented the working-out of ideas taken, as its director acknowledged, from the Rauhe Haus, at Hamburg. There were differences in the development of those ideas, and they were applied on a much larger scale; but this produced a more instructive illustration of them. The Mettray colony, when Mr. Letchworth saw it, could undertake the care of about eight hundred boys, on a domain which embraced fourteen hundred and eighty English acres of ground, in a region of country which his notes of the visit described as "charming." "The entrance to the institution," he noted, "looks more like that to a private villa. Vines and creepers seem to adorn every building. Gravel walks and roads are in every part of the grounds."

Mettray Colony for Reformation of Boys

The boys under correction at Mettray are

sent to it as culprits by a magistrate, or committed for discipline and training by the "Administration of Public Assistance," or received as ungovernable youths on the application of parents or guardians. Those in the first two classes are not received at ages above sixteen years. At the time of Mr. Letchworth's visit to the colony it had under treatment between forty and fifty of the boys of the third class, and they were kept in a "family" by themselves. Otherwise its inmates were all classified into "families" "according to age — not by moral or other standards." "The so-called families," he noted, "consist of forty to fifty boys who sleep and dine in the same houses, but work and go to school by other divisions, — *i.e.*, according to age and capacity.... The management of the establishment is of a military order. The boys wear a uniform of white trousers, blue blouses, and wooden shoes"; and their assemblages and marchings to and from work, school, etc., are directed by bugle calls. Each family had its "house-father," who slept in the dormitory of his boys, but, as Mr. Letchworth noted, did not dine with them. Attempts at running away from the colony were said to be rare, and almost never successful. Of punishments permitted Mr. Letchworth does not seem to have obtained much information, but a general claim of kind treatment was made.

Leaving France early in October and passing into Belgium, our studious tourist found a number of institutions at Brussels, Ghent and Antwerp which had suggestions of importance to repay his painstaking investigation of them. Moreover, the National Exposition then in progress at Brussels included a section devoted to exhibits, from several hospitals for the insane, of work done by their patients, and of the latest improvements of device and construction for use in connection with the treatment of the insane. These latter were shown in effective contrast with the brutalities of caging and shackling which had preceded them, not many decades before. *In Belgium*

An orphanage for girls, at Brussels, presented so many features of excellence in its construction, arrangement, and management,— in the amplitude of its rooms and corridors, the salubrity of its air and the general wholesomeness prevailing in it,— that extensive notes of the institution were brought away. At Ghent or Gand, too, Mr. Letchworth found a large orphanage for boys, of corresponding roominess and liberality of wholesome arrangement, together with a military discipline and order that seemed to be of good effect. But of Belgian institutions, the famous Colony of Gheel, not far from Antwerp, was the one which excited his deepest interest. To that and the insane asylum of Alt-Scherbitz, in Saxony, he gave the most extended description and discussion in his work on "The Insane in Foreign Countries."

A legend of the seventh century, narrating the persecution and martyrdom of an Irish Christian princess, Dymphna, by her own father, who pursued her when she fled from him and slew her at Gheel, gave rise to the belief that her grave was a place of miraculous healing, especially for disorders of the mind. It was said that St. Dymphna (for she was canonized) thought her father to have been insane, and became for that reason a special intercessor for all who were crazed. Hence, from an early time, demented persons were brought to Gheel, for prayers in their behalf at St. Dymphna's shrine, and increasing numbers of these were taken into the houses of the neighborhood for lodgement and care. Until about the beginning of the last century there was no supervision of the

Colony of Gheel for the insane

treatment of these unfortunates, and it was reputed to be heartless and ignorant in the last degree. Something of correction was then attempted by the communes which sent patients to Gheel, through inspectors of their own appointment, and it was not until 1850 that the Belgian Government took control of the colony. Even then it was not until 1862 that a central place of treatment was established, to fulfil "the functions of a central asylum, or observation station, through which all cases received into the colony must pass, and to which are returned such as are unsuited to family life."

At the time of Mr. Letchworth's visit to Gheel this central institution held but forty-six patients. The remainder of the sixteen hundred and thirty insane members of the colony were distributed in the dwellings of the commune, either as private boarders, whose friends paid for their keeping, or as paupers (who numbered fourteen hundred), the scant public allowance for whose maintenance ranged from two hundred and nineteen to three hundred and thirteen francs per year. As stated in his book, the primary aim of Mr. Letchworth in visiting Gheel was to make an examination of the condition of the

Opinion of the Gheel system

insane in these homes, and his three days at the colony were spent mostly in "going from house to house and from cottage to cottage, first through the town and afterward into the surrounding country." In his published account of Gheel he has described minutely the conditions that he found in many houses that he visited, and they tell their own story. Very seldom do they seem to satisfy the requirements of health and comfort even moderately well; and most commonly it is impossible to bring into association with them any thought of comfort or health.

In his summary of conclusions Mr. Letchworth finds some advantages in the home life, the occupations, the general freedom from restraint at Gheel; but against these stand results that come inevitably from (1) the fact that "the care of the insane is relied upon by the people of the place as their main business or means of money-making," and is therefore commercialized in spirit; (2) "the straining after economy, which regulates the rate of maintenance [for the pauper insane], affects the quality of the food, and also influences, prejudicially, the nature of the medical and other supervision." Lack of bathing facilities, ventilation and pure water, prevalence of damp floors, "too frequent proximity of stables and manure heaps to the farm cottages," and other marks of "a lamentable indifference to sanitary considerations," are among the results in question. A reader of Mr. Letchworth's chapter on the Colony of Gheel is prepared fully for his final remark that "the Gheel system is of little practical value to America, except as demonstrating that a great amount of freedom is possible in the care of certain classes of the insane."

In Holland Mr. Letchworth appears to have given attention only to the reformatory for boys, near Zutphen, which bears the name of the Netherland Mettray, *In Holland* and which thereby acknowledges the modelling of its organization and system on those of the French institution at Mettray, near Tours. Inasmuch as the latter had been formed upon principles that were worked out originally by Immanuel Wichern, at the Rauhe Haus, of Hamburg, this gave our American investigator one more exhibit of the working of the family scheme of life, in groups of cottage buildings, for young people under correctional training. The Netherland Mettray was founded in 1854 by a private individual, W. H. Suringar, and received no public support. The boys dealt with were sent by charitable societies or brought by parents, who paid fixed sums per year. None had developed criminality, but were inclined to evil ways. The only punishment ever given to them was confinement in a solitary chamber. The discipline, it was affirmed, "rests on love"; "a perverse boy is taken aside and spoken to kindly." The dormitories were not locked; there were no enclosing walls; the runaways were few. Each cottage had its "house-father," whose room adjoined the sitting-room of the boys. Mr. Letchworth was much pleased with the institution and wrote in his notes: "There is the look of a natural family life all about the place, very different from the stiff, military, cold appearance of everything about the Tours Mettray. The boys look healthy, contented, cheerful, animated in manner, and respectful. Seeing one of them, about thirteen years old, with a pipe in his mouth, I asked if the boys were allowed to smoke, and was answered, 'Yes, a little.' Far from recommending the same license to be given at other institutions, I would call attention to the fact that this permission shows how far the tone and feeling of familiarity between teachers and pupils is carried here." The final jotting in his notebook was this: "The boys are remarkably clean; had scarcely any odor about them."

Proceeding, about the middle of October, to England, where he ended his European tour, Mr. Letchworth remained in that country until early in January, visiting many insane asylums, juvenile reformatories, workhouses (corresponding nearly to our poorhouses), orphanages, etc., but also enjoying somewhat of English hospitality and indulging himself in a well-earned measure of recreation and rest. Of institutions for the insane that he inspected we have extended descriptions in his subsequent work on the subject; but his notes on other establishments seem never to have been rewritten, as most of those taken on the Continent were, and, being hasty jottings of the moment, pencilled with notebook in hand, they are sometimes quite illegible now, and yield scanty gleanings of information as to what he saw and with what effect on his views. *In England*

Generally, in the English asylums for the insane he found a spirit of humanity, an enlightenment of methods, a degree of freedom given to the patients, an absence of mechanical restraints, a cleanliness *English asylums for the insane* and an order which impressed him most favorably; but he could not approve the magnitude of most of them, — the swarming population they hived together, — the scantiness of their grounds, in most cases, and the limited number of attendants employed. Hanwell Asylum, seven miles from London, interested him as having been the place in which, under public auspices, Dr. Conolly, nearly half a century before, demonstrated the practicability of the non-restraint principle in treating the insane; and it pleased him to learn that the superintendent whom he met, Dr. Rayner, "had never resorted to mechanical restraints except by the use of gloves, . . . in exceptional cases, such as preventing a patient from tearing open a wound." But his observation of the workings of the institution led him to conclude that, "from overfulness, restricted airing-courts and grounds, and the presence of numbers too great for close individual inspection, the asylum could not reach those curative results which the enlightened principles governing it would seem to warrant." He found occasion to apply somewhat the same criticism to several others of the English asylums, but not to all. The Brookwood Asylum, one of three provided for the County of Surrey, and situated twenty-eight miles from London, drew from him nothing but praise. "Without architectural display," he wrote, "or other extravagance, comfortable and proper provision for the insane seemed to be here attained; and appropriate as were the fittings and furnishings of this institution, that which impressed me most favorably was the humane spirit pervading its entire administration."

In Mr. Letchworth's book on "The Insane in Foreign Countries" there are, in all, fourteen of the English institutions quite fully described. It is probable that the one to which he was carried by the strongest attraction and with the warmest feeling of interest was "The Friends' Retreat," near the City of York. "This," he said in a private letter written at the time of his visit, "was the first asylum in England, if not in the world, that dispensed with using means of restraint when patients are violent." In his book he wrote of it: "Projected in the spring of 1792 and opened in 1796, the York Retreat is memorable as the place where the non-restraint principle was first adopted in Great Britain — where William Tuke, on behalf of the Society of Friends, courageously renounced, as did Pinel at Paris, the use

"The Friends' Retreat"

of chains and manacles in the treatment of the insane. . . . The Retreat, a private institution, or 'registered hospital,' is still directed by those who are, for the most part, members of the Society of Friends. It has a yearly income of about $75,000. The buildings are old-fashioned, but wear an aspect of unpretentious comfort. In the oldest part some of the arrangements scarcely meet all modern requirements. . . . At the time of my visit the records showed one hundred and fifty-three patients — sixty-four men and eighty-nine women. . . . A full inspection of the Retreat, with its detached cottages, its artfully screened walls, its beautiful recreation grounds, and its wealth of flowers within and without, suffices to convince the visitor that this small and select institution, which well-nigh a hundred years ago proved such a powerful factor in educating and elevating public opinion in England, retains to this day much of that progressive spirit and humanity of purpose upon which its world-wide reputation rests."

Of English institutions for a reformative training of ill-doing children Mr. Letchworth visited a large number, in and around London, Bristol, Liverpool, Manchester, Wakefield, Sheffield, York, Birmingham, and other centres of population. Writing from London, of the week between October 18 and 24, he said that it had been devoted entirely to institution-visiting, and added: "I have collected a vast fund of information which I hope may be of use to the cause of humanity in some way at some future time." We may be sure that this fund of information went into the guidance and stimulation of his subsequent labors; but its sources, for the most part, are left undisclosed, so far as concerns other subjects than the treatment of the insane.

To Bristol Mr. Letchworth was drawn especially by his admiration of the work of the late Miss Mary Carpenter, who had been, for many years, with tongue and pen and personal influence, the leader of child-saving movements, not only in England, but widely elsewhere in the world. His estimate of the great importance of Miss Carpenter's labors was set forth in a sketch of her life and its results which he wrote in 1889. He has left in this an account of two of the reformatory schools which she established in Bristol, and to which he gave close attention while there. They were planned for the reclaiming of the more hardened class of juvenile offenders.

Miss Mary Carpenter's reformatory schools

Miss Carpenter's first undertaking to that end was in the establishment of the Kingswood Reformatory, which was opened in 1852, on property purchased and placed at her disposal by Mr. Russell Scott. This was intended originally for both boys and girls, but experience disapproved of the combination, as it has done generally throughout Europe, and a separate institution, the Red Lodge Reformatory, for girls, was established in another part of the town. The grounds and the building — an ancient Elizabethan mansion — for this latter institution were purchased and given to it by Lady Noel Byron, wife of the poet.

At the time of Mr. Letchworth's visit to it the Kingswood Reformatory held about one hundred and fifty boys, mostly engaged in the making of pressed brick. Some, however, were employed in farm work, some in a shop, mending farm tools, some in tailoring, some in shoemaking, some in household tasks. "The doors," he wrote, "were open throughout the building, and the place was not enclosed, nor were there any guards. Only two boys were found in confinement." In the Red Lodge Reformatory, at the same time, there were fifty-two girls, "all sentenced for grave offences, too serious for committal to the industrial school." They "were generally placed out after remaining in the institution two years, but could be recalled, upon any act of misconduct, to complete their sentence. Beyond this they were supervised for three years after their time had expired.... After three months' probation the girls received a portion of their earnings, according to their conduct and work.... Religious teaching and moral training were features in the institution; the rudiments of a common-school education were also taught." In the room which Miss Carpenter had occupied when personally superintending the institution hangs a framed government document which certifies that it was the first reformatory school for girls established in England.

Another of his inspections which he made with peculiar feelings of interest was at a reformatory for boys, near Gloucester, to which he alluded soon after, in his paper on "Classification and Training of Children, Innocent and Incorrigible," read at the National Conference of Charities and Correction, at Louisville, in 1883, — as follows: "When in England, not long since, I had the pleasure of meeting a remarkable person, a pub-

[margin: Hardwicke Court Reformatory]

lic-spirited magistrate, whose position on the bench gave him unusual opportunity for studying the question of juvenile delinquency. He was a gentleman of culture and refinement, as well as a philanthropist, and is now regarded as an authority on all matters relating to crime and correctional methods. Impressed with the importance of purifying the sources of evil with which he had officially to deal, he, of his own means and on his own estate, established a reformatory for boys, upon a basis which he had long deemed a right one, and placed it under the guidance of a young clergyman, who gave his life to the work without other emolument than the satisfaction derived from doing good. This institution has become a model of its kind, and it afforded me many avenues for study while there. I refer to the Hardwicke Court Reformatory, near Gloucester." As the guest of the gentleman thus mentioned, T. Barwick Lloyd Baker Esq., of Hardwicke Court, Mr. Letchworth spent two delightful October days, enjoying the opportunity, as he wrote to his sister, "of an interior view of the social life and habits of a genuine country squire, the owner of a Hall surrounded by thousands of acres"; and opening then a warm friendship which expressed itself in intimate correspondence until Mr. Baker's death.

Among the papers that have come into the hands of the writer of this biography is one entitled "Child-saving Work Abroad," on which Mr. Letchworth had endorsed the following note: "I cannot now (1907) recall upon what occasion the paper entitled 'Child-saving Work Abroad' was used." Probably it was written not long after his return from the investigations of 1880. It relates to what he saw and learned then, but mostly to the charitable rather than the reformative institutions for children, and almost wholly to his observations in the British Isles. His first remarks in it indicate the deep impression that was made on his mind by the stress which he had found to be laid on the importance of a careful classification of the children who came under treatment in public institutions, to discriminate between three characters in which they come, namely, (1) the homeless and destitute, who need maintenance; (2) those who are making wrong beginnings in life, through ill-training or endangering associations, from which they need rescue; and (3) those who have entered the criminal class or belong to it by birth. He had felt the importance of this before; but it seems manifest that he came home with a deepened conviction that such an assorting of the subjects of child-saving work in public institutions had a rational precedence of everything else.

He found in Great Britain a lamentable departure from this principle in one serious particular, although, otherwise, the principle had careful recognition. "The larger proportion of the children," he wrote, "belong to establishments in connection with the workhouse, or, as we would term it, the poorhouse or almshouse. In some cases the pauper establishments [for children] are on the poorhouse grounds; in others they are separately located. These remarks apply equally to England, Scotland, and Ireland." Then he describes one which he visisited, at Sutton, fourteen miles out of London, where fifteen hundred and seventy-four children were housed. They were in two departments, for boys and for girls, occupying "a large tastefully built structure," on a good site, with well-kept grounds; but the place seemed to him "cold, dreary and formal," bearing, "internally and externally," "certain well-marked features of a pauper establishment." He proceeds next to describe two other more recently created institutions for pauper children in England which gave a better impression. One of these, at Banstead, fifteen miles from London, he found to be arranged "on the cottage plan, which is growing in favor with large numbers of the intelligent and benevolent, who dislike the so-called pauper school." Here were eight two-story cottage buildings for boys, having twenty-six in each, and twelve for girls, each accommodating twenty-four. Other buildings comprised infirmaries, schools, workshops, chapel, superintendent's residence, and office. The other of these institutions which he visited, at Marston Green, near Birmingham, showed him fourteen cottages, arranged as on a village street, seven being for boys, seven for girls, thirty in each. "The boys," he tells us, "are under the charge of a 'father and mother'; the girls receive the attention of a mother. The male head of each household is a tradesman or mechanic, who imparts to the boys a knowledge of his craft. Work and schooling are taken alternately." Here, evidently, are ideas taken from Immanuel Wichern and Rauhe Haus.

On the practice in England and Scotland of boarding-out large numbers of orphaned and otherwise homeless children in the families of cottagers, which is strongly supported by many such philanthropists as the Misses Hill, of Birmingham, he says: "I was forced to the conviction that this system was an improvement upon institutional life as it exists in England." He found many of these boarded-out children " placed with people of good character, under good influences, well cared for, and fairly introduced into what may be termed family life. Nevertheless the fact of their being paid for by the authorities and consequently dependent seemed to prejudice their social position." In America the placing-out of such children in families which find their reward later, when their little guests have grown to an age of usefulness in the family work, has, in his view, a very different character, "almost unique."

The "boarding-out" of homeless children

The account in this paper of reformatories and industrial schools in Great Britain is entirely a general one and quite brief. " Any number of individuals may organize what are termed industrial schools," which are located generally in the suburbs of large towns. " Reformatories are situated in the country, are generally small, built on the open or cottage plan, and must be inspected or certified by a government officer." In England, Scotland, and Wales, when Mr. Letchworth wrote of them, there were about two hundred of the reformatories and schools, training upwards of twenty thousand children; besides eight government training-ships, to which boys are sent from the reformatories to be trained for the British merchant service. "Some of the reformatory schools," he thought, "might be regarded as models. They are generally devoid of high walls, institution aspect, or prison-like characteristics. The boys occupy cottages, under a male attendant or married couple. In fine weather they have outdoor work on the farm; in winter they work indoors at a trade."

In closing his summary review of "Child-Saving Work Abroad," as he had surveyed it, Mr. Letchworth touched a question so interesting that all readers must regret the reservedness of his reply to it.

During my tour of inspection [he said] the question was often asked me, " How do American institutions compare with those of Britain ? " It is a question somewhat difficult to answer. On a broad examination I am constrained to think that both have something to learn, the one from the other, and in my opinion an international conference or interchange of ideas could not fail to be of great mutual benefit. I have mentioned that the reformatory system abroad exhibits many features of interest to us; I am also bound to say that there is one part of that system as administered in England which will not commend itself to philanthropic people on this side of the Atlantic. I refer to the rule of law requiring the reformatory child to have been in prison at least ten days, before being admitted to a reformatory,— a system, be it observed, which closes the door of the industrial school to the juvenile offender. The spectacle — albeit it may be rare — of so-called "hardened criminals," only eight years old, on their way to a prison or reformatory, is very saddening, and I am glad to be able to state that in several places reformatory authorities have stood out against receiving boys under twelve years on a first conviction.

What he had learned in his tour of foreign investigation was not all that Commissioner Letchworth brought home when he returned from it, early in January, 1881. He was the medium of a highly important gift from the English Local Government Board to the New York State Board of Charities. In recent years that Board had acquired authority to control the planning of all buildings provided for paupers, and the experts it employed had been making great im-

Gift of English building-plans

provements in such plans. Commissioner Letchworth was permitted to examine these, and they interested him so much that Sir John Lambert, the head of the Board, caused copies of the most approved to be made and officially transmitted to the New York State Board, along with many important documents. A formal presentation of these to the latter Board was made by Mr. Letchworth at its meeting in March, 1881.

CHAPTER VI

CHILD-SAVING WORK: REFORMATIVE

FROM his observations abroad it is certain that Mr. Letchworth brought much that cleared his understanding, instructed his judgment, broadened and deepened his thought concerning the grave and difficult matter of so dealing with errant youth as to train it into better courses; but the cardinal convictions of his mind on this subject were those which the Rauhe Haus of Immanuel Wichern, at Hamburg, and its varied copies elsewhere had impressed upon him. For a time it became his chief mission to plead for the transformation of juvenile "houses of refuge" and similar so-called reformatories from grim prisons into systematized industrial schools; for the tearing away of their stone walls; for the transplanting of them into open country surroundings; for the grouping and cottage-housing of their pupil inmates, under some semblance of the associations of a common family life; and (before all else) for a careful classifica-

THE LAWN, GLEN IRIS

tion of juvenile delinquents, to part the uncorrupted from the corrupt.

It will be necessary, however, before taking up the record of his work for the betterment of juvenile reformatories at the point where it came to be influenced by his investigations abroad, to go back a little in time and make note of what he had been doing previously on approximate lines. Incidentally, while busied with his earlier tasks, he had been seeing and learning much of the workings of the penal and correctional institutions of the country and of their dealing with young offenders against the law. He had come into intimate relations with people who were leading the undertakings of social reform in that most important direction. He was already in coöperation with Dr. E. C. Wines, the distinguished secretary of the National Prison Association, and with Dr. Elisha Harris, corresponding secretary of the Prison Association of New York, exchanging suggestion and counsel with both. The pernicious unwisdom and carelessness of prevailing modes of dealing with vagrancies and the minor breaches of social order were then greatly exercising the minds of these earnest philanthropists and the associations with which they

The work of the prison associations

labored, and juvenile delinquency was involved gravely in the depraving influences found here.

In September, 1874, the second year of Mr. Letchworth's official service, Dr. Harris had submitted to the State Board of Charities a proposal of joint effort to secure in the State of New York a "suitable and effectual system of local workhouses, which shall be truly institutions or places of correctional treatment for the classes which now infest society by tramping, begging, hanging upon almshouses, as well as by practising various crimes and offensive courses of life." The objects sought were to suppress vagrancy; to save "the young, the innocent, and reformable classes" of persons who might be drifting into vagrancy from being brought "into the community and conversation" of the radically debased class; and, finally, to cure "the great evils that exist in the county jails, by affording means of immediate and effectual removal and suitable discipline for persons convicted of misdemeanors, and who under existing laws and usages remain in the jails, to expiate their offences by a moral and physical kind of slow death." The State Board of Charities was asked to appoint a committee for a conference with a committee of the Prison Association, looking toward a united undertaking to obtain proper legislation on these lines. The Board of Charities responded to the request, and Mr. Letchworth was a member of the committee named. His correspondence with Dr. Harris, intimate and extensive from that time, shows that discussion of the project of legislation went through a long period, to no conclusive action; and shows, too, that its inconclusiveness was because the time for so broad a reform was not yet ripe.

Mr. Letchworth's interest in the matter was fully aroused, especially in its bearing on the exposure of the young to corrupting associations, and his own observations soon confirmed all that was said of the seriousness of the evil by Dr. Harris and other investigators of our jails and other penal institutions. In December, 1875, he asked the secretary of his Board to bring the matter to the attention of Governor Tilden, and to request him, in his forthcoming annual message, to recommend legislation for securing the removal of children, not only from poorhouses, as had been done, but from common jails and from all association with adult paupers and criminals.

Children in jails and penitentiaries

The law of the last legislature [he wrote] requires this to be effected now in poorhouses and almshouses, and previously enacted laws require it to be enforced in penitentiaries; but for some reason, perhaps of defect in the law, it is practically disregarded. In nearly all of the penitentiaries in the state, as well as the state's prisons, considerable numbers are to be found under sixteen years of age. In the penitentiaries some are mere children. It seems to me that the law should be made, not only more restrictive, but to apply also to jails and lockups, and that the principle of dissociating children from adult paupers and criminals should be held as fundamental. When at Hart's Island, in October, I saw eleven children intermingled with a gang of sixty criminals emerge from the hold of the steamer belonging to the Department of Public Charities in New York.

Some slight and partial allusion to the subject was made by the governor in his subsequent message, but nothing that was likely to produce legislative results. Two years after this appeal to a right-minded governor for help in obtaining remedies of law for a most dangerous social infection there is evidence that no progress toward such remedies had been made. Mrs. Lowell, of the State Board of Charities, was heart and soul with Mr. Letchworth in this line of work. Two letters written by Dr.

Harris, of the Prison Association, on the same day, January 23, 1877, one addressed to Mrs. Lowell and the other to Mr. Letchworth, tell us what was the state of things at that time.

To Mrs. Lowell he wrote: —

Most people do not see our magistrates and police justices as I see them,— utterly indifferent to the questions, Is this offender a child? and Is the child under sixteen years old? From our city recorders and the supreme court I have seen boys under sixteen years old marched into Sing Sing. At Syracuse I found a child under eleven years old in the penitentiary, as a vagrant, sentenced for sixty days. There is no law to forbid such sentences, and even when a child is found in state prison the governor must act — if he can be induced to act — to order the child's transfer to the House of Refuge. . . . I have found children under sentence and serving out their term of punishment in *nearly every jail in the state, in every penitentiary, and in every prison.* Yet I might reiterate the facts for ten years, vainly hoping to induce action; but if a revision of all the statutes in a brief act is attempted I believe we could obtain the law now needed. The existing statutes readily permit the imprisonment of children, first, by not directly prohibiting the sentence of a child to any one of the three classes of prisons; second, by accepting the judge's decision as to the age of a juvenile offender; but, from 1826, 1830, 1846, 1850, and 1852, every allusion to juvenile offenders constructively implies that they are not to be sentenced to jail, penitentiary, or state prison.

In his simultaneous letter to Mr. Letchworth Dr. Harris wrote: —

I am soon to visit all the jails and penitentiaries and I shall closely record the cases I meet with; but no office, no officer, no records existing now can give us the facts you seek. A child eleven years old told your Buffalo police magistrate, "I don't know my age." I saw him in the penitentiary and talked with him. Captain Felton knew his age. He was only a homeless child, wandering all the way from London, England, to London in Canada, and to Buffalo. In Albany I saw a case fifteen years old; in Syracuse one nine or ten; in Rochester five cases under fifteen, all in for one year. . . . In fifty jails I have seen child convicts, and in the state prisons I have seen case after case.

According to what was told of conditions prevailing generally in the jails of the United States, within the period in which these statements were made, the placing of children in them was iniquitous beyond measure. Said Dr. Wines, in the report of the National Prison Association, adopted at its congress of 1874: "If by some supernatural process our two thousand jails

CHILD-SAVING: REFORMATIVE 217

could be unroofed, and the things they conceal be thus instantly exposed to our view, a shriek would go up from this congress and country which would not only reach every corner of the land, but be heard, in Scripture phrase, 'to the very ends of the earth.'" In 1877 a conference of prison keepers and observers, held at Newport, Rhode Island, adopted a report which said, among other things, this: "The system of county jails in the United States is a disgrace to our civilization. It is hopelessly bad, and must remain so as long as it exists under its present form. De Tocqueville, half a century ago, pronounced our county jails 'the worst prisons he had ever seen,' and there has been little marked improvement since."

Officially, Mr. Letchworth had no authority or any other standing than as a citizen for action against these abominations of the prison system. By joining hands with the Prison Association of New York he became a participant, not in the exercise of any actual power of reformation, but in the use of a right of inspection and criticism which had no small importance. In January, 1876, he was elected a member of the Executive Committee of the Prison Association, and thus

Work with the Prison Association of New York

came into close relations with its work. Later he was one of its vice-presidents. Little record of his personal action in those relations can be found; but we may be sure that it was no perfunctory performance, and that he bore as active a part as his official labors would permit in the counsels and the undertakings of the Association during some subsequent years. It worked against great obstacles, and the progress of prison reform was slow. It was not until 1895 that the administration of prisons in the State of New York was importantly changed, by the creation of the State Commission of Prisons; and that commission, in its third annual report, was even then compelled to give a bad account of the majority of the county jails in the state. It said of them that they "are relics of another generation, when the sole object was confinement, and no consideration was given to the health or reformation of the inmates."

Over juvenile reformatory institutions the State Board of Charities exercised a jurisdiction which included something of authority and much more of influence to correct mismanagement in them. Here, therefore, was his main field of child-saving work, when the rescue of the homeless from pauperism had been achieved, and his thought and labor could be turned to the ill-doing boys and girls, out of whom it is the need and the duty of society to make well-doing men and women if it can. This side of the child-saving appeal had been urgent to him from his first harkening to that call; and his earliest scrutiny of the facts to be dealt with showed him exactly what needed most to be done. We learn this from an undated memorandum, found among his papers, which probably was written in his later years. In this he says: —

In the early days of my examination of institutions and the means established for the reformation of juvenile delinquents, I was strongly impressed with the disregard of proper classification and the indifference shown to this subject. This was particularly the case in New York State. Massachusetts had largely broken away from the old system, by the establishment of a state agency, with a probation system. Ohio had established its reform school for boys on the cottage plan, at Lancaster, and for girls, on the same plan, at Delaware. Under the direction of Governor Bagley, Michigan changed its State Reform School, at Lansing, from the congregate plan to the cottage plan; afterwards founding the Lancaster School for girls, on the cottage plan at Adrian. Advances in other states might be mentioned, but, until a recent date, New York State has been signally apathetic on this subject.

When my attention was first directed to the matter I found that the innocent and the incorrigible were indiscriminately commingled in institutional life. Once, on entering the House of Refuge at Randall's Island, I found a group of boys who had just entered and were being registered, preparatory to being taken to their wards and cells, which were on the same plan as those in state prisons. . . . I asked one little boy, who was sitting with others on a wooden bench and swinging his legs in a "happy go lucky" way, what he had been sent there for? "Oh," he replied, with much gusto, "for stealing a horse." I found afterwards that he and some other boys, in a frolicsome spirit, had got into a grocer's wagon and driven off. He was arrested on a charge of felony and sentenced to imprisonment during the long years of his minority, his name forever branded with infamy — a brand which, by judgment record, time could never efface. . . .

Shameful conditions in New York

Once, on visiting a reform school, my attention was directed to a nice-looking lad, who was standing in the corner of the yard with his face against the angle of the brick wall, sobbing bitterly. The superintendent said he had been in the institution three days, during all which time he had been crying and had kept aloof from the other boys. This boy was in a mood to be reformed, and it saddened me to think that he could not be properly dealt with, in his repentant mood, instead of being subjected to close companionship with evil associates. . . . This lad was but a type of great numbers I have seen, who should never have been committed to such institutions. Many thousands of children in the State of New York who were simply wayward — whose parents, perhaps, were more at fault than the children — who were what they were because of evil environments, and who needed only mild correctional treatment — have been subjected to the great wrong of commitment to institutions which brought them into intimate association with the hardened, the incorrigible. In such establishments I have known of secret organizations of bad boys who taught the innocent newcomers all manner of criminal practices, including pocket-picking, house-breaking, and how effectually to commit rape.

Apparently, Mr. Letchworth's first public utterance of opinion on modes of dealing with juvenile delinquency was in 1877, at the National Conference of Charities and Correction at Saratoga. He was one of a committee which had been appointed to report on "Dependent and Delinquent Children"; but the committee had not been able to confer, and in a personal report that he submitted he limited himself mostly to a sketch of the history of the development, in the State of New York, of both charitable and reformatory institutions for children. To this historical re-

First expression on "Classification"

view he added a brief discussion of unsatisfied needs as he saw them. On the reformatory side he went no further than to endorse a resolution adopted at the last preceding State Convention of Superintendents of the Poor, in New York, which urged that "institutions of a correctional character, and intermediate between the orphan asylum and the house of refuge, are needed, and that those institutions will attain the best results the more nearly they conform to the family system." On this he said:—

In our orphan asylums it has been found that a class of children float into them who need a restraint and discipline that cannot be enforced in such institutions. The presence in orphan asylums of children who are uncontrollable under ordinary rules exercises an injurious effect upon the other children. . . . The interest, both of an ungovernable child and of the institution itself, requires its removal. To place such a child in a house of refuge, among incorrigible and hardened offenders, many of them mature in years and crime, is evidently unwise, and must result in an influence being exerted on him proportionately as injurious as his influence was injurious upon the children in the institution from which he was removed. There are also, in every county throughout the State, considerable numbers of children who have broken loose from parental control, who need some kind of reformatory training, and whom to send to houses of refuge would be impolitic and unjust. In these institutions, as at present constituted, proper classification is not practicable.

This seems to have been his first protest against the indiscriminate penalizing of all degrees of juvenile delinquency,—his first plea for a rational classification of offences and offenders amongst the young. It was a plea which became more and more urgent from him in subsequent years. From the months he spent abroad, in 1880, visiting institutions and studying methods of public benevolence, he came back with convictions and feelings on this point confirmed and intensified. He had gathered instruction on many lines from his questioning of foreign experience and practice, but none more decisive than this, of the importance of a systematic classification in the treatment of children with whom the law has to deal. He had found that, generally, this was recognized and acted upon more fully in other countries than in ours, and that thereby they were advanced a step beyond us. It now became one of his most earnest endeavors to create a right view and a right feeling on the subject in the American mind.

A flagrant illustration of the need of that enlightenment was afforded in the spring of 1882, when he discovered a bill making progress through the legislature of New York, which purported to have no other object than the changing of the name of the Western House of Refuge, at Rochester, but which actually was intended to increase in that prisonlike institution an already abominable disregard of grades and qualities in juvenile transgressions. Making haste to Albany, he secured a hearing before the committee which had the bill in charge, and made, in a brief but effectual address, such an exposure of its naked purpose that it seems to have died then and there. "Should this bill become a law," he said to the committee, "the anomalous spectacle would be presented of a heterogeneous collection in one institution of the following classes of children, embracing both sexes: first, the felon; second, the thief; third, the child arrested for assault and battery; fourth, the disorderly; fifth, the malicious; sixth, the truant from school; seventh, the child arrested for begging from door to door; eighth, the abandoned child; ninth, the neglected child; tenth, the street prostitute."

The case of the Western House of Refuge

The Western House of Refuge did obtain

CHILD-SAVING: REFORMATIVE 225

the better name desired for it, and it was saved from an atrocious misuse, to become one of the truest reformative institutions in the United States.

At the Tenth National Conference of Charities and Correction, held at Louisville, in September, 1883, in a paper entitled "Classification and Training of Children, Innocent and Incorrigible," he discussed the subject broadly and at length. *The innocent and the incorrigible* In this paper he quoted from correspondence he had had with the notable English magistrate, T. B. Ll. Baker, Esq., of Hardwicke Court, who had founded a reformatory for boys on his own estate, and whom he had visited while in England three years before. Among the observations of Mr. Baker was this: "The notion of putting a large number of boys together, of all sorts, seems very wild. Of course I cannot say that such a system may not answer with you; though if any man were to propose a similar plan here we should consider it equivalent to a certificate of lunacy."

For the basis of a proper classification of the children coming under public care, for either support or correction, Mr. Letchworth proposed the following fourfold division:—

(1) The homeless and destitute through death or poverty of parents.

(2) Truants from school.

(3) Children rebellious of parental control; those guilty of petty offences and unsuited to orphanages, including vagrants and those in danger of falling.

(4) Boys and girls of hardened nature or hereditary vicious propensities, who are guilty of felonious offences.

Orphanages for the first class, schools for truants for the second, industrial schools for the third, reform schools for the fourth, were the several agencies of care and discipline recommended. That reformatories for boys and girls should be, in all cases, distinct institutions was urged strongly as a conclusion to which all experience led. In the same paper Mr. Letchworth drew attention to legislation in Massachusetts which provides "for the appointment of a state agent, who, in a certain sense, acts as counsel for juvenile offenders." This officer must be notified of complaints in court pending against any boy or girl under seventeen years of age, and have opportunity to investigate the case as well as to attend the trial. On his request the court was authorized to refer the

CHILD-SAVING: REFORMATIVE

disposition of the child to the State Board of Health, Lunacy and Charity. Having given considerable time to a personal investigation, in Massachusetts, of the working of this system, Mr. Letchworth had secured the attendance of the Massachusetts State Agent, Mr. Gardner Tufts, at the meeting of the National Conference of Charities and Correction in 1880, with a paper on the working of the Massachusetts system, which awakened much interest, here and abroad.

As president of the Eleventh National Conference, at St. Louis, in 1884, Mr. Letchworth, in his opening address, put the emphasis of his thought on preventive aims in charitable and reformative work, as the primary rule. "Try to lessen the number of inmates in institutions of all kinds, rather than increase them, especially in institutions for children," he said. "The institution is something to be used only as a last resort. The Massachusetts plan of dealing with juvenile offenders appears to me worthy of general adoption." Briefly explaining the suspension of judicial sentence which this permitted, while the young delinquent was kept under surveillance by the state agent, he went on to say:

The Massachusetts system

"Meanwhile the agent influences the boy and his parents or guardians for his reformation, and reports to the court. If the delinquent improves, the sentence is still further suspended. . . . If it becomes necessary, however, to commit the offender to an institution, the agent is consulted as to what institution he shall be sent to; but the paternal care of the state does not cease here. It follows the delinquent to the institution, where, if it be found that his interest or that of the institution will be promoted by a change, he is transferred elsewhere, on the recommendation of the state agent."

Massachusetts, it will be seen, had conceived and acted on the idea of "probation" more than thirty years ago, and Mr. Letchworth was one of the first of the missionaries of its propagation. The Massachusetts State Agency, in fact, had been doing its work of assistance to the courts in dealing with juvenile transgressors of law since 1869, and other states had given little heed to the example. But that example was held persistently by Commissioner Letchworth before the National Conference of Charities and Correction, in addresses and papers which returned to it again and again.

At the meeting of 1886, in St. Paul, he

presented one of the ablest of his essays on social questions touching the young, entitling it "The Children of the State." In this he ventured "to hazard," as he expressed his undertaking, "the presentation of a plan [of dealing with juvenile delinquents] which is," he said, "the outgrowth of close study of the views of specialists in reformatory work in different countries, and of extended personal observation." His plan started, of course, with *classification* for its fundamental requirement, to discriminate with care between the truant, the homeless child, the wayward, the vagrant, the disorderly, the thief, and the felon. It demanded, too, the reformative training of boys and girls in entirely separate institutions. It condemned institutions of so great a size and congregating such large numbers that individuality is lost and children have to be known by number instead of by name. Beyond these radical principles he framed his plan essentially on the lines of the Massachusetts State Agency system, and a kindred system of county visitors in Michigan, which he had studied and referred to with approbation more than once.

<small>Mr. Letchworth's plan for dealing with juvenile delinquency</small>

A central unpaid supervising board, independent of political influence [he advised], should direct the work, with power to appoint a paid state agent, and an unsalaried agent in every county, who shall be one of a committee of visitors, likewise appointed by such board. It should have jurisdiction over all classes of children brought before the courts with a view to restraint or correction. The local committee should consist of persons residing in different parts of the county, who would look after the delinquent children that had been brought under state supervision, and report respecting them, from time to time, to the county agent, who should likewise report to the state board through the state agent.

The function and authority of the state agent, as contemplated in Mr. Letchworth's plan, would be substantially those of the Massachusetts state agent, already outlined, and he would have the proposed state and county boards and the county agents to assist and support him in his work.

For the disciplining of juvenile delinquency, in its minor exhibitions, when punitive discipline is found necessary, Mr. Letchworth favored a method that he found practised by the School Board of Liverpool, England, in the treatment of obstinate cases of truancy from school. Boys who will not attend school are sent to a house of detention a few miles outside of the city. For terms of from five to not more than thirty days they are kept there, —

under a solitary system, and subjected to the severest training compatible with their years and the preservation of their health. Food is taken to their rooms. They are marched in single file to the shops, where they work in small squads. No recreation except outside calisthenics is permitted. The rules forbid conversation or any kind of intercourse between the boys. This punishment having been administered once, it is rarely found necessary to inflict it again. . . . In this brief but sharp and severe punishment there is no lasting stigma upon the character nor injury to the person, nor is there danger of moral contamination from evil associates. Similar houses for the correction of juvenile delinquency might be established near our large cities, and prove useful in materially lessening commitments to our houses of refuge and reform schools, thus relieving them of much of their expensively conducted work. . . . In case the conduct of a boy could not be corrected by the influence of the county agent, or by holding him under suspended sentence, or in family care, he might be committed for a short term to a house of detention. If one or two repetitions of this kind of punishment should not prove effectual, a longer discipline in the reform school should be tried. . . .

The adoption of the preventive measures as suggested would make it necessary to commit but few to the reform school; and in the plan proposed this institution should be located on a farm removed some distance from the city, and organized and controlled, when practicable, by private benevolence. It should receive aid from the state, city, or county, but not sufficient to maintain it, so that public sympathy would be kept alive in the reformatory work. Parents, too, should be required to contribute, in accordance with their means, towards the support of their children in these institutions, in order that they may feel a due share of responsibility.

These schools should be small, such having proved the most successful. They should be examined by a central supervising board, and certified to as suitable for the care and training of delinquents, before being permitted to receive inmates, and this examination should be repeated and the certificate renewed each year as a condition to continuance. Should peculiar circumstances make it desirable that the institution receive more than one hundred inmates, the cottage plan should be adopted. The internal system of a reformatory school should be as nearly as practicable that of the family, with its refining and elevating influences; while the awakening of the conscience and the inculcation of religious principles should be primary aims. . . .

Every boy should be instructed in some useful trade

CHILD-SAVING: REFORMATIVE 233

or occupation, and his wishes consulted in selecting it. Trades should be taught under the Russian system of technologic training, whereby a boy, as Mr. Auchmuty in his trade school in New York has demonstrated, may be taught plumbing, carpentry, stone- and brick-laying, plastering, and other useful handicrafts, in from three to four months; and when so taught, although not having the expertness that comes with practice, is a better mechanic than if he had spent five years in acquiring a trade in the old way, because he has learned the principles of mechanics and chemistry that are applicable to his trade. Such as prefer farming and gardening, so far as season and weather permit, should be employed and instructed in those pursuits.

It is now a quarter of a century since this systematic plan of reformative treatment, to be applied to those differing disposi- *Present acceptance of* tions or ill-trainings of the young *these ideas* which tend toward an inveterate perversity, was worked out by the most careful student of the subject in that day. As a systematic plan, so far as the present writer has knowledge, it has never been instituted and put in practice anywhere, and perhaps it will never be, though every feature of the organization recommended in it appears to be soundly and practically designed; but the ideas, the experiments, and the experiences that were gathered together and constructively combined in it have substantially all been brought widely into recognition and acceptance within these twenty-five years. The careful classification of juvenile misdoings, the suspension of judicial sentences, the probationing of young transgressors, the farm-planting of reform schools, the cottage colony, the systematic industrial training, — these have all come now to be requirements which an enlightened community is expected to meet in the designing and conducting of its reformative institutions. The last decade, especially, has produced an extraordinary ripening in the public mind of the scientific and rational as well as philanthropic ideas which they represent. When Mr. Letchworth assembled them in his plan it is not to be supposed for a moment that he drew any of those ideas from his own originating mind. It was never his way to rest a recommendation that he offered to the public on a merely theoretical idea. All the problems in public philanthropy that he dealt with were studied in the light of such experiments and experiences as applied a sure test to the theory from which they sprang.

His investigations to that end were the most remarkable part of his work. No time, no labor, no travel, no sacrifice of his personal comfort was too much for him to give to the searching out and inspecting of institutions and of laws which had object lessons of method to offer, with conclusive provings of result. He was unmatched among social workers in that effectual study, and therefore unmatched as a public teacher on the vital subjects which he prepared himself to speak upon with high authority. The authority of his opinion on these matters was recognized, because the carefulness of the quest which went before the opinion was always plain. Hence, it can safely be said that the influence of Mr. Letchworth, beyond any other personal influence in the last generation, has entered into the producing of a wholly different public opinion at the present day, touching the public treatment of dependent and delinquent children, compared with that of the time when he began his work as a commissioner in the Board of Charities of the State of New York.

Effectual study of problems

Three years prior to his presentation of the above elaborated plan of dealing with juvenile delinquents, in a paper prepared, on the invitation of the Société Générale de Protection pour l'Enfance abandonnée ou coupable, for the Congrès International de la Protection de l'Enfance, held at Paris in June, 1883, he had submitted "Seventeen Propositions relating to Child-saving Work" which embodied the same principles, substantially, in an excellently condensed form. Later, in 1888, these "Seventeen Propositions" were laid before the National Conference of Charities and Correction, at its session in Buffalo, and discussed with much approval, in debate on the report of the committee on the care and disposal of dependent children. They are as follows:—

Seventeen child-saving propositions

First. There should be a proper classification, primarily into the following divisions: (*a*) Children thrown upon the public for support by misfortune or poverty of parents. (*b*) Truants from school subject to the compulsory education laws. (*c*) Children homeless, or with bad associations, who are in danger of falling, and who need homelike care and training rather than reformatory treatment. (*d*) Incorrigibles, felons, those experienced in crime, and the fallen needing reformation.

Second. Provision should be made for girls, except the younger class, in institutions separate from boys.

Third. The institution should be homelike in character, and its administration as nearly as possible that of family life.

Fourth. Small institutions on the open or cottage plan should be provided for boys, upon farms in the country, where agriculture and gardening may be combined with a thorough indoor and common-school system.

Fifth. The labor of children should, under no circumstances, be hired to contractors.

Sixth. Government supervision should be exercised over all institutions for children, and frequent examinations made as to sanitary and other conditions, annual approval by the Government being requisite to the continuance of the work.

Seventh. Power should be lodged in a central authority to transfer inmates from one institution to another, in order to perfect and maintain classifications; also to remove juvenile offenders from institutions and place them in family care during good conduct; also to remove from institutional care and to place permanently in homes all children suited to family life.

Eighth. There should be provided a governmental agency to act in the interest of juvenile offenders when on trial. The agency should be vested with power, with the approval of the judge, to take the delinquent into custody under suspended sentence and place him on probation in a family.

Ninth. Disinterested benevolence should control and direct work as far as practicable, the state or local Government contributing, if need be, but not to an extent sufficient to meet the whole expense.

Tenth. The coöperation of women of elevated character should be considered essential to the attainment of the highest success.

Eleventh. Parents able to do so should be made to contribute to the support of their children while under reformatory treatment.

Twelfth. When debased parents have demonstrated their inability or unwillingness to support their children, and the latter in consequence have become a charge upon the public, the interest of the child should be regarded as paramount, and the rights of the parent should cease, the state assuming control.

Thirteenth. Children who in their home life had been environed by vicious associations and adverse influences, should, on their release from institutional custody, be transplanted to new and, perhaps, distant homes with good surroundings.

Fourteenth. A study of the child's character and a knowledge of its antecedents should be considered essential to successful work.

Fifteenth. The delinquent child should be regarded as morally diseased, and a correct diagnosis of its moral condition should be made and carefully considered in applying remedies for the cure. This having been done the strengthening of character by awak-

CHILD-SAVING: REFORMATIVE

ening hope, building up self-respect, and inculcating moral and religious principles will be more easily effected.

Sixteenth. In the process of restoration, homes in good families should be made available to the utmost extent possible.

Seventeenth. Technological training should be given in juvenile reformatories where practicable.

The founding of an institution which accorded with Mr. Letchworth's ideas and enlisted his hearty interest was undertaken in 1885 by a gentleman, Mr. Frederick J. Burnham, who resided in New Jersey, but who planted his benevolent enterprise in the State of New York. A valuable estate of about six hundred acres, situated near Canaan Four Corners, Columbia County, New York, was devoted by Mr. Burnham to the establishment thereon of an industrial farm for unruly and delinquent boys. He had not the wealth necessary for endowing the institution, further than with the all-important estate of land, and he struggled for years with difficulties in securing sufficient help from others to put it on its feet. In those years it is evident that he was greatly upheld by Mr. Letchworth's influence, encouragement, and aid. "Mrs. Burn-

Burnham Industrial Farm

ham and I look upon you as the inspiration and the guide of this work," are Mr. Burnham's words in a letter of 1887, — the year after the Burnham Industrial Farm had been incorporated by legislative act. "For your constant and generous sympathy and kindness I can scarcely find words to express our gratitude" is the expression in another, two years later. How victorious the heroic struggle came to be in the end is reported by the same hand in a letter to Mr. Letchworth written November 14, 1904. "The work," wrote Mr. Burnham, "is now prospering. Eighty boys have been receiving care and instruction there during the past year, and the results are most encouraging. The news from the boys who have gone from our institution to find work and a place in the world are very gratifying. Most of them are doing well, and their letters show a manly spirit of self-reliance. Not one has asked for any help, and all express their affection for the Farm." Such fruit-reports from fields in which he helped the seed-sowing were among the rewards of which Mr. Letchworth had many.

That a juvenile reformatory should be, systematically, an industrial training-school, had become a clear conviction in Mr. Letchworth's

CHILD-SAVING: REFORMATIVE 241

mind when, at the National Conference in Louisville, in 1883, he discussed the subject of "Classification and Training," and much of his paper was devoted to that view. By personal visitation of reformatories and by correspondence with the people in charge of them he had acquainted himself with facts which determined his mind absolutely on one primary point, namely, in condemnation of the contract system of employment for the inmates of such reformatories. He had found that New York was in company with only three other states in maintaining the contract system; while fifteen of her associates in the Union had discarded it. He had found that under the contract system seven industries only were carried on, while twenty-two were proved to be practicable in the institutions which did not hire their boys and girls to contractors. He had found that "under the free labor system a full trade is frequently if not generally taught, and the boys become expert workmen in their particular line, while under the contract system no such opportunity is afforded, and but one operation or process is inculcated." He had found that "the contract system is peculiar to America"; he could not

[sidenote: Contract labor in reformatories]

find it existing in Europe,—"in any juvenile reformatory either on the Continent or in the United Kingdom of Great Britain and Ireland."

When abroad, "on the Continent," he wrote, "I was particularly struck with the thoroughness of the instruction and the skill attained by the pupils in every department. In summer the principal occupations are farming and gardening, and such other work as keeps the children out of doors and tends to make them strong and robust; while the inclement weather and winter months are selected for such industrial and intellectual education as may be afforded indoors. . . . At the Rauhe Haus, near Hamburg, established by Immanuel Wichern of revered memory, the following trades were being carried on: blacksmithing, carpentering, tailoring, shoemaking, printing, wagonmaking, gardening, etc." At the Netherlands Mettray and the French Mettray, near Tours, the industries taught and conducted were much the same.

The conclusive objections to the contract labor system in reformatory institutions were summed up by Mr. Letchworth in a few words, as follows:—

CHILD-SAVING: REFORMATIVE

It subordinates the reformation and improvement of the child to the interest of the contractor; introduces a foreign element into the institution, in the person of the contractors' employés, who have no sympathy with the cause of reform, but, on the contrary, exercise a vicious influence.

It also interferes with opportunities for intellectual instruction and recreation; imposes long hours of work, and makes the boy believe that he is part of a scheme for making money for the institution. He works grudgingly, and is encouraged to steal and misrepresent his labor in order to satisfy demands upon him.

The system is at fault as an industrial education, inasmuch as by its plan of teaching but one process in the operation, the boy does not learn a complete trade.

A winning fight

Already, in the previous year, with the coöperation of Senator Titus, representing the Buffalo district in the State Senate, Mr. Letchworth had opened attack on the contract system of labor in reformatory or correctional institutions. Senator Titus had introduced and given earnest support to a bill which would make it unlawful " to contract, hire, or let by the day, week, or month, or any longer period, the services or labor of any child or children under sixteen years of age"; and Mr.

Letchworth, in March, 1882, addressed an argument to the senate committee having charge of the bill, bringing a great array of testimony from officials in other states which trained their delinquent children to useful work, and did not put them to labor for hire. "I had no idea that such a thing was done anywhere," wrote one secretary of a Western state board of charities and reform. But the New York Legislature was not easily to be moved by mere argument and testimony on a question of reform, and the bill died in its hands.

Mr. Letchworth had become accustomed to pleading again and again in vain, at Albany, for such betterments of method in public benevolence, and accustomed likewise to winning his plea in the end. Next year, with Senator Titus, he returned to the attack; and this time he brought communications from "all the resident officers in charge of juvenile reformatory institutions throughout the United States," representing thirty-five institutions, in twenty-seven of which the labor was conducted on free lines. Still the influences in opposition were strong enough to smother the proposed reform. But in the third year of the campaign against contract labor, which Commissioner Letchworth

CHILD-SAVING: REFORMATIVE 245

reopened with unshaken faith, public opinion appears to have voiced itself, in a tone which Albany hears and obeys, and the desired law was enacted on the fourth of June, 1884.

Having secured the expulsion of contract labor from juvenile reformative institutions, Mr. Letchworth turned his exertions at once towards giving the best attainable quality to the industrial training undertaken in its place. *[Industrial training]* He had already been questioning experience in the matter, wherever it seemed instructive, and had learned that there came to the Centennial Exposition at Philadelphia, in 1876, an exhibit from Russia of methods in teaching mechanic arts which alert minds in Massachusetts and elsewhere had caught suggestions from and made practical trials of, with remarkable satisfaction. President John D. Runkle, of the Massachusetts Institute of Technology, had brought it into operation in the Mechanic Art School connected with that technical university. There our State Commissioner went, to make a thorough study of the system, procuring photographs, models used in giving lessons, and descriptions of whole courses of the lessons given, in their serial order, disclosing the end of an intelligent workmanship to which they were pursued. At the same time he studied the somewhat similar methods, having similar aims, which Mr. Auchmuty, a wealthy architect of New York City, had introduced in a school which he founded for the education of artisans in the principles that underlie their several trades.

From other sources of practical experience he gathered further illustrations, of the great and important educational results that are obtainable from an industrial training conducted on such lines as seemed to be worked out most perfectly in the system known as the Russian technologic. "Under this system," as he convinced himself, "not only does the boy learn a trade, but he learns it quickly; at the same time he is taught, by successive and natural stages, scientific principles underlying all trades, so that when he leaves school, whether he follows a trade in which he has been instructed or not, he can adapt himself to other pursuits, in which the knowledge he has acquired may be utilized."

Thus prepared for well-informed and clear discussion of the subject, he obtained a hearing on it before the board of managers of the Western House of Refuge, at Rochester, on the

26th of February, 1884. The facts and the exhibits he submitted were convincing, and in the following month the board adopted the report of a special committee to whom the question had been referred and who recommended a memorial to the legislature, asking for an appropriation of fifteen thousand dollars, to cover the cost of tools, fixtures, and instructors for one hundred boys. The legislature proved gracious, and made the appropriation, but the Governor found reasons for disapproving it and striking it out. This, however, meant no more than delay; it was not defeat. The needed appropriation was obtained a little later, and Commissioner Letchworth had the satisfaction of seeing the Western House of Refuge changed in name to the State Industrial School, in 1886, and changed in character, correspondingly, in the next year, by the installation of a fully worthy and scientific system of industrial education. The shops then established were for carpentry, lathe and pattern work, forging and foundry work.

Transforming the Western House of Refuge

In February of this important year the building occupied by girls was burned, and Mr. Letchworth became the leader of strenuous efforts to improve the opportunity thus afforded for establishing the girls in a different institution, entirely apart. In a long letter addressed to the speaker of the assembly he pleaded, not merely for a separation of sexes in the measure, but for the creation of a reformatory which should not be a prison,—for a reformatory on the farm and cottage or cottage and family plan, which trial had approved in Massachusetts, Michigan, Connecticut and Ohio. He accompanied his argument, as usual, with abundant supporting testimony, and illuminated it with plans and illustrations of the buildings and grounds of the Michigan State Industrial Home for Girls. The argument was unanswerable, but it was addressed to deaf ears. Sixteen years later Mr. Letchworth republished it, with the remark that "the reasons given herewith for establishing a separate girls' reformatory . . . are as pertinent to-day as when they were presented to the speaker of the assembly in 1887." The question had then arisen again, and half a generation of change in the public and the public mind of New York had brought so much enlightenment that legislative consent to the separate girls' reformatory was obtained. In the summer of 1904 it was established at Albion, under the name of the Western House of Refuge for Women. Three more years carried nearly to a full realization the ideals of a reformative institution for young delinquents which Mr. Letchworth had been pressing upon the attention of his state so long. In 1907 the boys of the grim old Western House of Refuge, at Rochester, were taken out of their walled prison and transferred to cottages, on a large country farm, a few miles beyond the city, in a place to which the fitting name of Industry has been given.

Under its new conditions the State Industrial School exercises its protégés and pupils in gardening, farming, and dairy-work, extensively, as well as in the shop trades of blacksmithing, carpentry, tailoring, printing, laundrying, baking, painting, masonry, etc. At last accounts its inmates occupied thirty-one cottages, each having accommodations for twenty-five boys.

It gladdens one to know that Mr. Letchworth lived long enough to see such perfected fruit as the present State Industrial School in one of the fields of his most earnest and ardent labor. It is to be hoped, too, that such an incident as the following, related in the Rochester *Post-Express* of April

An impressive incident

13, 1911, came to his knowledge in his last years:—

A few years before the school was closed [in its old place, at Rochester, but after the introduction of the better industrial training which Mr. Letchworth had fairly forced upon it], there walked into the office a silk-hatted, frock-coated man, who asked to be shown through the building. He seemed to be familiar with the halls, and finally stopped before a row of doors opening into the little rooms in the boys' building. His guide watched him closely and then asked, "Which room was it?" The man looked startled, and then slowly replied, "It was that little room, right there." The inspection continued until they came to the blacksmith rooms, when the man walked to a certain anvil and, kneeling beside it, prayed: "I thank Thee, O God, for giving to William Pryor Letchworth the vision of Thine understanding and of the need of Thine erring children." The man had been sent to the school as a boy, and had worked for hours over the anvil at which he had stopped. Leaving the school with an apprenticeship served, he readily secured employment, and, through the habits of study acquired at the school, soon mastered some of the technical details of ironworking. Eventually he became a large contractor, and is to-day a wealthy man. That was just one of the instances which came to the notice of the officers of the institution, of the tremendous factor for good that this work became.

In tracing the child-saving lines to which Mr. Letchworth devoted his work especially, during half or more of the years of his official service, we have passed by much that he did to other ends. In 1873-75 he was engrossed, as we have seen, quite entirely in his undertakings (1) to rescue homeless children from poorhouses and the like; (2) to ascertain the sufficiency of hospitality for them in existing orphanages; (3) to stimulate the passing on of such unfortunates from orphanages to family homes. In the next few years his chief interest and labor were given to that vitally important condition of a successful reformative treatment of juvenile wrongdoers which demands discrimination between the wayward and the depraved, and forbids their being mixed, as he found them mixed in the so-called reformatories and houses of refuge of the State of New York. When signs of a hopeful planting of this fundamental suggestion in the better minds of the state began to appear, he opened his campaign for the abolition of contract labor in reformative institutions; for the conversion of them into industrial schools, imparting to their inmates the most perfect knowledge of industrial arts by the most scien-

Successive objects of Mr. Letchworth's work

tific and effective methods that have been devised; and, finally, for the demolishing of their prison walls, transferring them to cottages in country fields. But, meantime, he had turned frequently to other tasks, and these, with some attending incidents of his life, must now be reviewed.

In 1876 he accepted the presidency of an association organized in Wyoming County, New York, to undertake the building, at Warsaw, the countyseat, of a monument to the soldiers and sailors of the war for the Union. There is evidence in his letter books that he pulled the stroke oar, so to speak, in this undertaking, and gave to it, for many months, a large measure of his thought and his time. It is almost needless to say that the project was carried to success.

Neighborhood tasks and home life

In October of that year he was borne down for a time by a shock of sorrow, which came, unlooked for, in a telegram announcing his mother's death. He was absent from home at the time, in New York, as he had been absent, in Europe, when his father died. His affection for his parents had been very warm, and it added to his grief that he could not have been with either father or mother in the last hours.

CHILD-SAVING: REFORMATIVE

The spring of the next year brought a glad change into the circumstances of his life at Glen Iris, by giving him the companionship there of his widowed eldest sister, Mrs. Crozer. Thenceforward until her death Mrs. Crozer was the presiding genius of his home, and his happiness in it was made more complete.

When this occurred he had just accepted (April, 1877), from Governor Lucius Robinson, a reappointment on the State Board of Charities for the term of eight years. Among the new commissioners who now came into the Board was Mrs. Josephine Shaw Lowell, of New York City,— the first woman to be chosen for this important service of the state. Mrs. Lowell had been active in the State Charities Aid Association, and was distinguished throughout her life for zeal and efficiency in social service. She brought a notable reinforcement of energy and sound judgment to the Board, and Mr. Letchworth, who became its president that year, on the death of Mr. Pruyn, had no counsellor and supporter more valued than she. His official cares and labor would, in any event, have been much increased by his advancement to the presidency; but such a consequence was doubled for him by the dis-

Reappointment on State Board

position to indefatigable thoroughness of performance and to unbelief in failure or defeat which he had carefully trained in himself.

In the course of this year, 1877, he made a thorough general inspection of all the charities in the Eighth Judicial District of the state,—the district which he specially represented in the State Board. This covered eight counties at the western extremity of New York. The institutions inspected and reported on to the Board were thirty-five in number, including poorhouses, hospitals, reformatories, asylums, and "homes."

Official tasks of 1877-79

In May, 1877, on the request of the state comptroller, the executive committee of the Board undertook an investigation of the management and affairs of the New York State Institution for the Blind, at Batavia, and the chief burden of labor connected therewith was accepted by Commissioner Letchworth. After twelve days with his associates of the Committee at Batavia, given to inspections and the examination of witnesses, he went personally to Boston, Philadelphia, Columbus, and Indianapolis, to visit other institutions for the instruction of the blind, in pursuit of information which the committee desired. The result was a highly impor-

CHILD-SAVING: REFORMATIVE

tant report of comparative facts, touching the management of four of the most highly esteemed schools for the blind. The findings of the investigation were not favorable to the administration of the institution at Batavia.

The most arduous of Mr. Letchworth's labors in 1878 was the preparation of a report on "Plans for Poorhouses," made in response to a request from the Board. He found, he said, in submitting his report, that "the absence in architectural literature of plans and descriptions of buildings adapted to a population so mixed and characteristic as that of county poorhouses" had rendered the task assigned him "more difficult and its necessity more obvious." From an inspection of poorhouses in all of the New England States and in a number of Western States, as well as in New York; from a careful examination of official plans that had originated in boards of state charities and boards of health, and from the opinions of a large number of experts, he brought an extensive mass of descriptive suggestions as well as illustrative designs. His own conclusions touching location, drainage, sewerage, building material, foundations, walls of superstructure, wainscoting, floors, flues, stairs, roofs, heating, ventilation, bathrooms, sun-exposure, etc., were clearly set forth, and with them he presented a sketch plan of the arrangement of poorhouse structures which his own judgment approved.

Another of his tasks of this year was an investigation of the Steuben County Poorhouse, consequent on the occurrence of a fire which destroyed sixteen lives. Twice before there had been fatal fires at the same institution, the first in 1839, when an insane pauper was burned, the second in 1859, when six lives were lost. Deplorable conditions of long standing were disclosed by the inquiry, and responsibility for them was traced quite plainly to the general public of the county, which had given no heed to facts often set before it.

Within this year the tireless Commissioner of the Eighth Judicial District repeated his visitation of all but one of the charitable institutions in that district, for the reason that "numerous improvements and extensions" had been made since his round of twelve months before, and he wished to see the changed conditions and report them.

On the dedication of the Soldiers' and Sailors' Home, at Bath, New York, January 23, 1879, Mr. Letchworth was invited to make the principal address. The president of the board of trustees of the Home, General Henry W. Slocum, introduced him with the following remarks: "While we do not admit that this Home is, in a strict sense of the word, a charitable institution, we realize the fact that it is hereafter to be supported by the state, and for this reason we have requested the State Board of Charities to visit us, to examine our work and our expenditures. This Board is one which, without compensation, is doing great good in our state. All of its members will at all times be welcome visitors to this Home. We want their advice and assistance. I take great pleasure in introducing to you Mr. Letchworth, the president of the State Board of Charities."

In Mr. Letchworth's address there was no taint of patriotic bombast. It was full of practical purpose throughout, especially describing the extent to which infirm and disabled veterans of the War for the Union were to be found in the poorhouses of the state, and appealing for exertions to remove them from that tainted association into the comradeship of the Soldiers' Home. At the same time he improved the opportunity for pleading the cause of the chronic insane in our poorhouses,—a barbarously wronged and suffering class, whose case was now beginning to appeal to him as strongly as that of the misused "children of the state" had done.

In this year, 1879, Commissioner Letchworth took part in two investigations, one concerning the insane asylum of the Onondaga County Poorhouse, in which the committee of the State Board acted with a committee of the County Board of Supervisors. The revelations in this, though less sickening than many which came to light later, were well calculated to deepen the feelings that were spurring our reformer to make the bettering of treatment for the insane the supreme object of endeavor for the remainder of his life.

The second investigation of the year, brought about by complaints and charges against the Society for the Reformation of Juvenile Delinquents, Randall's Island, New York, was conducted daily, at Randall's Island, on every secular day, from October 16 until and including December 22. The investigating committee was composed of Mr. Letchworth, as president, and Commissioners Donnelly and Van Antwerp, — the latter from Albany and the former from New York. The inquiry was searching;

the findings were unequivocal. Some of the managers could be lauded for devotion to their duty; but not more than half of the board of thirty were active in the work, and less than half attended the meetings of the board. The superintendent had the confidence of the managers; but testimony taken went to show that many things occurred in the House of which no record or report was ever made. The investigators made numerous recommendations, the most important being these: That the charter of the Society "be so amended as to confine its jurisdiction exclusively to the class of criminal commitments for the higher grade of crimes and to children over twelve and under sixteen years of age; that the work of reforming delinquent girls be carried on separately and in a distant locality. That such an arrangement of buildings and grounds be effected as will insure as thorough a classification of the inmates as is possible, according to their moral condition."

In November, 1879, Commissioner Letchworth, as president of the State Board of Charities, headed the representation of that Board and of other New York state and city officials, in a conference of grave importance with corresponding

New York at issue with Massachusetts

officials of Massachusetts, on the subject of the transfer of paupers from the latter to the former state. A cause of grievance in this arose from the fact that immigrants landed at New York City, but passing on into Massachusetts, and there becoming subjects of charity, were dealt with as belonging to New York, and sent back accordingly. Moreover, as the New York State Board complianed, " while in New York State paupers are removed only with their consent, and then to their places of destination, in Massachusetts no option is extended to them, but they are imperatively thrust out of her borders to burden this or other states." Controversy over these practices had been going on for two years, when the Massachusetts Commissioners of Health, Lunacy, and Charity accepted an invitation from the New York State Board of Charities to meet the latter in New York City for a thorough discussion of the questions involved. No definite agreements were reached at the conference; but the Massachusetts representatives, at the end of a spirited interchange of views, expressed the wish for another meeting in their own state, and their hope that it would lead ultimately to an amicable adjustment of differences.

Later national legislation, which began in

CHILD-SAVING: REFORMATIVE 261

1882, aiming to bar paupers and defective persons from admission to the country, has gone far, no doubt, towards extinguishing the question over which New York and Massachusetts were in dispute thirty years ago. The matter was one which had been exercising the mind of Mr. Letchworth ever since he began to acquaint himself with the conditions under which pauperism exists in the United States. At the National Conference of Charities and Correction, held in 1875, at Detroit, he took part in the discussion of a paper on "Immigration," read by Mr. Hamilton Andrews Hill, of Boston, and argued strongly against an indiscriminate hospitality to every kind of stranger from other countries who might seek or be sent to the open gates of our land. "Without care," he said, "we might be led to overlook the need of enforcing certain necessary measures of state policy"; his personal observation in various poorhouses having convinced him that "an organized system exists in other countries for shipping hopelessly dependent persons to this country." "Instead of relaxation in law, more stringent protective laws are demanded." In 1879 he proposed resolutions which were adopted by the State Board of Charities, asking Congress for legislation to this end; and he suggested similar action to the International Prison Congress that year.

The New York-Massachusetts Conference, in which Dr. Martin B. Anderson, President of Rochester University, bore a prominent part, was the last important occasion on which Mr. Letchworth was associated officially with that greatly esteemed colleague, between whom and himself the sympathies exercised in their common work were especially close. In April, 1880, Dr. Anderson was compelled, by the weight of his duties at the university, to resign from the State Board. In doing so he wrote to Commissioner Letchworth: "I should have resigned three years ago, had it not been for your earnest desire that I should remain longer on the Board. . . . You are kind enough to speak of assistance that I may have rendered you in the discharge of your duties as president of the Board. Permit me to say that whenever I can aid you in any way in your work in the future you may command me to the extent of my strength and ability. My associations with you have been among the pleasantest of my life, and I beg you always to consider me as a near personal friend."

CHAPTER VII

WORK FOR THE INSANE

A HORRIBLE condition of the chronic insane in the poorhouses of the State of New York was reported to the legislature in 1844, by Miss Dorothea L. Dix; then again in 1858 by a committee of the Senate; and still again, in 1865, by Dr. Willard, Secretary of the State Medical Society, after a personal investigation by him; and it was not until this last-mentioned revelation that anything was done to reform the shocking barbarity. The legislature was moved then to action which resulted in the establishment of the Willard Asylum, at Ovid, for the reception of the pauper chronic insane, previously caged in the poorhouses like wild beasts. The Willard Asylum was not ready, however, until 1869, and the State Board of Charities, created in 1867, and making its first examination of the poorhouses in 1868, found the chronic insane "in the same wretched and deplorable condition as had been described in the several reports before." According to the report of the Board, "the number of such insane then in these institutions was 1528. Of these, 213 were found chained or confined in cells. It was learned that nearly all of these had been for long periods thus chained or confined. A large proportion were violent and destructive, untidy and filthy in their habits and persons, and several were observed entirely nude."

It became apparent very early that the accommodations of the Willard Asylum would not suffice for the numbers required by the law to be removed, and in 1871 the legislature passed an act authorizing the State Board of Charities to grant exemptions from the law to counties whose buildings, etc., were found fit and adequate for the retention of their chronic insane. This became a source of much troublesome hindrance to the undertaking of reform.

Such were the conditions at which the State of New York had arrived in the care of its chronic insane when Mr. Letchworth became a member of its Board of Charities. He made acquaintance with them almost as early as with those conditions in the poorhouses which were educating children to pauperism and vagrancy and criminality, and they summoned him to strive against them by as urgent a call; but his

"ROCK-BOUND BATTLEMENTS"

WORK FOR THE INSANE

enlistment in the cause of the children had come first, and it engrossed his time and effort during the early years of his service on the State Board. Even from the first of those years, however, he began the championship of the insane in the part of his special district of the state which came most immediately under his eye. In October, 1873, he reported to the State Board the results of an investigation that he had made of the insane department of the Erie County Almshouse, showing its inmates to be kept in an intolerable state. They numbered one hundred and sixty-eight, and so crowded the quarters provided for them that "two patients in most instances, and sometimes three," were "compelled to occupy a small cell measuring but five feet four inches by seven feet two inches." Thus "the unfortunates were literally packed into the asylum. The cells were, of course, originally constructed for one inmate, though even then they fell far short of sanitary requirements. They had each but one bedstead, and the additional occupants had to be provided for by spreads on the floor, which filled up almost all the remaining space in the cell." There was no provision for hospital wards. The water supply was inadequate,

Beginning investigations

the main supply being brought in tubs from wells in the pauper department. There were no bathing facilities.

By presenting the facts to the County Board of Supervisors (who had been grossly neglectful of duty if they had not known them before, and heartless if they had known them), Commissioner Letchworth obtained action from that body which provided means for some remedial measures; but the committee charged with the undertaking soon found that expenditure on the existing buildings would be wasted, and the situation remained unchanged for another year. Meantime the state commissioner was consulted in the preparation of plans for a new building, which relieved and improved the situation considerably, but not to the extent that right feelings of humanity required. Official action in the county halted again until it was pushed, in 1876, to the erection of a wing, which the original building had contemplated, and to the promise of a second wing, for which there was still an urgent need. The promise was tardily fulfilled, after more official expostulation, in 1879. Two years later, in September, 1881, when Commissioner Letchworth made another inspection of the poorhouse, and especially its insane department, he found generally good conditions, but a serious inadequacy in the water supply, with defects in the sewerage, and was compelled to say: "It is a matter for regret that expenditures have been made in connection with this asylum not in accordance with the original plan, approved by the State Board of Charities, nor in keeping with true economy. . . . The consequence is that the plan of the asylum is incomplete and one of its primary aims [the effective separation of the sexes] defeated."

Knowing that conditions even worse than those he dealt with in Erie County were existing in other parts of the state, he was manifestly distressed by his inability during this period to expose them in a more general way. In January, 1876, he addressed an earnest letter to Miss Dix, imploring her to come again, if it might be possible, into the field of her noble exertions more than thirty years before, and strive to rouse the conscience of the country on the subject of the still barbarous treatment of the insane.

In 1878 he accepted the chairmanship of a committee appointed by the State Board of Charities to investigate, conjointly with a committee appointed by the Onondaga County Board of Supervisors, the condition and management of the county insane asylum in that county, concerning which serious complaints had been made. The investigation, in December, 1878, produced a report in which both committees agreed, condemning the asylum buildings entirely; finding the heating inadequate, the lighting imperfect, the sewerage defective, the water supply insufficient, the bedding and the clothing of the inmates insufficient for winter, the use of dungeons unjustifiable, the number of attendants too small, and, finally, "that the opinion entertained and practised by the chief attendant and others, that it was proper to inflict punishment upon the insane by striking them with a strap, showering them,— that is, dashing water in their faces while they are held on the floor,— depriving them of food for a time, and confining them in dungeons, was founded in the grossest ignorance and was inhuman in the extreme." Before this report reached the State Board of Charities, in the following March, the Onondaga County authorities had introduced steam-heating throughout its poorhouse and insane asylum, demolished the dungeons in the latter, put in new water-closets, as well as bathing conveniences, appointed a resident physician, and discharged all of the old force of attendants.

What has now been related shows substantially all that Mr. Letchworth, before his investigating tour of European countries in 1880, had been able to make of effort toward suppressing the heartlessness and instructing the ignorance which went, still, into so much of the treatment of the insane in our country, especially in the county institutions provided for them. The investigations of that tour, as we have seen, added largely to his preparation for labors in this line, as they did likewise to his preparation for endeavors to improve the aims and the working of our institutions for child reform. He came back from his travels, we may assume, with a well-determined intention to divide himself between these two missions, so far as official duty permitted him to specialize his work. The ideals of reformative training for the young which he strove to introduce have been indicated in the previous chapter. The ideals of treatment due to demented human beings, which actuated his work in the interest of those most pitiable of the afflicted, were elaborately set forth in the final chapter of his subsequently published work on "The Insane in Foreign Countries." Pending the publication of that work, he indicated them briefly in his address as president of the National Conference of Charities and Correction, at the meeting in St. Louis, October, 1884.

Alluding then to his "recent personal examination of a large number of European hospitals for the insane," and stating his conclusion "that there were many features in transatlantic systems superior to ours," which it gladdened him to see that "we are rapidly adopting,"—expressing at the same time his belief that "the way is open for European alienists to learn something from us,"—he touched on what had been done in late years to better the treatment of insanity, and proceeded to say:—

<small>Statement of aims and ideals</small>

I think we are now entering upon an era of still broader beneficence, and that the improvement to come will embrace the highest aims of philanthropy and the soundest principles of science,—a time when our laws respecting committal and discharge will be so perfected that violations of personal liberty will not occur; when the persons and property of the mentally diseased shall be fully protected; when the doors of an asylum shall open outward as freely as inward; when there will be no more reluctance to place those

WORK FOR THE INSANE

suffering from mental ailments in a hospital for the insane than in any other; when popular views respecting these institutions will not stand in the way of early treatment and consequently more hopeful cure; when the gloomy walls, the iron gratings, and prison-like appearance now characteristic of many of these institutions will disappear, and simpler, homelike structures, with a more natural life and greater freedom for the patient, with healthful outdoor employment and recreation diversified with indoor occupation and simple entertainment, will take their place; when the truth that "the laborer is worthy of his hire" will be recognized, and patients performing labor shall feel that they have some recompense, however trifling, for their services; when in every hospital shall be trained nurses and women physicians for female patients; when the moral element shall be coequal with the medical element in treatment; when gentleness shall take the place of force, and the principle set forth by the founders of the Pennsylvania Hospital, that the insane "should be regarded as men and brethren," shall become universal; and, finally, a still more blessed time, when there shall prevail throughout society an intelligent idea as to the causes which produce insanity, and prevention shall largely obviate the necessity of cure.

To contribute what he could to the stirring of a desire in the public mind for these reforms, by revelations of the stress of need for them and by demonstrations of their practicability, was now the main business of his life for something more than ten years. On the educational side of these endeavors his most important and effective undertaking was the preparation of his notable work on "The Insane in Foreign Countries," which he began soon after his return from abroad; but a number of years passed before it went to print. Investigations to expose the existing sufferings of the insane had more immediate urgency, and required much time. Labors for the promotion of wiser systems of reformative training for delinquent children consumed more; and when the general duties of his laborious office and his extensive correspondence had had their due of attention, not much of time or strength remained for such painstaking literary work as Mr. Letchworth's had to be.

Account of European institutions

He lost no time in setting on foot the investigations that would point and give motive to everything else that could be done. Three months after his arrival home he had obtained from the State Board of Charities (at its meeting in May, 1881) the appointment of himself, with two other

Investigation of poorhouse care of the insane

commissioners of the Board, Mr. Devereaux and Miss Carpenter, as a committee to visit and report on the condition of the insane department of poorhouses in counties exempted by the Board, under the Act of 1871, from the statute requiring the chronic insane to be transferred to the Willard Asylum. Commissioner Devereaux was unable to serve, and the investigation was made by Commissioners Letchworth and Carpenter. The institutions visited were in sixteen counties, and the conditions found in them were fully detailed. Nothing like the barbarities so common before 1869 were found; but the provision of apparatus for applying physical restraint to the patients (such as shackles, handcuffs, restraining chairs, "muffs" and "camisoles") was regarded by the committee as suspiciously large. "While it appears from the examination," said their report, "that few of the insane were under restraint, the presence of so large a number of restraining appliances within the institution, in the absence of strict rules and regulations on the subject, may lead to great abuses. Attendants find it much easier to manage and control excited and violent patients, for the time being, by placing them in restraint, rather than by seeking to overcome their violence and excitement by personal attention in the wards. This mode of dealing with them is quite likely to be resorted to during the night, to secure the ease and comfort of the attendant."

In the final summing of their conclusions the committee say: "A retrospective glance over the whole of the examination shows that, with few exceptions, the care of the chronic insane in the counties does not attain to a just and proper standard. In some of the counties the deficiency is lamentable." This would have been a too gentle condemnation of the conditions described in the committee's report if they could fairly have taken for their "just and proper standard" of comparison the best of the institutions that Mr. Letchworth had but recently seen. They had found, for example, the county insane establishments provided generally with but small yards for the airing and exercise of the patients, and these shut in, in all but two instances, by close board fences, from ten to fourteen feet high. Only four counties afforded any kind of outdoor recreation to the inmates, two of these furnishing swings, one allowing quoits to be pitched, and two permitting games of ball.

Report of committee

Defective sewerage, inadequate water supply, and offensive closets were facts often noted. Proper warmth during the winter season in many badly constructed buildings was thought questionable by the committee; but they had no thermometrical record to judge from. Few counties had provided a hospital ward in the insane department. In but one was an open fire found in any room. "In some instances, cases of acute insanity had been retained in the county establishments contrary to law," and both county physicians and superintendents of the poor were ignorant of the fact. "It frequently happens," said the report, " that the certificates of insanity are meagre and vague, and the officers to whose custody the patient is committed are unable to determine the duration of insanity, or to obtain other knowledge necessary to a proper disposal or treatment of the case." In two of the counties visited by the committee they found the insane departments locked, all of those supposed to be "in charge" absent — the keys with them — and the insane inmates left entirely to themselves.

Somewhat in extenuation of these conditions and to show the difficulties of prompt correction for them, the committee in their conclusions observed: "It must be kept in mind that many of the counties applied to the Board for exemption from the operation of the Willard Asylum Act as a *temporary measure*, intending to provide for their chronic insane at the poorhouse until such time only as the state should receive them under its care. It would therefore, perhaps, be unjust to exact as large an expenditure on buildings, under such circumstances, as would have been proper had permanent provision been contemplated. It must also be remembered that, at no time since the Board was empowered to grant these exemptions, has the state been able to accommodate the insane of the exempted counties in its institutions."

Recommendations urged by the committee were:—

(1) That "the enlargement of state provision, by means of plain, inexpensive buildings, with good sanitary surroundings and located upon tracts of good arable land, should be sufficient for the accommodation of all counties desiring to place their chronic insane under state care."

(2) That the chronic insane should not be retained by counties in groups numbering less than two hundred and fifty.

(3) That counties having smaller numbers

WORK FOR THE INSANE

should be permitted to unite and establish district asylums.

(4) That the control and management of all county and district asylums should be placed under a small board of uncompensated managers.

(5) That in all cases the chronic insane should be placed under the immediate charge of a resident medical superintendent.

(6) That "violent and disturbed cases should be provided for in appropriate state asylums."

(7) That all county asylums should be separated in management and in finances from the poorhouse establishments, and that no asylum building hereafter should be located on the poorhouse farm.

This important report was transmitted to the legislature in January, 1882, but was kept in the hands of the official printer, and not, therefore, made public, until February, 1883. It received good attention from the press when published, and the facts set forth in it appear to have excited a degree of public feeling which went beyond the proposals of the committee in its demand for reform. An agitation was started which grew and gathered force until it had compelled the state to take on itself, wholly

Care of the insane assumed wholly by the state

and exclusively, the care of the insane within its borders, and to equip itself adequately with institutions to that end. This was stoutly resisted by partisan political interests and influences in the counties, such as operate with vicious activity on the treatment of all public questions. To the managers of party, who exercise a power that controls official bodies too often, the creating and maintaining of a public institution means nothing else so important as the making and keeping of an instrument for the supplying of salaries and jobs to the henchmen of their party. In this view they fought the endeavor to perfect a system of treatment for insanity, by unifying it under the management of the state.

Meantime, while this conflict between public and party interests — between altruism and selfishness — between knowledge and ignorance — was going on, Mr. Letchworth found opportunities for effort to improve the working of the system as it was. In 1882 he was in coöperation with two of his colleagues of the State Board of Charities, Mr. William Rhinelander Stewart and Mrs. Josephine Shaw Lowell, leading a movement which had success in establishing a farm colony for the insane of New

York City, to relieve the overcrowding of the Ward's Island Hospital, on plans similar to those of the colony at Alt-Scherbitz, in the Prussian Province of Saxony. As was said by one who wrote to Mr. Letchworth about that achievement, some years later, they "initiated the Central Islip project and practically forced the city government to carry it through,"— establishing the insane on a farm of one thousand acres at Central Islip, Suffolk County, Long Island.

In the same year, "having become fully convinced," as he said subsequently, "that the interests of the state would be advanced and the welfare of the inmates of our charitable and correctional institutions promoted by a representation of women on each of the boards of managers," he set about securing legislation to make that representation a requirement of law. He began by setting forth in a printed circular, from the office of the State Board of Charities at Albany, a brief summary of reasons for the measure proposed. In this circular he cited the success of the administration of many public charities by men and women associated in their boards; declared that the state suffered a pecuniary loss

Women on boards of managers

by not availing itself of woman's superior knowledge of domestic economy; asserted that "female delicacy on the part of teachers, nurses, attendants, and servants in public charitable institutions, prevents them from communicating to men . . . information necessary to the protection of the inmates," and that to deprive women, suffering from mental or bodily disease in public institutions, of the benefit to them of a representation of their sex in the management, is an "arrogant assumption of power, often eventuating in unintentional cruelty."

Early in his campaign for this measure Mr. Letchworth counselled with Mrs. Abby Hopper Gibbons, of New York, an energetic woman, closely identified with charitable reform work and of large experience in reform movements, and received potent assistance from her, as well as excellent advice. Mrs. Gibbons's influence appears to have enlisted a number of men of weight in both branches of the legislature, including Senator Brooks, of Long Island, who introduced the desired bill. In an account which Mr. Letchworth, some years afterwards, gave of Mrs. Gibbons's exertions in behalf of the bill, he credited the measure to her entirely and related the outcome as follows:—

WORK FOR THE INSANE

It is hardly worth while to follow the course of this sad experience, sometimes hopeful, sometimes disappointing, except to record, for the example to others, the disappointment which noble reformers like Abby Hopper Gibbons must encounter, [in efforts] to protect and better the condition of the unfortunate. Mrs. Gibbons did not succeed in securing the desired legislation during the session in which she introduced the bill; but in the following session, nothing daunted, she introduced it again. In her old age and in an enfeebled condition she appeared before the legislative committee at Albany, and so clearly and forcibly did she present her arguments and make her appeal that the bill was accepted and passed by the legislature. Shameful to relate, however, a single word in the bill had been so changed as to absolutely nullify its intent. This was the word *may*, which was substituted for the word *shall*, leaving it optional with the governor, instead of obligatory, to make a representative appointment of women on the boards, thus leaving the statute the same as before. But the beneficial effects of the discussion were not lost, and the principle has come to be accepted in the administration of our state charitable institutions.

Mr. Letchworth's agency in bringing about the acceptance of this principle was not confined to the movement in which he worked with Mrs. Gibbons. He advocated it strenuously before the National Conference of Charities and Correction, in his presidential address, in 1884. In 1887 he entered earnestly into a movement initiated by the Women's Educational and Industrial Union of Buffalo, for the appointment of two women on the board of managers of the State Hospital for the Insane, at Buffalo. In an earnest letter to Governor Hill he bore testimony, from his long experience in the supervision of charitable institutions, to the great value of the participation of women in their management, and his entire conviction that the state should give them representation in all boards of its own creation for humane purposes, and especially in the case of asylums for the insane, where the reasons for doing so became peculiarly strong.

In 1886 the state hospitals for the insane were seven in number, namely: at Utica, existing since 1843; at Ovid (the Willard), opened in 1869; at Poughkeepsie (the Hudson River State Hospital), opened in 1871; at Middletown (the Homœopathic), opened in 1874; at Binghamton (converted from a former inebriate asylum) in 1881; and a state asylum for insane criminals at Auburn. They provided, under

Locating an asylum in Northern New York

overcrowded conditions, for scarcely more than four thousand of the thirteen thousand five hundred insane reported that year to be under institutional care in the state. Excepting a small number in private asylums the remainder were under county care. The pressure of the demand for less dependence on the counties for this care, and a larger provision of it by the state, had now become weighty enough to impel legislation which authorized the governor "to appoint five commissioners to select a suitable site in northern New York on which to erect an asylum for the insane." Happily for the result, Mr. Letchworth was one of the five named by Governor Hill, and was chosen to be the chairman of the commission. During the next six months he gave much time to this duty, making long trips through the northern counties of the state. Among his colleagues on the commission was Dr. P. M. Wise, superintendent of the Willard Asylum, and Dr. Wise and himself arrived at the same conclusion of choice between the various sites proposed, preferring one at Airy Point, Ogdensburg, before every other. Without much doubt they were the members of the commission who were best prepared to exercise an intelligent judgment in the matter; and it is possible that they were the most single-minded in considering what would be best for the proposed institution. However that may be, their three associates arrived at a different choice, and agreed in recommending a site at Plattsburg, which Mr. Letchworth and Dr. Wise regarded as utterly unfit, in itself and in its geographical location, for the purpose in view. A majority and a minority recommendation were accordingly reported to the legislature, early in January, 1887, and a hard-fought battle over them was waged until the following May. Powerful political interests appeared to be back of the majority recommendation; but the arguments and the exhibit of facts submitted by Mr. Letchworth and Dr. Wise proved more powerful, rallying to the support of the minority view a movement of opinion from the press, from medical bodies, and from the public at large, which carried the day.

An act authorizing and making appropriations for the purchase of the Ogdensburg site and for beginning the construction of buildings was passed before the close of the legislative session. Unfortunately, the expert knowledge and single-minded motives which had successfully controlled the location of the new hospital for the insane seem not to have won equal control of the constructive planning. The counsels of science and experience in the matter were not listened to; the most approved models were disregarded; and when the resulting buildings were approaching readiness for use, and a medical superintendent was sought, to prepare for opening it, one prominent alienist who refused an offer of the position is reported to have said to the managers who came to him: "You could have had an asylum that the world would have admired, at half the cost of the commonplace institution you will now have, and that will scarcely be known."

It had now become necessary for Commissioner Letchworth to call on the authorities of Erie County for a new and greater undertaking than hitherto to provide for the proper care of its insane. In conjunction with the Secretary of the State Board of Charities, Dr. Hoyt, he addressed a letter, in February, 1887, to the proper committee of the County Board of Supervisors, directing attention to the overcrowded conditions that had arisen again in the insane department of the county poorhouse, and showing that it would be impossible, on the limited farm

An embarrassment in Erie County

occupied by the poorhouse, to give such treatment as was needed to the large and increasing numbers of the Erie County insane. That "employment is of vital importance to the chronic insane," especially outdoor employment, and that a low rate of maintenance is best secured " by the possession of a liberal acreage of good arable land," were two facts specially emphasized in the communication. As examples of the recognition of these facts, it pointed to the recent purchase by the County of New York of a thousand acres for the farm settlement of its insane at Central Islip, Long Island, and the similar action of King's County in establishing its county farm at St. Johnsland. Hence the opinion was submitted to the Erie County Supervisors that "it is not wise to enlarge the buildings at the almshouse, or to erect more cottages on the almshouse grounds; but that it will be better for the county to purchase a farm of not less than five hundred acres of arable land, adapted to purposes of market gardening and easily tillable with hoe or spade."

The communication was referred to a special committee, between whom and Mr. Letchworth there were conferences and correspondence for some time. The latter's argument for the purchase of a tract of land contemplated no radical sudden changes at the poorhouse, nor expensive new building on the farm for the insane, but proposed " to utilize any comfortable buildings on the acquired property for the care of the excess of insane men over present accommodations, and as the numbers increased, or as further building space is required for sane paupers at the poorhouse, to erect plain, inexpensive buildings on the new farm." At the same time he admitted that "if it were possible for the county to send the excess of its chronic insane to the Willard Asylum it would certainly be advisable to do so"; for he believed " there is no question that state care is better than county care," and cheaper, for the reason "that it is administered by uncompensated non-partisan boards, whose members are appointed for long terms," and who acquire an experience which cannot be obtained by the county boards. The outcome of long discussion and inquiry by the supervisors' committee was a report from it, on the 13th of December, 1887, unanimously recommending the purchase of a tract of farm land, not less than five hundred acres in extent, for the colonizing of the county insane. The report was adopted by the board of supervisors; a specially appointed committee made choice, in due time, the next year, of the desired land, and it was bought.

In the circumstances, this was unquestionably a wise measure. The local need of enlarged accommodations and of conditions for a better treatment of the insane was urgent and fast increasing; there seemed in sight no prospect of adequate preparation by the state to relieve the situation; duty to the insane was clearly calling for county action to give them all possible alleviation of their affliction and all possible chances of cure. But now, at this juncture, an unexpected, quick change of circumstances occurred. The State Charities Aid Association, by proposing to the legislature a bill to provide for the transfer of both acute and chronic cases of insanity from county almshouses to the care of the state, freshened and stimulated the movement in favor of that important change of policy, and, with effective support from the medical profession, intelligent journalists, and intelligent people in general, the desired enactment was secured during the legislative session of 1890. This "State Care Act," as it was known, abolished all those exemptions from the Act of 1865 which the State Board of Charities had been

WORK FOR THE INSANE

authorized to grant to numerous counties, and restored full force to the earlier measure, with three exceptions: New York, Kings, and Monroe counties were now exempted from the requirement to transfer their insane to state care, because, as explained by the recently created State Commission in Lunacy, each of these counties "had provided separate institutions for its insane, apart from its poorhouse. Their asylums were fully organized and equipped institutions, and were managed in all substantial particulars like the state asylums."

Erie County was preparing to do the same, and, probably, under Mr. Letchworth's influence, in a more perfect way. He had a reasonable hope of securing the construction of this county hospital on the cottage plan, modelled on that at Alt-Scherbitz, in Prussian Saxony, which he had found to be so admirable in its working, and of which he had obtained complete building plans. Much as he approved of the adoption by the state of the entire care of the insane, it was a sore disappointment to him to miss the opportunity for exhibiting an example of the superiority of the cottage system, in economy and efficiency alike, as compared with any big construction of the hotel or palace type. In view of the completed purchase of an ample and excellent country site for its intended new hospital, he could not oppose the desire of Erie County to be included with New York, Kings, and Monroe in exemption from the State Care Act; and there were carping critics who found an inconsistency in this attitude, as well as other critics who, when the exemption was refused, held him blamable for leading the county into a purchase of lands which it could not use. His own consciousness of a consistent view and a justified motive withheld him from any reply to such criticisms, and public confidence in his wise guidance of public charity was not weakened in the least. Had his plans for Erie County been carried out, a model institution would have been created, which the state, in a few years, would have adopted as its own; for that is what occurred in the case of the institutions exempted in the counties of Monroe, New York, and Kings. Between 1891 and 1908 these were all brought under the immediate control of the state. As to the Erie County purchase of land, that came in the end to the use for which it was bought. The state took it and established on it the Gowanda State Homœopathic Hospital, opened in 1898.

WORK FOR THE INSANE

The recommendations and the action of Mr. Letchworth in the matter of county institutions for the insane, as in the exercise of his official duties touching every other subject, were adjusted reasonably to circumstances in each case. Thus, while urging the supervisors of Erie County to plan largely for a farm colony of the county insane, he went at the same time, in February, 1888, to a meeting of the supervisors of Allegany County to oppose the building of a new county asylum for the chronic insane. The circumstances were entirely different, and the consistency of his course was in his recognition of the difference.

In that year, 1888, he was urging a very important improvement of building arrangements at the Buffalo State Hospital for the Insane, by the erection of cottages, to provide for the most approved system of treatment. His recommendations, addressed to the board of managers of that institution at a hearing given him, and made public soon after, represent his matured views so succinctly and clearly that they seem to claim full quotation here: — *(Hospitals for acute insanity: matured views)*

After making extended examinations of hospitals and asylums for the insane, I have become convinced that small reception cottages, to which insane patients may be first taken upon admission and where they may remain for a short time under observation, before being assigned a more permanent place, are highly desirable in connection with all hospitals for the insane. The shock to many sensitive patients on being ushered, without preliminary explanation, into the formal-looking ward of a strange edifice, having more or less prison-like characteristics, is fearful. On the contrary, if the patient is first received in an ordinary dwelling, where a friendly interview is had with the physician and possible apprehensions allayed, and where the case can be more closely studied because of the home-like surroundings of the patient, great mental disturbance is frequently avoided, and the way is opened for more effective treatment.

I believe it is now universally conceded that, in the treatment of acute insanity, it is found desirable to transfer the patient from one ward to another, the change having a salutary effect. Some alienists go farther than this, having found it of greater advantage to remove the patient, when convalescing, from the painful associations attending the first stages of his disease and from what Miss Dix has termed "the terrible monotony of the wards," to a pleasant residence entirely removed from the asylum, where the work of restoration is rapidly accelerated. I think the most successful of these experiments is seen at Dr. Clouston's asylum at Morningside in Scotland, where, in the Craig House, situated at least a quarter of a mile away and embowered amid grand old trees, we behold highly satisfactory results from this course of treatment.

In pursuance of the same idea and in the line of moral treatment, is the providing of seaside summer cottages for the convalescing insane, now a feature of numerous foreign asylums, and also of the McLean Asylum in Massachusetts and the Friends' Retreat in Pennsylvania. While we have near Buffalo no seaside resorts, we have healthful change of air and scene with delightful surroundings on the near shores of our magnificent lakes and rivers.

This homelike provision and means of recreation to which I have briefly referred having proved of great advantage elsewhere, I earnestly ask your careful consideration of the question, whether it is not desirable to ask the legislature for the following appropriation: —

First. To erect and furnish two cottages, one for men and one for women, on opposite sides of the asylum grounds, but entirely apart from the asylum, of sufficient size to accommodate, say ten or twelve patients each, the structures to have the semblance of ordinary dwellings, and to be used as reception and observation cottages.

Second. To erect and furnish two cottages, one on each side of the asylum grounds, one for men and one for women, each to accommodate, say from twenty to thirty convalescing patients, the building to have the semblance of ordinary residences and to be likewise entirely apart from the asylum.

Third. To provide for the payment of the services of an assistant male physician to reside in one of the two houses for men, and for the payment of the services of an assistant female physician who shall reside in one of the two houses for women.

Fourth. For means to control by rental during the summer months, for a term of, say three experimental years, a small tract of land at some retired point upon Chautauqua Lake, or other desirable locality near Buffalo, to and from which certain quiet and convalescing patients may be taken at proper seasons and sheltered in hospital tents or temporary structures, possibly such as are known as the Ducker portable barrack and field hospital.

Change in official relations to the insane The official relations of Mr. Letchworth, as a commissioner and president of the State Board of Charities, to the institutions for the insane in his state, were now to undergo much change. By an act which passed the legislature in May, 1889, a large part of the duties, powers, and responsibilities concerning the care of the insane which had been vested in the State Board of Charities was transferred to a State Commission in Lunacy. "There is very little left for the Board to do regarding the insane," said Mr. Letchworth in a letter written to a friend at the time. It was a measure, however, which he fully approved. This approval is expressed in a historical account of "The Care of the Insane in New York State, compiled from Notes made by William Pryor Letchworth," which was one of the works of his last years, and left in manuscript, though it ought to be in published print. There had been since 1873 a state commissioner in lunacy whose duty was to examine and report to the State Board of Charities the condition of the insane and idiotic in the institutions receiving them. "It had become evident," said Mr. Letchworth, in the manuscript just referred to, "that a more comprehensive system of lunacy supervision, not only for the welfare of the insane, but for the interest of the state, was requisite. The framing of a law for this purpose was delegated to Dr. Stephen Smith." Dr. Smith had been the state commissioner in lunacy from 1882 to 1888, and had been, also, for many years, a commissioner of the State Board of Charities. He was, as Mr. Letchworth, his close friend, remarked, "eminently qualified for this task, through his experience as an author, a medical practitioner, and a psychologist, and by knowledge acquired through long experience in the inspection of state hospitals for the insane." The bill he prepared created a State Commission in Lunacy, composed of three members, — one to be a reputable physician, " who has had experience in the care and treatment of the insane and in the management of institutions for the insane"; another to be a reputable member of the bar, and the third a " reputable citizen."

As Mr. Letchworth had said of this act, it left little for the State Board of Charities to do, touching the insane; and that little appears to have been so undefined as to become a cause of some questions, between the Commission in Lunacy and the State Board of Charities, as to their respective duties and powers. Mr. Letchworth, however, was able still to find openings of service to the cause which appealed to him so pitifully.

He had now finished his elaborate and important report on the care and treatment of the insane in European institutions, as investigated by him in 1880, and it was beautifully published in 1889, by the Messrs. Putnam's Sons, New

Publication of "The Insane in Foreign Countries"

York, forming a large royal octavo volume of 374 pages, illustrated by Mr. Elias J. Whitney, of New York, with historical pictures as well as with views and plans of buildings and grounds. "The Insane in Foreign Countries" was the title given to the work. During the period of its preparation there had been many trying hindrances, wearisome interruptions, and actual disasters, which stretched the labor over about seven years. He had been called to long halts in it by other tasks, and he had never been able to give himself to it undividedly. At one time a large part of it was in print and destroyed by a fire at the printing establishment which had it in hand. Then, finally, time was taken to procure statistical and other facts dealt with down to the latest attainable date. But if the literary performance was slow, it was painstaking and exact; in securing which quality the author had effective assistance from his secretary, Miss Caroline Bishop, and from his always helpful friend, Mr. James N. Johnston. To the latter he owed many translations from German and French books, documents, and letters, as well as the suggestion and advice which he sought in most matters and trusted greatly from this source, characterizing it as "the wise counsel and unerring judgment of the 'lang heid.'"

Almost simultaneously with the completed printing of the book an act consolidating the English lunacy laws and making important changes in them was passed by parliament. This called for a revision of the treatment of English legislation on the subject and the early issuing of a new edition of the work.

The subjects of the descriptive part of this work have been indicated quite fully in what has been told of Mr. Letchworth's European tour and the inspections then made. His purpose was to present a clear showing of the best of the institutions that he found in other countries, setting them in comparison with each other and with those in the United States, and exhibiting all their features, of construction, arrangement, surroundings, management, methods, and governing ideas of treatment for the insane, which offered anything of suggestion or instruction. This is done with careful exactitude, and with enough of detail for its purpose. It is a part of the work which had more educational value at the time of its publication than now; but there remains to it an interest of history that cannot be lost. The lasting and great worth of the book is in the "Résumé" of its final chapter, where the author has exhibited, so to speak, the harvest of his own mind from the studies he had made, setting forth the conclusions he had drawn, not alone from these wide special examinations abroad, but from all his many years of official observation of methods and conditions attending the treatment of the insane.

Of buildings and their location, furnishings and decoration, grounds, sewage and water supply, the discussion is full and very informing. Equally so is that which follows, bearing on the freedom that can be given to the demented with happy effects; the possible disuse of mechanical restraints; the importance of thoroughly trained attendants; the curative influence of appropriate amusements and employments, with small payments for work performed — and many other topics which must necessarily enter into any organization of care for insane patients that is heedful at all of the most advanced knowledge and practice of the present day.

The admirable quality of the treatise, the supreme importance of the matters with which it dealt and the high value of the enlightenment it threw upon them, were recognized at once by those qualified for the recognition.

<small>Welcome to the book by alienists</small> Leading alienists at home and abroad gave it a specially cordial reception. Letters of commendation came to its author from Dr. Albrecht Paetz, director of the Prussian-Saxon Provincial Asylum of Alt-Scherbitz; Dr. John Sibbald, of the General Board of Lunacy, Edinburgh; Dr. Samuel Wesley Smith, New York State Commissioner in Lunacy; Dr. Stephen Smith, formerly in the same office; Dr. Clark Bell, president of the Medico-Legal Society; Dr. P. M. Wise, medical superintendent of the Willard Asylum, and other specialists in the medical profession. The book was reviewed at length by Dr. W. W. Ireland in the London *Medical Recorder;* by Dr. Frederick Peterson in the *Medical Analectic;* and without signature by writers of evident authority in all the leading medical journals of the United States. In the daily newspaper press of the country it received more interested attention than is given commonly to works of its kind.

But the best proof that the work had secured a high place in the literature of its subject appeared in 1905, when Dr. Kálman Pandy, principal physician of the State Insane Asylum at Budapest, published in the Magyar language a work on the "Insane in Europe," which (with careful credit) drew extensively from Mr. Letchworth's pages and gave a flattering consideration to his views. Two years later a German translation of Dr. Pandy's book was published, the translation having been revised by Dr. H. Engelken, of the Alt-Scherbitz staff, and it was dedicated to Dr. Paetz, the head of the famous Alt-Scherbitz institution, which all the world was coming to regard as the model to be copied in caring for the insane. The standing of Dr. Pandy's book was thus guaranteed by the imprimatur of Alt-Scherbitz, and there was weight, therefore, in the remark with which he opened his preface to it: " Since the appearance of the standard work of Tucker ('Lunacy in Many Lands,' Sydney, 1887), and the excellent studies of Letchworth ('The Insane in Foreign Countries,' second ed., New York and London, 1889), no book to my knowledge has appeared that has treated these highly important matters relating to humanity and the social life with a larger grasp." In a review of Dr. Pandy's book the *Journal of Insanity* remarked: "It is very interesting to observe how closely his conclusions confirm the painstaking accounts given by our own countryman, William Pryor Letchworth, who did so much by his admirable work to bring the methods of foreign hospitals for the insane to the knowledge of alienists in this and other English-speaking countries. It can but be most gratifying to him, in reviewing the incidents of a life devoted to the betterment of the care of all sorts and conditions of men, to feel that his self-denying labors in behalf of the insane are so widely known and appreciated both at home and abroad."

Late in 1890 it would seem that Mr. Letchworth had not yet been released by the legislation of the previous year from the inspection of institutions for the insane, for he wrote in a letter of October 14: "Last night I returned home, having just completed a visitation of all the state institutions for the insane, as also those vast county receptacles for this class in New York and Kings." No published report of this visitation has been found. Probably it was his last survey of state asylums and hospitals. His periodic inspection of other public charities in his judicial district, which he performed with fidelity to the end of his official service, brought him for some years

Final services to the insane

WORK FOR THE INSANE 303

yet, at the poorhouses, into county insane asylums which lingered in existence, waiting for the state to be prepared to take their inmates away. It was not until 1894, for example, that the insane of the Erie County Poorhouse were removed to the Willard Asylum.

What appears to have been the last recorded service of Mr. Letchworth as an official guardian and advocate of the interests of the insane was rendered in February, 1892, when he addressed a memorial to the legislature "embodying reasons why the asylum for insane criminals at Auburn should not be made a receptacle for the non-criminal insane." The insane criminals at Auburn were soon to be removed to the new institution for that class of the demented which the state was then establishing at Matteawan, and serious consideration was being given in the legislature to a bill which provided for utilizing the buildings vacated at Auburn Prison by their conversion to the purposes of a state hospital for the non-criminal insane. This, too, in the face of the fact that, both in their own structural unfitness and in their situation as part of the prison establishment, they had been condemned by the commission on whose recommendation the Matteawan Hospital was being established. The flagrancy of the project was exposed by Mr. Letchworth with a force which must have been most influential in bringing it to an end. The next legislature (1893) repealed the original act which established the State Asylum for Insane Criminals at Auburn.

Throughout the years (say in the decade 1880–90) in which the greater energies of his work were expended by Mr. Letchworth on two endeavors, — to better the dealing with errant children and to better the care and treatment of the insane, — these specialties of his labor were far from absorbing his time or his thought. He spent much of both in the service of other causes, and very little in indulgences of any sort to himself. Social as he was in his nature, and keenly as he enjoyed gatherings of his friends at Glen Iris, he had become too busy a man to maintain the large, open hospitality of former years. Not that he became recluse in the least, and not that Glen Iris lost anything of its hospitable atmosphere; but invitations and visitings were necessarily cut down by the frequent and often long absences of the master and by the work that tasked him when at home.

General official labors of 1880–90

WORK FOR THE INSANE

In 1882, along with his arduous inspection of and report on the insane departments of poorhouses in the state, he was giving laborious help to a movement in Buffalo for the rehabilitation of a Children's Aid Society that had not realized the intentions with which it was formed. He had been one of the prime movers in the organization of the society ten years before, when the impulse to it was given by a public Thanksgiving Day dinner to the newsboys and bootblacks of the city, at which he was the principal speaker to the boys. Now the officers of the society were endeavoring to revive activity in its undertakings, and applied to him for advice and instruction as to the methods of work they should take in hand. He might easily have thought it sufficient to refer them to some of his published writings on the subject of "preventive work among children," but that could not satisfy his wish to serve them to the utmost of his power. He made the reference, to be sure, but he added, in writing to them from Albany: "With the view of putting you in possession of the most recent experience, I have visited, since receiving your letter, several institutions illustrative of the points in reference to which your interrogatories are propounded. The following sketches are submitted in the hope that they may offer useful suggestions." This introduced an extended description of the various undertakings, "for newsboys, street children, and needy and ignorant girls," conducted by the Brooklyn Children's Aid Society, at its Newsboys' Home and Evening School, its Industrial School, its Sewing-Machine School, its Special Relief Department, its Day Nursery, and its Seaside Home, at Brighton Beach. Then followed accounts of the Home for Street Boys carried on by the Brooklyn Society of St. Vincent de Paul; the broad work of the New York Children's Aid Society, which maintained twenty-one industrial schools and twelve evening schools, besides its home for boys; and the homes, shelters, and nurseries of the American Female Guardian Society. Finally, the writer narrated some interesting and instructive incidents of his visit to the headquarters of the New York Society for the Prevention of Cruelty to Children, and the first of the recommendations which closed his letter was "the establishing on a sound basis of the work for the prevention of cruelty to children." All this represented the labor of many days, performed at a very busy time in Mr. Letchworth's official service, and quite outside of that.

Three years afterwards, on the 22d of May, 1885, he was present and spoke at the opening of a new Home which the Children's Aid Society of Buffalo had bought and fitted and furnished for its newsboy and bootblack guests. In his address he congratulated the society on the success it had thus far achieved, and extended his especial congratulations to "the first mover in the attempt to elevate the newsboys and bootblacks of this city, in the person," he said, "of our modest friend, Mr. David E. Brown." In closing, he remarked: "In this city we have real noblemen,—men blessed with generous natures and honestly acquired fortunes. It would not be strange if from some of these should at no distant day come the gift of a stately edifice for the carrying on of the beneficent work for poor children." Before he died he saw the faith that was expressed in these words justified by the opening, in 1908, of a new, larger, and better Home for newsboys, bootblacks, and their class, representing a bequest to the society, not by a man of the city, but by a generous woman, Mrs. Helen Thornton Campbell.

Of other doings and writings of Mr. Letchworth in these years, 1882–85, apart from what has already been told of his labors in the interest of delinquent children and the insane, some cursory mention will suffice. They include a report in 1882 of two inspections of the Thomas Orphan Asylum on the Cattaraugus Indian Reservation; a paper on the "Dependent and Delinquent Children of the State of New York," prepared in 1883, in response to a request, for the Congres International de la Protection de l'Enfance, held at Paris in June; an address introducing Bishop Ireland, at a great meeting in Buffalo for temperance, in 1884; an address on "Poorhouse Administration," at a state convention of county superintendents of the poor, in 1885.

In that year he received, from Governor Hill, his second reappointment on the State Board of Charities, as Commissioner from the Eighth Judicial District. But the Governor, in his next annual message to the legislature, recommended the abolition of the Board, and the substitution of a single "official to be known as the Commissioner of Charities, who shall be vested," said the Governor, "with substantially all the duties now exercised by such Board, as well as those performed by the Commissioner

Third appointment on the State Board

in Lunacy." The argument supporting the recommendation was this: "A board consisting of eleven persons (aside from its ex-officio members), scattered in various parts of the state, and which only occasionally meets, is a cumbersome and unwieldy body. It cannot perform its duties as efficiently or satisfactorily as a single responsible head. Its functions cannot be discharged as economically or expeditiously as when in the hands of one controlling executive officer."

In attempting to uphold the governor's argument, his party organ at Albany, the *Argus*, made statements so grossly incorrect that they drew a letter of expostulation from Mr. Letchworth.

Repelling political attacks on the Board

From the official figures [said the *Argus*] it is shown that the daily personal expense of each commissioner averages twenty-nine dollars, and that for three days' services the sum reached nearly ninety dollars for each commissioner. With eleven members on the Board the citizen and taxpayer, who desire to see the affairs of state government economically administered, can readily see that $319 per day for the personal expenses of the Board is a sum far in excess of what it should be, and agree with Governor Hill that a single commissioner, at a stated salary, will not only insure a saving of public moneys to the state, but that the work will be performed fully as well. It is to be admitted that the state is rich, but many will object to eleven commissioners in session, say in New York, stopping at hotels where the daily rate for each commissioner is five or six dollars.

To this Mr. Letchworth made answer: —

It has been customary, in consideration of the large charitable interests centring in New York and Brooklyn, and for the greater convenience of those having business to transact with the Board, to hold one of its stated meetings during the year in New York City. The last one held there was on the 15th, 16th, and 17th days of December, 1885, which was attended by eight members, together with the secretary and assistant secretary. According to your estimate, the expenses of this session of three days for ten persons at thirty dollars per day would have aggregated $900. The actual expenses, however, including the travelling expenses of the commissioners and secretaries in going and coming, according to official figures, was $136.38, making a discrepancy in your statement of $763.62. . . . The expenses of the Board from its organization in 1867 to October 1, 1885, for the travelling expenses and hotel bills of its commissioners, committees, and officers, in the inspection of institutions and in attendance upon its meetings, for

WORK FOR THE INSANE

clerk hire, printing, office expenses, and contingencies, have never exceeded the legislative appropriation, which in no instance has been more than $5000 per annum. Considering the time spent by the commissioners in the performance of their duties, and the saving results to the state, many will doubtless admit that it has not paid dearly for the unsalaried service of the comissioners.

Of course Mr. Letchworth made no mention of the important fact that, personally, he had never drawn payment from the state treasury for even the travelling expenses of his service as commissioner, much travel as it involved. *His personal gift of both service and expenses* It was a fact known to few; and he was still to continue the fact; for he and his associates of the State Board of Charities were not deprived of the privilege of giving unpaid labor and time to the discharge of the very gravest of the obligations of the state. Public opinion proved unfriendly to the recommendations of the Governor, and the State Board was not set aside.

The incessancy of the strain of work on him in this period may be inferred from a remark in one of his letters to a friend, dated in October, 1886: *The severe strain of work* "I am now," he said, "for the first time in years, at the bottom of my correspondence, both home and foreign; have my public work well in hand, and D.V., shall take hold again of my foreign notes [on 'The Insane in Foreign Countries'] and with hammer and tongs go at them with a right good will." Two months later he was indulging himself in a rare respite from official duties, going with one of his neighbors of Livingston County to the Blue Grass region of Kentucky, and spending two or three weeks in visiting its famous herds of shorthorn cattle, selecting purchases for his farm, as he wrote home, "from some of the very best families of cattle in Kentucky." "We have paid some high prices," he added, "and must take our chances upon getting our money back. If we do not we shall have the satisfaction of feeling that we have done something that may improve the herds of western New York."

Sorrow came to him in May of the next spring, when his brother George died. There had been hopes of recovery from a stroke of paralysis, suffered a year before, and the invalid had been taken to England under the care of his wife and daughter, but only to end life in a strange land. Within less than a year there was grief brought again to Mr. Letchworth by

WORK FOR THE INSANE

the untimely death, in February, 1888, of David Gray, to whom he was most warmly and tenderly attached.

In these two years (1887-88) he was putting aside more resolutely the exterior calls and lesser tasks which had burdened him so much, and applying himself as closely as possible to the completion of his book on the insane in foreign countries. No doubt he had been influenced by the wise advice of his friend Johnston, who wrote to him in May of the former year: "I wish you could lighten your work a little. Other men ultimately must take your burden; why not begin now to let them do so? Your supervision, suggestions, assistance would be better than taking so much detail work on yourself. Reserve your strength for the larger work, occasional and national, where a wider influence is exerted and less routine labor would be required from you." Evidently this was what he was now beginning to attempt, and with some degree of success, though not complete.

In October, 1887, he felt it necessary to decline a request from his English friends to contribute a paper to the General Conference of the National Association of Certified Reformatory and Industrial Schools, in England, which would be held at London in the following March.

On the 10th of April, 1888, he addressed to the State Board of Charities his resignation of the office of president of the Board, in which he had been kept by repeated elections for eleven years. At the meeting of the Board which received it he was not present, and the resignation was not accepted, but he was reëlected with unanimity for another term. He wrote at once: "I shall decline again at next meeting," and he did. The Board then respected the earnestness of his wish to be released from the responsibilities and labors of the office, and Mr. Oscar Craig, of Rochester, was chosen in his place. It was a post of dignity and honor, which some men might be able to enjoy without feeling that it laid much else upon them; but Mr. Letchworth had certainly found in it a heavy addition of duty and weight of care. To become again just Commissioner for the Eighth Judicial District of New York on the State Board of Charities was an undoubted relief.

Resignation of the presidency of the State Board

In the next half-dozen years, which brought his official service to its conclusion, Mr. Letchworth's writings, in reports, addresses, and

WORK FOR THE INSANE

other published papers, included reports on the poorhouses of the Eighth Judicial District in 1891, 1893, and 1896; reports on the New York State Institution for the Blind in 1892, 1894, and 1895; *(Official reports of 1890–96)* a general report on the institutions conducting charitable and reform work in the Eighth Judicial District, in 1893; a report (in conjunction with Dr. Stephen Smith, one of his colleagues in the State Board of Charities) on plans for the then projected Eastern New York Reformatory, in his studies for which he visited prisons in four states during the summer of 1894; reports of investigations made of institutions at Lockport and Jamestown, in 1894; reports of inspections of the Thomas Orphan Asylum, on the Cattaraugus Reservation, in 1894, 1895, and 1896; a carefully studied paper on "Poorhouse Construction," read at a New York State Convention of Superintendents of the Poor, in 1890; a paper in 1892 for the annual National Conference of Charities and Correction, on "State Boards of Charity," one of the most valuable of his essays, critically discussing the organization, duties, and powers of such boards and tracing their development historically; a "History of Child-saving Work in the State of New York," prepared on request for the Conference of Charities and Correction at Chicago, in connection with the Columbian Exposition of 1893, and praised enthusiastically in letters to Mr. Letchworth by Miss Clara Barton.

The Columbian Exposition at Chicago opened what seemed to Mr. Letchworth to be an opportunity for setting on foot a governmental undertaking in the interest of public charities which had long been in his thought. Acting as a member of a committee appointed at a conference of state boards of charities, in 1874, to formulate a plan of coöperation in the collection of statistics, he became persuaded that a bureau of the general government was the agency needed for this statistical work. As he remarked in writing of the matter subsequently, "such a bureau might include information on all subjects affecting the dependent and criminal classes, in other countries as well as our own, and include plans and models of buildings, descriptive of different systems for the care and treatment of these classes, and all valuable literature relating to these subjects." He found no favorable opportunity for urging this important project until the closing of the Columbian Exposition at

WORK FOR THE INSANE

Chicago, in 1893. He then made an effort to bring about a transfer of the extensive exhibit of charts, plans, models, etc., there collected, to Washington, to become the foundation of a permanent governmental undertaking. Unfortunately this proved to be one of the few important endeavors of Mr. Letchworth which did not attain success.

In 1892 President Craig and Commissioners Letchworth and Walrath formed a committee of the State Board of Charities, appointed under an act of the legislature, to select a site " on which to establish an institution, on the colony plan, for the medical treatment, care, education, and employment of epileptics." This was a subject which had now become deeply interesting to Mr. Letchworth, and it gave direction to the most important of his subsequent work. What he did in behalf of the epileptic, as formerly in behalf of the insane, will be told in the next chapter.

The term of Commissioner Letchworth's reappointment in 1885 having expired in 1893, he received on the 16th of January in that year his fourth consecutive appointment to the State Board of Charities, from Governor Flower. *Fourth appointment on the Board*

A little later, on the 9th of February, a mark of distinction so high that few have ever received it came to him from the University of the State of New York, by vote of the Regents of the University, conferring on him the degree of LL.D., "in recognition of his distinguished services to the State of New York, as a member and president of the State Board of Charities and as an author of most valuable literature pertaining to the dependent classes." In the one hundred and ten years of its existence at that date the Board of Regents had conferred this honorary degree only twenty times, and always after long preliminary notice of intention and on the unanimously favorable report of an inquiring committee. Not many titular honors have been guarded so jealously, — dispensed so sparingly; but all voices acclaimed the justice and applauded the propriety of this award of it.

Degree of LL.D. from the University of the State of New York

In the honors of the year, however, there was no medicine for the sore affliction that befel him on the 23d of November, when Mrs. Edward H. Crozer, his eldest sister, died. She had been his companion at Glen Iris, — the presiding genius of his home, — for many years, and her death was not only the wounding of

WORK FOR THE INSANE

tender affections, but a grave dislocation of his life. A tablet to Mrs. Crozer's memory was placed by Mr. Letchworth in the vestibule of the new building then being erected for the Women's Educational and Industrial Union, at Buffalo, and unveiled on the day of the opening of the building, October 29, 1894. Mrs. Crozer had been a member of the Union and much interested in its work.

The presidency of the State Board of Charities became vacant in 1894, on the death of Commissioner Oscar Craig, and was filled by the election of Mr. William Rhinelander Stewart, of the City of New York, who had been a member of the Board since 1883. Mr. Letchworth was engaged that year, with Dr. Stephen Smith, in the examination of plans and estimates for the development of the institution which the state had undertaken to establish for the treatment of epileptics, and to which the name of Craig Colony had been given. Ill health in the early months of 1895 not only interrupted the preparation of a paper that he had promised for the next National Conference of Charities and Correction, but detained him from the meeting, in May. He had missed very few of these important meetings since he entered the New York State Board of Charities.

In these final years of his official service Mr. Letchworth became deeply interested in the introduction of the rain-bath, or shower-bath, into various public institutions, most especially into poorhouses, to replace the uncleanly and unsanitary tub-bathing practised commonly in such places, so far as bathing might be practised systematically at all. He gave the subject much investigation, and gathered a quantity of practical information as to the best modes of construction and arrangement for it, which he put in form for communication to the officials whose interest in an improvement of such great importance might be enlisted. None of this seems to have gone into print, but it was used, no doubt, in personal ways, of correspondence and otherwise, and remains in manuscript form.

The year 1896 was his last in the service of the state, though his enlistment in the service of suffering humanity did not end till his death. Age and unsparing labors were beginning to wear down the energy of spirit which had replaced in him so much of the lack of a vigorous constitution. He was forced, no doubt, to feel that he must lighten his cares and his tasks. He declined the invitation to prepare a paper for presentation to

Last year of official service

WORK FOR THE INSANE 321

an International Congress for Children which met in 1896; but he wrote for the State Board of Charities an extended report on the "Erie County System of Placing Dependent Children in Families," which has been quoted from in a previous chapter; he made and reported his final inspection of poorhouses in his district; and he took part in the preparation of a report by the standing committee of the Board on Craig Colony for Epileptics. To this latter report was appended the following note, signed by the two colleagues of Mr. Letchworth on the committee, Dr. Enoch V. Stoddard and Peter Walrath: "Immediately subsequent to the completion of this report, Commissioner Letchworth, feeling compelled to lay down the work which he had followed during so many years and with such distinction, tendered his resignation to the governor and severed his relations with colleagues who part with him with the deepest regret."

His resignation had been tendered to the Governor on the 14th of November. The next meeting of the State Board of Charities was held on the 8th of December following, and it then received from him a letter announcing it and making known in these words his reasons for

Resignation from the State Board of Charities

withdrawing from the service he had performed so long: —

> While grateful for a degree of health and strength that would permit me to continue in the discharge of my duties, and duly regretting the severance of my official relations with the Board, I nevertheless feel that my private affairs, which have long suffered for lack of my personal supervision, now demand more attention than the proper discharge of the duties devolving upon me as a commissioner will permit. I was first appointed a commissioner by Governor Dix, in April, 1873, and was reappointed successively by Governors Robinson, Hill, and Flower, the last appointment expiring in March, 1901.

He then reverted briefly to the great improvements made within the past quarter of a century in the public care and treatment of the dependent and offending classes, and congratulated the State Board of Charities on its agency in the promotion of these advances. Also on the wider field now opened to it under the powers granted to it by the new constitution. In conclusion he expressed his grateful sense of the uniformly harmonious relations that had existed between himself and his colleagues and the unnumbered kindnesses and courtesies he had received at their hands.

The feeling of the Board, as expressed in its published records, went beyond a mere utterance of regret, to pay this tribute: —

Entering into this office well equipped by nature and research for the efficient discharge of his duties, Mr. Letchworth has, without remuneration, devoted the maturer years of his life to the amelioration of the condition of the suffering, unfortunate, and dependent classes in the State of New York. Every branch of the work devolving upon the State Board of Charities has felt the uplifting impulse of his wise and persistent efforts. The insane, the poor in county houses, the blind, the orphan and destitute children, the juvenile delinquents are all now more intelligently and humanely cared for in consequence of his initiation and unfailing and practical support of measures instituted for their relief.

By his conservative and painstaking discharge of official duties and intelligent application thereto of his wide sociological knowledge, Mr. Letchworth early won and has steadily retained the confidence and respect of the people of the state. These qualifications also led to his successive annual elections to the presidency of the Board for the period of ten years from 1878 to 1887. During this whole period his disregard of all selfish ambition and his many lovely qualities of heart and mind have gained for him the affection and esteem of his colleagues and hosts of friends.

By his resignation the people of the State of New York have lost the services of a tried and useful official, and the State Board of Charities the assistance and advice of one of its most valued members. Into the retirement which he has sought our earnest wishes for his future happiness accompany him.

More significant than this formulated expression of feeling by the Board on parting company with its senior member were the remarks made on the occasion by some of its members. These, for example, by Commissioner Dr. Stephen Smith:—

Mr. President: My acquaintance with Mr. Letchworth extends over a period of fifteen years, or from the date of my first entrance into this Board, in 1881. I recall gratefully the kind and sympathetic words with which he, as president, welcomed me to a membership with this body. I early recognized his large and comprehensive knowledge of every phase of public charities and his eminently judicious and conservative views of their administration. From him, therefore, I was accustomed to seek that information necessary to the proper performance of my duties, and I take great pleasure in acknowledging my obligations to him for whatever useful work I have accomplished among the charities of the state. His fraternal counsels were always inspirations to greater efforts to do better and still better service, and to fre-

WORK FOR THE INSANE 325

quent aspirations to attain to that high plane of consecration to the relief of human infirmities which he had reached. . . . The vast reforms in our public charities during the last thirty years have been effected with his coöperation and often with his initiation. The annual reports of the Board abound with most valuable contributions by him to nearly every branch of private and public charity. In the wider field of philanthropy represented by the National Conference of Charities, Mr. Letchworth has won a national reputation, as one of the foremost reformers of the methods of dealing with the dependent, defective, and criminal classes. But it is probable that in the distant future his great work on Hospitals will prove to be the most enduring monument of his self-sacrificing service in the cause of humanity. In the retirement of Mr. Letchworth from this Board we have lost a congenial companion and a wise counsellor, and the state an honest and most efficient public official.

In anticipation, perhaps, of his retirement, which may have been intimated at the beginning of the year, a letter requesting his portrait had been signed in the previous February by all the members of the Board.

Not only in the State of New York, but widely through the country, the retirement of Mr. Letchworth from his long official labors for the bettering of the institutions of public philanthropy was recognized as an event of public importance. "He is, perhaps," said the New York *Tribune*, "more widely known in this country and Europe in connection with his special work than any other living American, and might be fairly called the Lord Shaftesbury of the United States." The same journal remarked: "It is intimated that, in consideration of his long and useful public service, Governor Morton allowed Mr. Letchworth to suggest the name of his successor." The successor appointed was Mr. Harvey W. Putnam, a young lawyer of Buffalo.

CHAPTER VIII

WORK FOR THE EPILEPTIC

AFTER Mr. Letchworth's withdrawal from the service of the state there were years of work in his life, performed in the same field. He had surrendered official authority, but needed none to maintain the power of influence with which he could still labor for the unfortunates of mankind who need public care. He was released from tasks of supervision and inspection which had occupied great parts of his time, and could devote himself more to studies and discussions of the large problems of public philanthropy, where his long experience, his wide knowledge, his well-trained good judgment, could be exercised more usefully than on the mere scrutiny and criticism of particular institutions. He was now in the position which his friend Johnston had long urged him to assume. Several years before this time, Mr. Johnston, in a letter, had said to him with eloquent earnestness: "You have accomplished nearly all you can accomplish in New York State. Your ideas have been before the people nearly a score of years. A good deal has been done, and what has been done is an incentive and teaching to others, and the work will go on. But there is a continent — yes, a hemisphere — in which you can work (I might have said a world) and where germs of reform planted would in time give seed enough for great harvests. These continents are the fields into which you should carry your work. It matters something if five hundred paupers are more healthily, comfortably, economically housed; but it matters much more if some new state officials are taught how to save the young or to care for the insane. How I do wish that you would give the balance of your life to introducing your ideas more widely into places where they would be helpful."

He recognized the wisdom of this counsel; but the ties of his long connection with the state service were undoubtedly hard to break, and difficulties were in the breaking which others could not know. The severance, however, had now been accomplished, and William Pryor Letchworth, Doctor of Laws by the pronouncement of the highest organ of the academic authority of the state, was free from the routine of official duty which may, perhaps, have en-

DEH-GA-YA-SAH

WORK FOR THE EPILEPTIC 329

grossed too much of the time of Commissioner Letchworth of the State Board. Now that he had been divested of his official title it would be strictly proper, no doubt, to affix the honorary title to his name, and to speak of him as Dr. Letchworth throughout the remainder of this book. To do so, however, would seem like the introduction of a stranger into the narrative, and the writer feels that it is best to speak of Mr. Letchworth still, in the old familiar way.

The most important labors of the later years of Mr. Letchworth were in behalf of the victims of epilepsy, — a large class of pitiful sufferers who had experienced, in our country especially, more and longer neglect than any other whose affliction appealed as painfully to the sympathies of their fellow men. In one of his writings on the subject he has depicted most graphically the situation which makes this appeal: —

Pitiable state of the epileptic

The epileptic [he wrote] holds an anomalous position in society. As a child he is an object of solicitude to his parents or guardians. The street to him is full of danger, and if sent to school he is liable to seizures on the way or in the classroom. At school his attacks shock his classmates and create confusion. He cannot attend church or public entertainments, nor participate in social gatherings with those of his own age and station. In consequence of his infirmity, the epileptic grows up in idleness and ignorance, bereft of companionship outside of the family, and, friendless, he silently broods over his isolated and helpless condition. If the epileptic succeeds in learning a trade, business men are reluctant to employ him, and artisans will not work with him, especially if sharp-edged tools are used. . . . In such cases there is but one result, — the breaking down of all hope and energy. The epileptic workman having a trade, but unable to find employment, gradually sinks into a condition of public dependence. Frequently he is sent to the poorhouse . . . where there is no special provision for his care or proper medical treatment. Here he is regarded with aversion and distrust, and is a cause of unhappiness and sometimes of danger to others. Not infrequently the wrong is committed of sending him to an insane asylum.

With this description of the wretched situation of the sufferers from epilepsy went an estimate of their numbers, which assigned considerably more than 100,000 to the United States, for only a small fraction of whom had any provision been made, when this was written, of such care as they need. England and the United States had both been slow in recognizing their claim to special insti-

<small>Neglect in the United States</small>

tutions for treatment and maintenance, while some countries of Continental Europe had seen and accepted the duty long ago. Apparently it was not until 1868 that official attention was given to the subject in any American state. In that year the Ohio State Board of Charities recommended to the legislature of that state some better provision for the epileptics in the poorhouses; and in the next year it repeated the recommendation more urgently and with a definite plan, proposing a distinct asylum, with an ample farm, on which the inmates could be employed. The legislature was deaf to this counsel, renewed again and again, until 1877, when it made a beginning of action which, finally, in 1893, brought into existence the Ohio Hospital for Epileptics, at Gallipolis, — the first to be opened in the United States.

The next state to acknowledge its duty to the epileptics was New York. In the first report (1874) of its first Commissioner in Lunacy, Dr. John Ordronaux, he called attention to the fact that four hundred and thirty-six epileptics were being improperly kept in the lunatic asylums and poorhouses of the state, and declared to the legislature that "a state hospital for epileptics is an imperative necessity." In eight succeeding annual reports he continued the admonition without effect; and the appeal was taken up by the State Board of Charities with no better result. According to Mr. Letchworth, who became the historian of the reform, "in seeking for the germs of the movement for colonizing epileptics in this country we must look in another direction. Dr. Frederick Peterson, while assistant physician of the Hudson River State Hospital for the Insane, had a considerable number of epileptics under his charge, and became specially interested in the treatment of this class. In 1886, in pursuance of their interests, he visited the colony for epileptics at Bielefeld, in Westphalia, of which little, if anything, was known in this country. After his return home he wrote a full description of this peculiar and highly successful work, which was published in the New York *Medical Record* in April, 1887. The article attracted much attention and was republished in England. Dr. Peterson, in his zeal, continued to write upon the subject for medical and other journals, and his whole-souled devotion to the cause he had espoused laid broad and deep in the public mind the conviction that a state colony for epileptics was an immediate and pressing necessity. He presented the subject in charity conference meetings, at state conventions of superintendents of the poor, and elsewhere. He also urged the matter upon the attention of the State Charities Aid Association."

An attempt in 1890 to obtain legislation in New York, providing for the selection of a site for the desired colony, came to naught; but in 1892 it had success. A bill prepared by the State Charities Aid Association and introduced on its request, directing the commissioners of the State Board of Charities to select a suitable site for the purpose stated, became law. As mentioned in the preceding chapter, the State Board delegated the duty of making this important selection to a committee composed of its president, Mr. Craig, and commissioners Letchworth and Walrath. The committee was not only to inspect sites, but to examine plans and ascertain facts " relative and important to the object of the statute, namely, the establishment in a proper situation, with a proper organization, of a colony for epileptics." Many sites were proposed, and the members of the committee, either collectively or separately, spent a large part of the summer of 1892 in examining tracts of land and collecting desired information. But singu-

First movement in New York

larly favoring circumstances offered one piece of property to them which had so incomparable a superiority to every other, in advantages of every kind, that the selection was easily made and put quite beyond reasonable dispute. It was in the beautiful Genesee Valley, near Mount Morris, — the seat of a settlement of the religious people known commonly as Shakers, but named by themselves the United Society of Christian Believers. They occupied a large tract (eighteen hundred acres) of very valuable land, on the site of an old Indian village which bore the name of Sonyea, the name signifying a "sunny or warm place." They had erected many buildings that would be more or less readily convertible to immediate use for the contemplated epileptic colony. "One of the original purposes of the society was to receive and maintain orphan children, some of whom would take the place of deceased members; but the multiplication of institutions for homeless children in Western New York stood in the way of thus increasing their numbers, which their practice of celibacy also restricted. The members were mostly advanced in years, and, as their numbers were gradually but surely diminishing,

The Shaker settlement of Sonyea

WORK FOR THE EPILEPTIC

they decided to sell their home at Sonyea and unite their fortunes with a similar society at Watervliet, New York." They could have sold the splendid property in parcels very readily and with much pecuniary gain; but they wished it to go as a whole to a charitable use, and offered it at a moderate price. The State Board of Charities adopted the report of its committee recommending the purchase of the Sonyea domain; a bill which authorized and made the needed provision for carrying out the recommendation passed the legislature of 1893; but, to the consternation and disheartenment of a multitude of citizens, it was vetoed by Governor Flower, on the ground that the state could not afford the expenditure, and that some particulars of the plan of government of the intended colony did not meet his approval. Fortunately the rare opportunity which the Shakers of Sonyea had offered was not thrown away by this, as it might easily have been. They gave a new option, and a modified enactment, pressed by a strong public sentiment on the legislature and the Governor in 1894, was secured in April of that year. The general design of the institution authorized was set forth in the following language of the act: —

The objects of such colony shall be to secure the humane, curative, scientific, and economical treatment and care of epileptics, exclusive of insane epileptics, to fulfil which design there shall be provided, among other things, a tract of fertile and productive land, in a healthful situation, and an abundant supply of wholesome water, sufficient means for drainage and disposal of sewage, and sanitary conditions; and there shall be furnished, among other necessary structures, cottages for dormitory and domiciliary uses, buildings for an infirmary, a schoolhouse and a chapel, workshops for the proper teaching and productive prosecution of trades and industries; all of which structures shall be substantial and attractive, but plain and moderate in cost, and arranged on the colony or village plan.

To an extraordinary extent this design was fulfilled at once by the mere purchase of the Sonyea domain. Fertility of soil, healthfulness of situation, abundance and purity of water, easy drainage and sewerage, all went with the land; and there went also thirty buildings of various kinds, which were estimated in value by Commissioner Letchworth and an architect, before the purchase was made, at $75,000. The state appropriation for the purchase of the whole property was $115,000. The largest of the buildings then

Craig Colony established

on the ground — a massive brick structure — underwent ready conversion into a dormitory which accommodates one hundred and thirty female patients, and is named Letchworth House. There was much at the place, it can be seen, to facilitate the preparation of it for its humane use, and the preparation went rapidly on. Dr. William P. Spratling, previously first assistant physician at the Morristown, New Jersey, State Hospital for the Insane, was chosen for superintendent of the colony, by competitive examination, under the civil service system of New York. He received his appointment in November, 1894, beginning duty in the following May, having visited, meantime, the famous Bethel Colony for Epileptics, at Bielefeld, Germany, to study methods and arrangements there. Dr. Spratling had already made special studies of epilepsy, and he received the highest marking in the examination. The colony was in readiness to begin receiving patients and was formally opened on the 20th of January, 1896. It had been named Craig Colony, in memory of the late president of the State Board of Charities, who died on the 2d of January, 1894.

A documentary history of the whole course of proceedings connected with the founding of this first colony for epileptics in the State of New York was compiled by Mr. Letchworth in his last years. The record shows him quite distinctly to have been the persisting spirit in the movement, throughout; pricking it to action when it lagged, and rousing it to fresh aggressiveness when it had been stricken with discouragement by the Governor's veto in 1892. Until some months after its opening he was in official relations to the colony, first as chairman of the Standing Committee of the State Board of Charities on the Construction of Buildings for Charitable and Correctional Institutions, and finally as a member of the special new Committee of the Board on Craig Colony. The duties of the first-named committee brought him into coöperation with Dr. Frederick Peterson, who had been made president of the board of managers of the colony, and Mrs. Charles F. Wadsworth, chairman of the executive committee of that board, in studying and determining plans for utilizing the buildings already in place on the estate, and for the new buildings which would need to be provided at once. The report of this work, by himself and Dr. Stephen Smith, was made to the Board in January, 1895. The report of the

Mr. Letchworth's interest in the colony

later committee, made on the 13th of November, 1896, was Commissioner Letchworth's last official act. It recorded the experience of the institution in the first ten months of its operation. The comparatively small number of patients thus far admitted had been selected from the various institutions of the state by Superintendent Dr. Spratling, assisted by Dr. Hoyt, secretary of the State Board. The report, in its conclusion, expressed congratulations to the managers of the colony "upon the very satisfactory results accomplished in the face of so many difficulties."

As Mr. Letchworth's interest in Craig Colony was not of the mere functional kind it did not expire when his official commission was resigned; nor was he allowed to drop out of its affairs. His private correspondence shows how much he continued to be counselled with by those in charge of its work; how often his visits to it were solicited and how welcome they were. But his sense of duty to the victims of epilepsy was far from satisfied by what had been done in the establishment of this one institution by his own state. It was the second of its kind in the whole country. Massachusetts had been giving good treatment and care to a number of epileptic children, in a group of cottage hospitals at Baldwinsville, established by private benevolence in 1882, but maintained latterly by the state; and the state had taken action in 1895 by consequence of which a general hospital for epileptics was in process of creation. In a few other states there were movements on foot which promised some adequate provision for this afflicted class; and in a somewhat larger number there was more or less of imperfect provision for it in private institutions or in improper connection with asylums for the feeble-minded. But inquiries pursued by Mr. Letchworth in all parts of the country found practically nothing done for epileptics in a large majority of the states, or nothing that was fitting to their case. He recognized, therefore, an extremely urgent need of information to the public of the nation, as to the dreadful extent of this neglect, and what it meant of suffering to thousands of individuals and of grave consequences to society at large. The situation was one of which few people, even in the medical profession, appear to have had clear knowledge. The facts of it had never been gathered up and put forth collectively, in a form to be impressive in effect. He determined now to take on himself the task of assembling this needed information from its many sources, printed and unprinted, and making it available for use in stirring public feeling on the subject. He had done something in that direction already, as set forth in two papers prepared for the National Conference of Charities and Correction,—on "Provision for Epileptics," read at Nashville in 1894, and on "Care of Epileptics," read at Grand Rapids in 1896. He now undertook a work of thoroughness on the lines that were sketched in those essays.

He entered deeply into this new task soon after his release from the State Board of Charities, and, while turning frequently to other matters, it was his main occupation until its completion, late in 1899. By laborious correspondence he drew from officials and professional men, from governments and from institutions, in reports and other documents or in personal letters, the information and the expert opinion that went into his book. He was attempting no original treatise, but simply producing as authentic and complete a compilation as could be made of the knowledge and experience of that time in the matter of the care and treatment of

Facts and studies embodied in a book

epileptics. He was preparing a book which Mr. O'Conor, of the Rochester *Post-Express*, characterized subsequently, at the close of three columns of review, as "a complete history of the care and treatment of epileptics — a handbook of all that had been done in their behalf," and he "spared no pains in collecting information or in putting it into convenient shape for instruction or for reference." His inquiries extended to many foreign countries, as well as to all the states of the American Union. The result was a mass of information which men of scientific light and leading in the medical profession hailed with grateful satisfaction. In this work, as in the preparation of the volume on "The Insane in Foreign Countries," he had much and very valuable assistance from his friend, James Nicol Johnston, as well as from Miss Bishop, his secretary.

The book, entitled "Care and Treatment of Epileptics," was published in the same admirable style as that of "The Insane in Foreign Countries," with appropriate and interesting illustrations, by the Messrs. G. P. Putnam's Sons, New York and London, early in 1900. Reviews of it in the medical journals at home and abroad were universally commendatory. In

Brain, the organ of the Neurological Society of London, Dr. William Aldren Turner gave an extended account of its contents and a discussion of the colony system of epileptic treatment as presented in them. The work, it said, "gives a complete account of the epileptic colonies in Europe and America, and a valuable chapter upon the general principles which should guide those more immediately concerned in the development and management of such institutions. The work has required an immense amount of investigation and care in its construction."

In the *Bulletin of the Medical Society of Belgium* the book was even more fully described and discussed. "All who desire to study seriously the hospitalization of epileptics," said the writer, "will find in this large volume, containing a mass of beautiful views and phototyped plans, much information that one would vainly seek elsewhere. It is on this account that we have endeavored to make known the fine work of the great philanthropist, Mr. Letchworth."

One of the first books of the year [said the *Medical Record,* of New York] will doubtless be one of the most useful and practical in the coming century, for the reason that it is the summing-up of methods and theories, with a practical solution of a medico-social problem. . . . It is not the extolling of a philanthropic scheme [Craig Colony] that makes this book valuable; it is the practical discussion of site, labor, buildings, restrictions, diet, training, supervision, economics, nursing, and treatment of epileptics that illustrates what has been done in this beautiful Genesee village, with its farm-lands and orchards, to make the epileptic a useful, happy member, in spite of his fits. . . . The chief value of Mr. Letchworth's historical sketches and descriptions of methods of work is that it is now possible for every state in the Union to establish just such a colony, without the labor of breaking the ground of new ideas and untried philanthropy.

To the same effect the *Medical News* of Philadelphia spoke of Mr. Letchworth and his book: —

As one of the foremost students of philanthropy and sociology in the state, his voice upon the subject combines the tone of authority and experience. His book is not the plea of a dreamer of social reforms; it is a keen, practical, detailed account of how to bring about and accomplish what most people only talk about. To care for the dependent classes without pauperizing them, and without overtaxing the community, and to care for the hitherto almost uncurable epileptic in such a way that he may be benefited without sedative drugs, but by the skilful appreciation of the laws of nature, is the problem which Mr. Letchworth has solved in his work; and every state in the Union, and every private sanatorium for epileptics in the country, could not do better than study the question from his standpoint.

The foremost of European authorities on epilepsy, Dr. Wildermuth, of Stuttgart, wrote of the work to Mr. Letchworth:—

Rarely has a book given me as much pleasure as your fine and complete work, which, indeed, is the only one of its kind in literature. When I began to interest myself actively in the care of epileptics, over twenty years ago, there was very little interest taken in the question by physicians, even by nervous specialists. The great progress made since those days is well shown in your book. Any one who has done work of a similar nature will be able to appreciate the amount of patient labor that your book has cost you. The rich material you have collected is presented in a very clear and finished manner. ... The chapter on general principles is of special interest to me and has given me much pleasure, as here, too, you have treated the subject exhaustively, clearly bringing out all essential points.

Early in the undertaking of this literary task on behalf of the epileptic, if not somewhat prior to it, Mr. Letchworth, in conjunction with Dr. Peterson, Dr. Spratling, General Brinkerhoff, of Ohio, and other leaders in the movement of feeling on behalf of those neglected sufferers, took steps toward bringing about the organization of a national association for the study of epilepsy and the care and treatment of its victims. At a meeting brought together in the City of New York, on the 24th of May, 1898, such a national association was organized, with William Pryor Letchworth, LL.D., for its president; Frederick Peterson, M.D. (New York City), first vice-president; Professor William Osler, M.D. (Baltimore), second vice-president; William P. Spratling, M.D. (Craig Colony), secretary; H. C. Rutter, M.D. (Gallipolis, Ohio), treasurer, and an executive committee of five, Dr. Peterson, chairman.

National Association organized

The first annual meeting of the Association was not held until three years later, when a highly satisfactory body of members was assembled at Washington, on the 14th and 15th of May, 1901. In the interval there had been much well-directed exertion by the officers of the Association and their helpers to extend its membership

First meeting of the Association

WORK FOR THE EPILEPTIC

and to secure contributions to the reports and discussions that would make the meeting profitable and interesting. It goes without saying that the president of the Association took his full share of this arduous work. He is quite likely to have done more than his share. General Brinkerhoff, at least, thought that he did; for writing to him afterwards, with reference to the published proceedings of the meeting, he said: "I wish now to congratulate you on the results of that conference, which owed its existence to your tireless industry in getting it together and securing so many valuable papers which are given to the world in this report."

How wide a ground was covered by the papers presented to the meeting is indicated in the following passage from a brief address by President Letchworth at the opening of its proceedings: —

Through the kind courtesy of Secretary Hay, valuable service has been rendered the Association. By his assistance and the benevolent coöperation of our foreign ministers and ambassadors we have information relating to this strange disease from different countries of Europe, including Sweden in the north and Italy in the south. We have valuable papers and communications from Mexico, South America, India, and Japan, also hints of progressive work in Australia. From other reliable sources we have a review of the work for epileptics in Great Britain, including an interesting account of the development of the useful and beneficent work of the National Society for Employment of Epileptics, at Chalfont, St. Peter, England. We have late information concerning the progress of the great work at the Bethel Colony, near Bielefeld [in the Prussian Province of Westphalia], and much that is suggestive from Belgium and Switzerland. We wait expectantly, hoping for more light from the wide expanse of Russia, including the wine-growing region of the Caucasus. From all these various sources we have matter for study and reflection. The history of the special work for epileptics will be brought down to the present date in Ohio, New York, Massachusetts, Pennsylvania, New Jersey, Texas, and elsewhere in the United States.

The "Transactions" of this first annual meeting of the National Association for the Study of Epilepsy and the Care and Treatment of Epileptics were edited for publication by President Letchworth, and produced from the press before the close of the year. At the next annual meeting of the Association, held at New York in October, 1902, the following resolution was adopted: "That this Association has great pleasure in extending to the Honorable William Pryor Letchworth, LL.D., its most cordial thanks for his valuable, painstaking, and laborious work in preparing for publication the transactions of the Association's first annual meeting, held in Washington, D.C., in May, 1901, and for his generous gift of a sum of money sufficient to pay the cost of printing and binding one thousand copies of the same." The volume, beyond question, was a most valuable supplement to that which Mr. Letchworth had published, two years before, as his personal compilation on the subject of the "Care and Treatment of Epileptics." Dr. Wildermuth was one of many who gave it a very earnest welcome.

The Association had now a list of two hundred and sixty-eight regular and eighteen honorary members, the latter being scientists of distinction in other countries. It represented a widely wakened interest in the study and the social duty which it had been organized to promote. Those who labored to arouse that interest could now take rest in some degree; and for him whose work is the subject of record here the rest was a clear necessity. He would still be a laborer in the vineyard that had tasked him so long, but with a slower hand; and the finishing touches were being given to his handiwork in its various directions, here and there. Practically he had done what he could for the epileptics, and would attempt no more, except in the way of suggested action, at times, by the Association in its annual meetings. Beyond the first one, he was unable to attend these meetings, but his interest in them, and in Craig Colony, and in all the work for epileptics, was never lost.

In other arenas of public benevolence he had been continuingly active since his retirement from official service, and would continue so for a brief term still. In June, 1897, he had, for the last time, addressed the Superintendents of the Poor of New York State, sketching the history of their conventions, showing the good that had come from them, and pointing out the lines on which more could be achieved. In July of the same year, at the National Conference of Charities and Correction, held at Toronto, Canada, he read the paper on "Dependent Children and Family Homes" which has been spoken of in a former chapter.

Incidental labors

That year he found bits of leisure and op-

WORK FOR THE EPILEPTIC 351

portunity for renewing attention to those claims of historical duty which he had always felt to be urgent on the people of the Genesee Valley. Among the incidents of General Sullivan's expedition to the Valley, in 1779, was one which touched his feeling peculiarly, and it had long been his wish to have the scene of it marked memorially. A detachment of Sullivan's troops had been ambushed by the Indians and slaughtered, the two officers of the company, Lieutenant Thomas Boyd and Sergeant Michael Parker, being cruelly tortured to death. In a letter addressed to the President of the Livingston County Historical Society, Mr. W. Austin Wadsworth, March 19, 1897, he suggested the propriety of action by the Society to secure possession of the two spots hallowed by these tragedies of patriotism, and to mark them in some enduring way. During the following summer, in company with Mr. Andrew Langdon, president of the Buffalo Historical Society, he visited and studied the ground, to assure himself of the accuracy with which the points in question could be identified. From the data in hand that assurance was made clear to them, beyond question. The place of ambush was found in the town of Groveland and the place of torture near Cuylerville, both spots being in Livingston County. By subsequent action the Livingston County Historical Society acquired title to the Groveland site and erected on it a plain monument, appropriately inscribed. Unfortunately, the other site could not be secured.

Early in the next year a project of sordid menace to Glen Iris came to light, and the peace of the Glen's good master and devoted lover was tormented by it thenceforward until his death. Avaricious capital had planned to exploit the falls of the Genesee for electric power, and the legislature, in the spring of 1898, had before it a bill which granted the needed authority. Later on there will be a story to tell of painful experience from this cause; for the present we will pass it by.

Menace to Glen Iris

In the midst of the anxieties which now became ever present in his mind, Mr. Letchworth could still give thought to the old subjects of his care, and in the spring of 1898 we find him contributing his influence to a movement in Erie County for separating the poorhouse from the county hospital, and establishing the latter on a large country farm. In December of that year he was grieved by the death of Dr. Hoyt, who had been secretary of the State Board of

WORK FOR THE EPILEPTIC 353

Charities from its organization in 1868, and with whom he had worked throughout his whole service in the Board. Soon after this he suffered an illness which caused some anxiety, but it did not disable him for the hard work of 1899 on the "Care and Treatment of Epileptics." How onerous and trying that work had been may be inferred from what he wrote to a friend in May, 1900:—

My desk is a mass of papers in unutterable confusion. I think I must have at this moment fifty or more unanswered letters on it, among them several from Professor Barnard, formerly Commissioner of the United States Bureau of Education, asking a list of questions that will take me a week to answer. He and his daughter press me for replies. . . . What am I to do? And how can I go to Topeka [to the National Conference of Charities and Correction]? The conference convenes on the 18th inst. and lasts until the 24th. Then there is the convention of medical superintendents of institutions for the feeble-minded, to be held the last of the month at Polk, in western Pennsylvania, to which I am urgently invited and which I would like to attend.

He attended the meeting at Polk, and on the 10th of June, after his return, was able to write: "Am getting my papers pretty well in hand." But on the 21st he must be at an important meeting of the Epileptic Association, in New York, for which he had preparations to make.

Later that year, in November, Mr. Letchworth was called to Albany, to attend the First State Conference of Charities and Correction, as its president, and to make an opening address. For the main theme of his address he reverted to his old urgency of the fundamental need of a carefully discriminating classification in all treatment of the dependent and offending classes, and most carefully in the treatment of the young. Much had been done in that direction, as he showed, but the principle must be carried further, and for reasons economic as well as humane. He looked to the future with a robust faith and hope. The address was one of the wisest counsels he has left. Excepting the brief address which he made on opening the First Annual Meeting of the National Association for the Study of Epilepsy, held at Washington in the next May, it was his last deliberate and formal utterance on the subjects which had occupied his mind during half of his life.

He attended the second of the State Conferences, in November, 1901, and took a little part in one of the discussions on that occasion, speaking with unwonted bitterness, in denunciation of the county-jail system, as administered in his own county for the personal profit of the sheriff of the county. His remarks were called out by one of the committee reports presented to the conference, in the course of the discussion of which he said: —

Bitter denunciation of the county-jail system

Since the building of the old jail in that county [Wyoming] — I do not know just how many years ago — fifty, sixty, or seventy years ago — we have suffered under a grave abuse there. Young men and lads committed to this jail have been brought, under the system there, into intimate association with the most hardened offenders, — those who have been discharged convicts from state prisons, — and these have the opportunity of teaching them all the vices and the crimes and the very worst features of criminal life. Thus, in that county, through these years, we have been educating lads and young men for the penitentiary, where they have to be supported at the expense of the state. But a plan for a new jail comes up, and I was among those interested in getting the jail constructed on the principle that is now adopted in Ohio and Minnesota, whereby there is a complete separation of the prisoners. A prisoner might come in and remain until his term expired and not see another. Now it would seem as if that was very desirable. It was practicable. It was shown beyond any question that the jail part of the prison could be built that way without any additional expense. And why could not that be carried? It was because the sheriff said: "I object to that. It affects my income. I can't afford it. It reduces my income." That was the objection, stated boldly. And he carried his point.

Now, I felt deeply interested in this. . . . I went before the board of supervisors, myself, and I pleaded. I asked that I might be humored in the matter, in consideration of my long service to the state. I asked for that favor to those young men. I tell you, friends, it was denied me, and it was denied to those young men. And what was the objection? No objection but the influence of that sheriff whose pocket was affected. There would be a less number of prisoners in the jail under this system, and so he could not make as much out of it. This is a great wrong. How are we going to remedy it? I would say further, and I say it with great respect, that an appeal was made to the Prison Commission of the State; but the Ohio plan and the Minnesota plan were set aside, and the jail was so built that we shall go on for sixty or seventy years more under a system that ruins young men. It is a pity.

Excuse me for speaking with so much emphasis; but this is something that I know of my own knowledge, and it goes to my heart. How are we going to save these young men? How are we going to set aside this abominable system? It is feasible, if we choose to do it, in the smaller counties. I do not speak of the large jails, such as those of New York and Brooklyn. I speak of the small jails throughout the country.

Death came once more into Mr. Letchworth's family in the summer of 1902, when his sister Hannah — Mrs. William Howland, of Sherwood, New York — died. Six months later, on the 14th of February, 1903, a stealthy forerunner of the dread angel crept into the home at Glen Iris and touched its master with a paralyzing finger, leaving him maimed and weakened for the remaining seven years of his life. That night Miss Bishop made this record in her diary of what had happened: — [sidenote: Stricken with partial paralysis]

After supper this evening Miss McCloud [a cousin of Mr. Letchworth, who had lived with him and conducted his household since Mrs. Crozer's death], sister Ellen, and I went to the library, and soon after Mr. Letchworth came in and asked for a volume of Tennyson. He wished to look for a quotation in which occurred the expression "an ancient tale of wrong." He opened the volume to "Lord Burleigh," which I read aloud at his request; and then Mr.

Letchworth took the book and began to read "Lady Clare." He had read but a few words when his speech grew inarticulate; a strange expression came over his face, his head bowed, and his book dropped to the floor. But while Miss McCloud and I went to summon assistance, Mr. Letchworth looked up and spoke naturally to Ellen. This was about 7.15 o'clock. We assisted him to the couch, when he said something indistinctly about paralysis, and requested us to look in a medical book and find out what to do.

Dr. Miller, of Castile, was called at once, and later in the evening a message was sent to Dr. Roswell Park, of Buffalo, who arrived Sunday evening, bringing a nurse.

After three weeks had passed, Miss Bishop, in a letter to Dr. Stephen Smith, the long-time colleague of Mr. Letchworth in the State Board of Charities, gave the following account of the stricken man's state: —

From the first, Mr. Letchworth's mind has been active. He is still confined to his bed, except for brief periods two or three times each day, when he sits in his easy chair to rest. The entire left side is somewhat disabled and he has as yet but little use of his left arm; but his face is natural. It has been very difficult to keep him as quiet as the doctors desired, and, until some of the work which was on hand when he was taken ill was cleared away, he could not rest. Only three days after the stroke he said: "The doctors say I must not think about my work, but I can no more help it than I can stop the flow of the Genesee River. If you will bring a pencil and some paper and take down a brief dictation my mind will be relieved and I can rest." The distressed look on his face compelled me to yield to his request. He dictated two brief letters and soon after fell asleep. Dr. Park says that it is better sometimes to give him an opportunity to relieve his overburdened mind than for him to be so disturbed because his work is not done.

Not long after this was written the invalid was made happy by an expression to him of the affection with which he was regarded by the whole community of Craig Colony. It came in the form of a beautiful loving-cup, to the purchase of which nearly a thousand of the patients, attendants, and officials had contributed, none of the former being allowed to give more than five cents, while some had pleasure in giving one. On one of its faces the cup bore the following inscription:— *Loving-cup from Craig Colony*

Presented to the Honorable William P. Letchworth, LL.D., by the officers, assistants, employés, and patients of the Craig Colony for Epileptics, at Sonyea, Livingston County, New York, in recognition of his noble and unselfish devotion to the public charities of the state, and especially in appreciation of his untiring zeal in helping to found the Craig Colony, and for his faithful and continued interest in its welfare. March 10, 1903.

It had been intended to make the presentation of the cup an occasion of some ceremony at the colony; but the givers were profoundly grateful for so much improvement in Mr. Letchworth's condition as permitted it to be done quietly by Dr. Spratling at Glen Iris.

Late in April Mr. Letchworth was able to receive a visit from his friend Johnston, who wrote to him on returning home: "I am encouraged by my visit. . . . My hope is that you will soon feel much more comfortable and better. One serious word in conclusion: God needs no man's work; yet He has been so good as to allow you these long years of work for Him and His poor helpless children. Nor did He prevent you until your work was well rounded up, and its effect being felt all over the world. So, sit and think with joy of the good He has permitted you to do, and how you have been favored and beloved by Him and by your fellow men." A little later the same good counsellor wrote: "What is un-

Slow and imperfect recovery

done is so little; what has been done is so much and so satisfactory; it would be wrong to worry over the completed." In such words Mr. Johnston expressed the general feeling of Mr. Letchworth's friends, — that he had nothing of an incomplete lifework to give him grief.

By the middle of May he was beginning to be wheeled about the grounds of Glen Iris, and to be driven out to some of his fields; but he was not able, on the 4th of July, to attend the dedication of the Wyoming County Soldiers' and Sailors' Monument, at Warsaw, in bringing about the erection of which he had taken an actively leading part. A few days later he rejoiced in the ability to write a short letter with his own hand. But when November brought to Buffalo the Fourth State Conference of Charities and Correction he could not attend it. That he was in the thought of those present was assured to him by the following expression from the conference, communicated to him by its secretary: "That the conference greatly regrets the absence of the Honorable William Pryor Letchworth, of Portage, and the fact that his absence is caused by illness. Dr. Letchworth was the first president of the conference, and his long and distinguished services for the poor have won the respect of and greatly endeared him to the members of this conference, who desire to place upon its records this testimonial of their esteem."

During the next two years he was making slow gains of strength and recovering a limited use of his limbs; the capabilities of his mind never having been much impaired. Gradually he became busied again, not with any new undertakings in the former lines of his public work, but in some endeavors to enlarge the fruitfulness of what he had done, as well as in renewed attention to his private affairs, and in attempts to reduce his enormous accumulation of letters and papers to an orderly state. In September, 1904, he was bereft again in his home by the death of Miss McCloud, and thereafter had none of kinship to him in his household, but was affectionately and thoughtfully cared for, especially by Miss Bishop, who had been his secretary and confidential assistant for nearly twenty-two years. He was surrounded, moreover, as he had been throughout his life, by the devotion of all who came into his service.

In the spring of 1906 the danger to Glen Iris,—to its safety and its beauty alike,—which had been threatening it for several years and afflicting Mr. Letchworth with grievous anxiety, became acute. Its causes and the immediate results to which it led are now to be told.

CHAPTER IX

THE GIFT OF LETCHWORTH PARK TO THE STATE OF NEW YORK

IT may be that when Mr. Letchworth made his first purchases at Glen Iris there were undefined thoughts in his mind of some ultimate dedication of the beautiful place to a public use. There is no warrant for such a conjecture, but the suggestion of it comes reasonably enough from a general observation of the motives that ruled his life, and the forethoughtfulness that went into everything of importance that he did.

All, however, that we can know of the entrance of that thought into his intentions is, that it had grown to a certain maturity of purpose within the first ten years of his possession of the Glen; for he made it manifest in 1870, by procuring from the legislature (chapter 479, Laws of 1870) the passage of an act of incorporation which provided as follows: —

The Wyoming Benevolent Institute

SECTION 1. John B. Skinner, Edward H. Letchworth, Henry R. Howland, George J. Letchworth, and Josiah Letchworth, and their successors, to be duly appointed as hereinafter specified, are hereby constituted and appointed a body corporate for the purpose of establishing and maintaining in the County of Wyoming an institution for the support and education of indigent young persons.

SECTION 2. Said corporation shall be called the Wyoming Benevolent Institute, and under that name shall have perpetual succession and be capable of taking and holding, by purchase, gift, grant, devise, or bequest, any real or personal estate for the purpose aforesaid.

That the Wyoming Benevolent Institute was organized with an intention to identify it with the future of the Glen Iris estate, or with some important part of that property, is left in no doubt by the few incidents of its later history. Nothing that even attempted the fulfilment of its declared purpose ever came from it; but the purpose itself, " of establishing and maintaining in the County of Wyoming an institution for the support and education of indigent young persons," does not appear to have undergone any change for many years. Its full realization cannot have been expected or intended to occur until after Mr. Letchworth's death, when bequests, sometimes mentioned in his letters to the trustees, would make a provision for the institution which he could not make during his life. It is doubtful if he ever thought of being able, with his own means solely, to establish and maintain, even by bequest, an institution that would be worthy of the setting which Glen Iris would give it. Aside from what went into that noble estate, in purchase money and improvements, his fortune was certainly not large, and the drafts on his income during all the years of his service, officially and personally, to afflicted humanity, grew heavier as time went on. He counted on the enlistment of others with him in a due endowment of the homes and schools for homeless girls and boys which he would plant in his lovely valley.

The Wyoming Benevolent Institute is, therefore, to be regarded as an instrument of organization made ready, with wise precaution, in advance, for employment whenever there should come to it the legacies provided for its ultimate work. It may be that Mr. Letchworth contemplated originally some small beginnings, under his own eye, of the "support and education of indigent young persons," and hoped to see the institution thus planted and in growth while he lived; but if we remember that when he organized the Institute he had nothing of the knowledge of such undertakings which he began to acquire soon afterwards, we may easily believe that the more he learned of the problems involved the more he felt cautioned against haste in his designs.

Correct or incorrect as our explanations of the fact may be, there appears to have been nothing done by the Wyoming Benevolent Institute between 1870 and 1883, when, on the 15th of October, Mr. Letchworth addressed to the trustees a letter, relating at the outset to some contemplated buildings and other improvements, on property which he had conveyed to the Institute, and then proceeding as follows: — *Original plans for the Institute*

In the mean time I desire that a limited work on behalf of unfortunate children be carried on. There are so many ways in which this can be done that I do not wish to bind the trustees to an exact method which subsequently, under changing conditions, might be found inconvenient to carry out. My private idea is, however, in the main to take healthy and intelligent children, suitable to family care, who are thrown on the public for support, either through loss of parents, destitution, homelessness, or other cause, and to provide for such a temporary home, preparatory to placing them as soon as may be in family homes, in the usual course. A cherished thought with me is that of giving temporary support to poor girls while giving them a thorough training in domestic housekeeping, graduating them with certificates of competency; also of giving a like opportunity to poor boys, while making good gardeners and florists of them. The work for boys and girls should be separately carried on, — the one at Glen Iris homestead, perhaps, for girls, and the other at Prospect Home Farm for boys.

Nothing of an extended character can, of course, be carried on until there has been an aggregation of funds affording a yearly handsome income. I have strong hopes, however, that liberal donations will be made by the benevolent to carry on the work, as soon as they see it fairly inaugurated, and that the institution will soon be placed on an independent footing, and enabled to carry on its work on a reasonably large and generous scale. I have given all I have to accomplish this. I can do no more.

These hopes were not realized. The Institute was still, for a long time, to be scarcely **Later sug-** more than a name. Evidently Mr. **gestions** Letchworth had not enlisted the cooperation of others in his undertaking, and his view of the practicabilities in it had undergone some modification at last. On the 14th of September, 1900, he wrote again to the trustees,

VIEW FROM PROSPECT FARM, LETCHWORTH PARK

revoking his letter of October 15, 1883, and asking that his present writing be substituted therefor, as an expression of his desires concerning the future use of the bequest he had made to the Institute. In this letter he said: —

Considering the rare advantages the property possesses, for affording the opportunity of quick recuperation to delicate children who may be brought here from crowded cities in the summer, especially during the heated term, — children who may be benefited by country air, a change of diet, happy surroundings, — it has seemed to me that for the present, and perhaps for some years to come, the greatest good can be dispensed, with the means at hand, by bringing needy children to Glen Iris from the cities and caring for them during the summer months. Eventually it may be found practicable to extend to boys some kind of industrial training, to include gardening, agriculture, and instruction in different branches of mechanic arts; and to girls domestic science and floral culture.

Attempts, inspired by selfish motives, have already been made, as you are aware, to gain control of the waters of the Genesee River in this locality and, by placing a dam across the river, to utilize it for the advancement of mercenary schemes. Should such a project or projects ever succeed, the consequences would be deplorable. A philanthropic enterprise that I have been laboring for over forty years to place on an enduring foundation would be jeopardized if not overthrown, and one of the most beautiful and health-giving resorts in the state would be deprived of its attractiveness and means of affording happiness. I entreat you to use every honorable means to defeat such attempts.

In this letter Mr. Letchworth expressed again his "hope that liberal gifts will eventually be made by the benevolent to aid in carrying on the work of the corporation on a reasonably large and generous scale," and added: "Should no outside aid be received, however, I believe by prudent management the invested fund of the corporation may be increased from year to year, and at the same time the charitable work may be so conducted on a prudent scale that great good may be dispensed through its instrumentality."

The threatening scheme referred to in this letter was one which planned the construction of a dam above the upper fall of the Genesee, to control the waters for a development of electric power, and it gave, ere long, an entirely changed destiny to Glen Iris, setting aside all prior intentions concerning its future use. For a few years, however, these last suggestions of Mr. Letchworth to the trustees of the Institute were carried out. He deeded to them the piece of property known as " Prospect Home," containing fifty-nine acres of ground, with a comfortable house, possession to be given on the 1st of April, 1902. After that time children from the orphan asylums of Buffalo were invited each summer, in parties of ten at a time, for a three days' visit to Prospect Home, and to be entertained on one of those days at the Glen Iris home. These were outings that gave great happiness to little people who have scant shares of real happiness in their early lives.

At about the same time a small, carefully chosen library of books and current periodicals was opened, under the auspices of the Wyoming Benevolent Institute, for circulation in the neighborhood.

These kindly attempts to make some beginning of the benevolent uses of Glen Iris, which the Institute had been organized to conduct, were soon brought to an end, by the menace which electric science had inspired in the last decade of last century against all cascades and cataracts, as exhibitions of an idly wasted force. For some years prior to the pointing of that menace directly at the section of the Genesee River which traversed Mr. Letchworth's domain, there had been projects of a storage reservoir on the river for purposes con-

Menacing project of water storage on the Genesee
nected with the Erie Canal. It was suggested in the annual report for 1889 of the state engineer and surveyor on canals that a supply of water from the Genesee River, immediately available, by means of such storage, would be of great value in case of any serious accident to the canal west of Rochester. On this suggestion the legislature directed the state engineer to investigate the matter and report. He did so, and his report for 1890 recommended the construction of a storage dam at a point a short distance above Mount Morris. This placed it near the lower end of the continuous gorge through which the Genesee runs from the Lower Falls of the Portage section to Mount Morris, thus establishing the storage reservoir within that gorge, entirely below Glen Iris. In recommending this the state engineer declared the location to be "peculiarly adapted to the construction of a stable and safe dam."

In 1892 the legislature, by concurrent resolution, created a commission of three persons to consider the project and report on it. This commission reported favorably, approving the

GIFT OF LETCHWORTH PARK 373

Mount Morris site. In his report of the next year the state engineer renewed his recommendation; and in 1894 his report was accompanied by a special report on the subject, by George W. Rafter, engineer in charge of the water-storage investigation. This, too, was urgent in support of the undertaking to establish a storage of water in the gorge below the Glen Iris falls, by a dam near Mount Morris. Four possible locations of the dam had been investigated, all in the vicinity of Mount Morris, at distances ranging from one to eight miles; but one or the other of the lower two was preferred. Thus far no other sites had been considered; and the project was still regarded as a public enterprise for the state to take in hand, primarily for the benefit of the Erie Canal, with incidental benefits to the city of Rochester.

In this view the legislature of 1895 passed an act declared to be "for the construction of a dam on the Genesee River for the purposes of the Erie Canal, and for restoring to the owners of water power on the Genesee River the water diverted by the state for canal purposes." This enactment was vetoed by Governor Morton. In his veto the governor recited the fact that the bill required the dam to be constructed at one of three sites, "all in a gorge in the Genesee River near Mount Morris," and admitted that "if a dam is to be constructed upon the Genesee River for the purpose of water storage, this gorge is the most available place." "Civil engineers and others," he added, "agree that the opportunities for storing a large quantity of water at this point are unsurpassed if not unequalled." His objections to the measure were on the ground that the existing condition of canal business did not justify the heavy expenditure involved, and that no provision was made for any contribution towards that expenditure by the localities interested. In his view the project should wait until the people had voted on the then pending proposition to deepen the Erie Canal to nine feet.

But speculative capital was now beginning to be excited by demonstrations of practical success in the conversion of water power into electric power, and in the transmission of it over considerable distances for profitable use. The tapping of the Falls of Niagara for this purpose was in progress, and its grand success was realized in 1896. This may have brought a change of motive into the project of water storage in the Genesee,

Sinister change in the project

GIFT OF LETCHWORTH PARK 375

and an access of new ideas into the minds of the officials who planned for it. They discovered themselves to have been in error when they recommended the location of the dam at Mount Morris. They now saw that it should be placed at Portage, above the Upper Fall. "Of the several available sites for storage reservoirs on the Genesee River," said the state engineer in his report for 1896, "completer surveys show that the Portage site is preferable to all others, because of affording the greatest possible storage at the smallest cost per unit volume." He omitted to mention the further fact that the water to be stored would be five hundred feet higher at Portage than at Mount Morris, and afford a development of much more power. That was left for casual mention in the accompanying report of Mr. George W. Rafter, the engineer in charge of this part of the state engineer's work.

From Mr. Rafter's report we learn that the surveys and investigations at Portage were made without legal authority, and expended an appropriation which the legislature had specifically provided for further surveys at Mount Morris. "The provision in question," said Mr. Rafter, "apparently limited the additional investigation to the site formerly considered at Mount Morris. On second thought, however, it appeared clear that this was a technical error which had no significance." And so, on this " second thought," the other " second thought," of a dam at Portage, was brought forward with the needed preliminaries of survey and investigation.

The situation was now well prepared for making the storage of water and water power on the Genesee River an undertaking of private enterprise, relieving the state of cost and responsibility and securing an opportunity of profit to the promoters of the enterprise. More than a year passed, however, before the formal assent of the state to that treatment of the project was secured. Then, by an act which became law April 29, 1898, a " Genesee River Company " of five persons, Mr. George W. Rafter being one, was incorporated, and authorized to build a main dam or reservoir on the Genesee River near Portageville. The ostensible purpose, as set forth in the preamble of the act, was that "of improving the sanitary condition of the Genesee Valley, of checking floods in the Genesee River by producing as far as possible an equable flow

The Genesee River Company

GIFT OF LETCHWORTH PARK

therein, of supplying necessary water to the enlarged Erie Canal, and of furnishing pure and wholesome water for municipal purposes." No hint in this of a development of electric power for industrial employment, as being among the purposes of the dam. That was secured by subsequent provisions of the act, but as though it were no more than an incident or accident that would attend the carrying-out of a public-spirited undertaking on the part of the people incorporated for it. The right to accept and make use of this trifling by-product of its beneficent enterprise was conferred on the Genesee River Company in these words:—

Said corporation shall have the right to utilize all the water power *incidentally created* by the construction of said main dam or reservoir, and, for the purpose of such utilization, said corporation may construct, maintain, and operate in and upon the Genesee River and its tributaries within one mile of the mouth of each of such tributaries and along the line thereof, at any and all points below the location of the aforesaid main dam or reservoir, all necessary power dams, subsidiary reservoirs, sluices, gates, trunks, irrigation canals and distributaries, hydraulic power raceways, and all other necessary appliances for the purpose of utilizing the water and water power of said river for the development of hydraulic and electrical power, and for the purpose of making and transmitting compressed air, and for other purposes.

By the terms of the act they were required to begin, "actually and in good faith," "the work of constructing the said main dam or reservoir on the Genesee River near Portage," "within five years after the passage of this Act," and to expend on such work at least ten per centum of the minimum ($3,000,000) of capital stock authorized by the act; in default of which work and expenditure within that period "the said corporation," it was declared, "shall be dissolved." The legislature, in its grant of rights and powers to these incorporators, had spared nothing that could help to make their franchise highly valuable and attractive to enterprising capitalists. They could take property, even of cemeteries, by condemnation. They could acquire property belonging to the state or other authorities; they could use public streets and highways; they could fix their own charges for power, light, etc., and, as shown above, there was seemingly nothing that they could not do in and along the shores of the Genesee River. And yet, with such a franchise, they were not able to raise

Expiration and revival of charter

GIFT OF LETCHWORTH PARK 379

$300,000 for expenditure on their project within five years. That period expired on the 29th of April, 1903, and with it the charter of the Genesee River Company expired.

For some time after this occurrence Mr. Letchworth, and all lovers of that paradise of the Genesee over which he held wardenship, had relief from immediate anxieties. But in the winter of 1906 the supposedly dead Genesee River Company reappeared before the legislature, asserting itself to be still in life, inasmuch as the provisional mandate of dissolution in the Act of 1898 had never been enforced against it by any official authority, and asking for legislation to so amend the Act of 1898 as should extend to five years from July 1, 1906, the time allowed for beginning the construction of the Portage dam or reservoir. Despite strong opposition the legislature listened favorably to this remarkable proposition, and passed the desired amendatory act, reviving the dangerous franchise of the Genesee River Company, unless the courts should declare that the legislature had no power to breathe life into a corporation which it had commanded to die on a given day.

Mr. Letchworth now despaired of saving his

wonderful part of the river and its enclosing valley from vandal seizure for industrial exploitation, by any other means than that of making it the property of the state. Having long been ready — perhaps ready from the beginning of his ownership — to give it to a public use, he was quite prepared, in existing circumstances, to make the gift direct to the State of New York. Besides the hope of thus securing the beauty of his place from spoliation, there were other incidents of the situation which moved him to the same resolve. He indicated them to his nephew, Mr. Ogden P. Letchworth, president of the board of trustees of the Wyoming Benevolent Institute, in a letter bearing date September 20, 1906, when he wrote: —

Glen Iris to be given to the state

It has doubtless become patent to you, as it has to me, that the carrying-out of the original purposes of the Wyoming Benevolent Institute is now utterly impracticable. Not only has the capital that I intended for this work become so lessened as to greatly reduce my income, but the expenses of carrying on the work here are greatly increased, through the necessity of paying larger wages and the employing of a larger number of men to do the same amount of work. It is a large property, and the repairs on everything perishable are constant and very great. . . . As I cannot carry out my first intention, it now appears to me that greater good will come to mankind from the devoting of my property here to a public park, embracing some educational features, than from any other disposition of it.

Before deciding finally to make the proffer of his superb domain to the state he studied how best to secure for it a faithful caretaking in future years. In doing this he became attentive to the mission and work of the American Scenic and Historic Preservation Society, founded by Andrew H. Green, the father of New York City's Central Park, and incorporated in 1895. What the society had done in defending Niagara Falls and in saving the Palisades of the Hudson, Watkins Glen, etc., gave him confidence in the efficient public spirit and influence embodied in it, and in 1906 he sought the advice of its trustees. The results of the consultation are told in the Twelfth Annual Report of the Society, as follows: —

Consultation with American Scenic and Historic Preservation Society

Upon his invitation the trustees appointed from among their number the following committee to confer with him and coöperate in carrying out his benevolent purposes: George Frederick Kunz, Ph.D., of

New York, the mineralogist and gem expert, and president of the society; Professor L. H. Bailey, of Ithaca, head of the College of Agriculture of Cornell University; the Honorable Charles M. Dow, of Jamestown, New York, President of the Commissioners of the State Reservation at Niagara; Mr. Francis Whiting Halsey, of New York, the well-known writer on Indian subjects and literary adviser to Funk & Wagnalls, publishers; the Honorable Thomas P. Kingsford, of Oswego, a commissioner of the state reservation at Niagara; Henry M. Leipziger, Ph.D., educator and supervisor of lectures of the Board of Education of the City of New York; the Honorable N. Taylor Phillips, deputy comptroller of the City of New York, and trustee of many philanthropic organizations; Colonel Henry W. Sackett, of New York, a trustee of Cornell University and counsellor to many public bodies; and the writer of this paper [Edward Hagaman Hall, Secretary of the society].

After several conferences with these gentlemen, Mr. Letchworth concluded to give the title to his property to the State of New York, with the proviso that he should retain a life use and tenancy, with the right further to improve the property, and that upon his death the American Scenic and Historic Preservation Society should have the control and management. Having resolved upon this course, he asked the committee to communicate his purpose to the Honorable

GIFT OF LETCHWORTH PARK

Charles E. Hughes, governor-elect, and to ask him, if he approved, to transmit the offer formally to the legislature.

On December 14, 1906, the committee called upon the governor-elect. After listening to their mission, Mr. Hughes expressed his high appreciation of the generosity and public spirit of Mr. Letchworth and said: "In the midst of so many calls from people who are asking for something *from* the state, it is a novel and delightful sensation to have some one offer to give something *to* the state. This is certainly a most generous benefaction." Governor Hughes communicated the tender to the legislature in his inaugural message to that body, January 2, 1907, in the following words: "It is my privilege to lay before you the public-spirited proposal of the Honorable William Pryor Letchworth to convey to the people of the State of New York one thousand acres of land, approximately, situated in the town of Genesee Falls, Wyoming County, and the town of Portage, Livingston County, upon which Mr. Letchworth now resides. He desires to dedicate the land to the purposes of a public park or reservation, subject to his life use and tenancy and his right to make changes and improvements thereon. If it is your pleasure to provide for the acceptance of the gift, the state will thus obtain title to a tract of rare beauty, the preservation of which for the purposes of a public park cannot fail to contribute to the advantage and enjoyment of the people."

Within little more than a fortnight after the reception of this message the assembly had passed a bill to accept title to the lands proposed to be given, on the terms and conditions stated in the deed, "namely, that the land therein conveyed shall be forever dedicated to the purpose of a public park or reservation, subject only to the life use and tenancy of said William Pryor Letchworth, who shall have the right to make changes and improvements thereon." The bill provided further: "All lands described in and covered by said deed of William Pryor Letchworth shall be deemed to be in the actual possession of the comptroller of this state, subject to such life use and tenancy of said grantor. After the death of the grantor the American Scenic and Historic Preservation Society shall have control and jurisdiction thereof for the purposes stated, unless the supreme court shall determine otherwise for good cause shown upon application of the comptroller, or some other duly authorized official of the state."

Acceptance of the gift by the state

In the senate some opposition to the acceptance of the gift was developed, and it prevailed on the senate finance committee to report an amended bill, omitting the clause giving cus-

GIFT OF LETCHWORTH PARK

tody and control of the property, after Mr. Letchworth's death, to the American Scenic and Historic Preservation Society. In the course of the debate which ensued the following telegram from Mr. Letchworth to the chairman of the finance committee was read: —

Mr. Letchworth respectfully requests your honorable committee to report its approval of the bill as passed by the assembly to accept his deed now in the hands of Governor Hughes, and to withdraw the amended bill now before the senate striking out the Scenic Society, because, to expend a large amount in changes and improvements contemplated by him requires that his plans be known, and he has made them known to the Scenic Society, who approve and will be in a position to carry them out with funds provided by him if the state shall not disapprove and the bill passed by the assembly shall become a law.

With all due respect, Mr. Letchworth cannot accept your amended bill, but must regard a vote for it as a vote not to accept his gift, which he thinks should be accepted upon the reasonable conditions he states, if the gift is otherwise acceptable, his main reason being that if the state could afford to buy and pay for Watkins Glen last year and make the Scenic Society the permanent custodian thereof, it can afford to accept Mr. Letchworth's gift now of much more valuable scenic and historic value, and make the Scenic

Society the temporary custodian thereof, to complete Mr. Letchworth's work with his funds, the state obtaining absolute title to the property and the right to permanently occupy and control it.

On this the opposition gave way, and the bill as passed by the assembly, reported now favorably by the finance committee, was passed by the senate, — forty ayes to four nays. It was the first act signed by Governor Hughes, and on signing it, January 24, 1907, he filed with it the following memorandum: —

This bill provides for the acceptance of a deed of gift made by William Pryor Letchworth to the people of the State of New York, conveying lands of about one thousand acres in extent, situate in the town of Genesee Falls, Wyoming County, and the town of Portage, Livingston County. The deed is made upon the condition that the lands shall be forever dedicated to the purpose of a public park or reservation, subject only to the life use and tenancy of Mr. Letchworth, who shall have the right to make changes and improvements thereon.

This gift to the people is an act of generosity which fitly crowns a life of conspicuous public usefulness, and entitles the donor to the lasting regard of his fellow citizens. The people of the state cannot fail to realize the advantages which will accrue from their acquisition of this beautiful tract and by means of its perpetual dedication to the purpose of a public park or reservation. CHARLES E. HUGHES.

A few days later, January 28, the Governor sent a copy of the act to Mr. Letchworth, with the following note: —

It gives me pleasure to state that an act has been passed, of which I enclose a copy, providing for the acceptance of the deed of gift executed by you under date of the 31st of December, 1906, to the people of the State of New York, conveying to them certain lands, approximately one thousand acres in extent, in the town of Genesee Falls, Wyoming County, and the town of Portage, Livingston County, upon condition that they shall be forever dedicated to the purpose of a public park or reservation, subject only to your life use and tenancy and your right to make changes and improvements thereon. I also enclose a copy of the memorandum filed by me upon the approval of the bill.

In accordance with your request I have delivered to the comptroller of the state the deed executed by you, together with the affidavit and other documents, which you placed in my hands.

Permit me again to express my appreciation of your generous and public-spirited gift and of the lasting benefits which will thereby accrue to the people of the state. I remain, with respect,

Very truly yours,
(Signed)   CHARLES E. HUGHES.

On the day on which the bill became a law Mr. Letchworth made this public acknowledgment: —

To my friends, especially those of the press, who have sympathized in the measure to secure to the people for all time a public park at Portage, I desire to convey my cordial thanks for their warm interest and potent influence. In the development of a higher civilization, let us continue our efforts to preserve for the enjoyment and elevation of mankind those places in our land possessing rare natural beauty, the charms of which, once destroyed, can never be restored.

Very respectfully,
WILLIAM PRYOR LETCHWORTH.

The new state reservation named "Letchworth Park"

By concurrent resolution of the senate, February 4, and of the assembly, February 5, it was declared that the lands conveyed to the state by Mr. Letchworth, for use as a park or reservation, should hereafter be known as "Letchworth Park," "to commemorate the humane and noble work in private and public charities to which his life has been devoted, and in recognition of his eminent services to the people of this state." On receiving a certified copy of this resolution, Mr. Letchworth expressed to the presiding officers of the two chambers of the legislature his "grateful appreciation of the distinguished honor."

At an early stage of the proceedings which thus transferred the entire Glen Iris property to the possession of the state, for perpetual use as a public park (named Letchworth Park by legislative resolution), but under the control and jurisdiction of the American Scenic and Historic Preservation Society, Mr. Letchworth had addressed a communication (December 15, 1906) to the trustees of the Wyoming Benevolent Institute, announcing the conclusion to which he had come, and submitting to them a request for the conveyance to him of "the real estate belonging to the Wyoming Benevolent Institute which is surrounded by and was formerly a portion of the Glen Iris estate, and thereby make possible the transfer of the entire property to the state intact." He added as further suggestions that the treasurer of the Institute be authorized to pay over to him certain funds in the treasury, to be applied by him to the perfecting and carrying-out of improvements and developments of the property, and that the small library of the Institute be transferred to the Cordelia A. Greene Memorial Library, at Castile, New York.

Action in accordance with these requests and suggestions was taken by the trustees at their annual meeting, December 18, 1906.

General recognition of the importance, the value, the generosity of the gift of Letchworth **Importance** Park to the public was manifested, **of the gift** not only throughout the State of New York, but widely in the country at large, by the comments of the press, and by letters to Mr. Letchworth from others than personal friends. Of its kind it is doubtless the most notable gift that a citizen of this country has ever made to the public of his state. Its value and importance are not measured by the area of the estate conveyed, but by the fact that one of the most remarkable exhibits of rare scenery in America was contained wholly in that area. The American people hold many such beauty-spots of the continent in public possession; but what other, of equal distinction, has become public property by a gratuitous surrender of private rights?

The distinction, moreover, of this tract of valley and river is not alone in its varied picturesqueness, but also in its geological significance. As long ago as 1837 it gave its name to the group of rocks which have a singularly instruct-

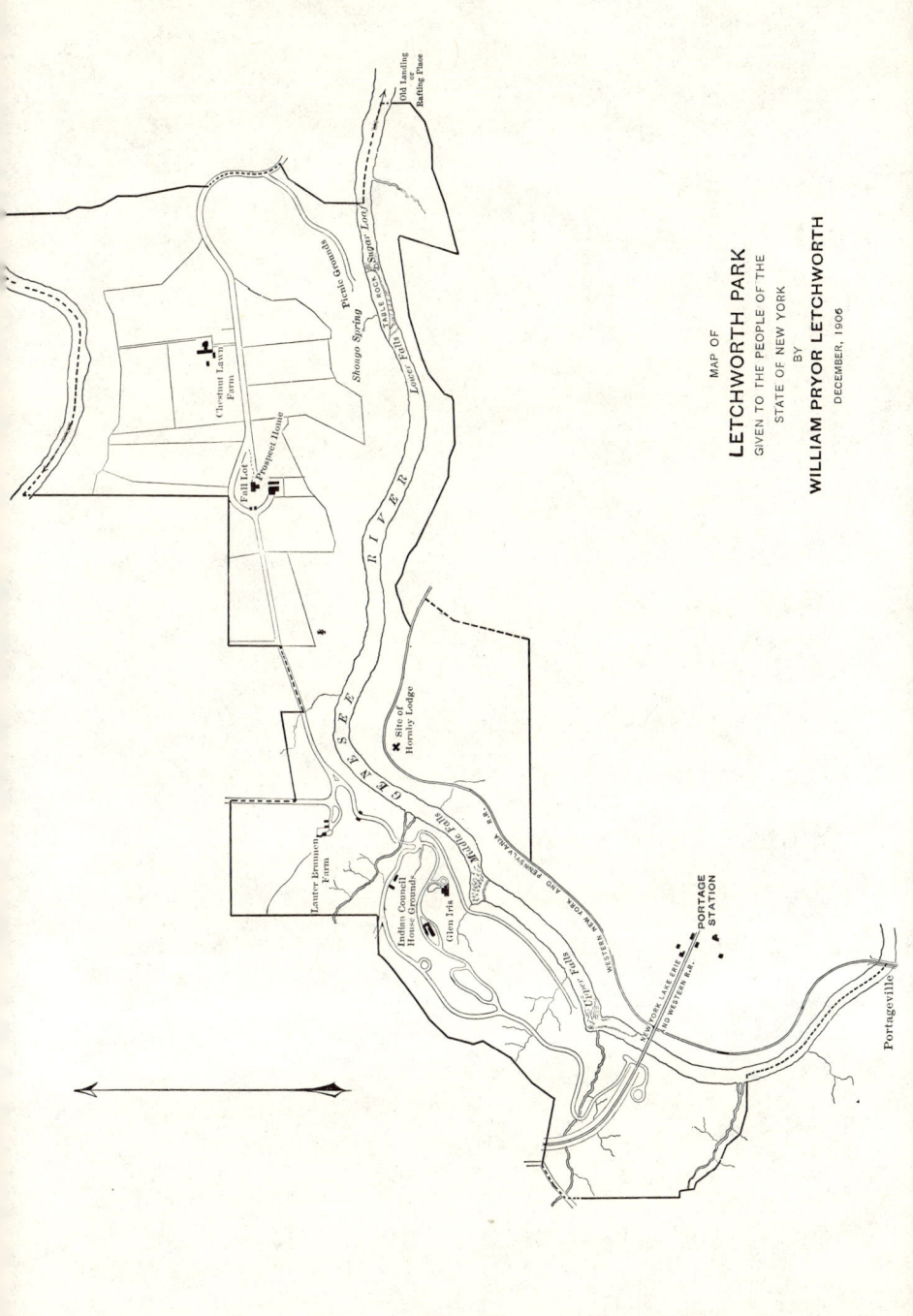

GIFT OF LETCHWORTH PARK

ive exposure in the gorge of the Portage Falls. In geological nomenclature this series of rocks, traceable from Cayuga Lake westward into Ohio, bears the name of the Portage Group, given to it by Professor James Hall. The exceptional character of the rock exposure in Letchworth Park is described as follows, in the inscription prepared in 1908 for a tablet to be erected in the park by a number of geologists to the memory of Professor Hall: —

This gorge, embracing the three Portage Falls, exhibits the typical expression of Hall's Portage Group, whose rocks carry an assemblage of organic remains more widely diffused throughout the world than that of any other geological formation.

The whole geological history of this section of the Genesee Valley has been found to be uncommonly interesting, and has been studied with care by Dr. John M. Clarke, state geologist of New York, Dr. A. W. Grabau, Professor of Palæontology at Columbia University, and others. Professor Grabau discussed it in an address descriptive of the interesting features of Letchworth Park, at a meeting of the section of Geology and Mineralogy of the New York Academy of Sciences, March 4, 1907. It has been treated more fully by Professor H. L. Fairchild, of Rochester University, in a paper on "Glacial Genesee Lakes," published in volume VII of the *Bulletin* of the Geological Society of America. A synopsis of this geological history, prepared by Mr. Edward Hagaman Hall, secretary of the American Scenic and Historic Preservation Society, is presented in the Twelfth Annual Report of that Society, as the third chapter of Appendix B. It is touched upon, also, in Appendix C of the same report, wherein the general "Educational Possibilities of Letchworth Park," as bearing on art, geology, botany, bird life, Indian history and archæology, and model farming, are discussed by Dr. George Frederick Kunz, president of the American Scenic and Historic Preservation Society.

This, the scientific view of Mr. Letchworth's gift to the state, led the New York Academy of Sciences, at a meeting on the 4th of February, 1907, to express its estimate of the importance of the gift in the following preamble and resolutions : —

WHEREAS, The New York Academy of Sciences has learned of the generous gift to the State of New York of a public park known as Glen Iris, at Portage, by Mr. William Pryor Letchworth, and its accept-

GIFT OF LETCHWORTH PARK

ance by the state legislature, under the condition prescribed by Mr. Letchworth, that this beautiful reservation be placed in charge of the American Scenic and Historic Preservation Society:

Resolved, That the Academy of Sciences expresses its recognition of the value to science of this reservation, which, in addition to its exceptional interest from the point of view of scenery, botany, and glacial geology, contains an important part of the standard section of the Upper Devonic formations of North America;

Resolved, That the Academy hereby expresses its sincere appreciation of this gift, which will give pleasure and be of important educational value for all time to the people of the State of New York and to visitors from other states and countries; and

Resolved, That the thanks of the New York Academy of Sciences be and hereby are tendered to the distinguished and public-spirited donor.

By passing into the possession of the state, Letchworth Park had not escaped from the besieging commercialism which covets the "power going to waste" in mere production of the beauty of a waterfall. Practically it seems to have been made safe as against the Genesee River Company, since the doubtfully revivified charter of that company was allowed again to expire, on the 1st of July, 1911, with no attempt to test its validity. But the authority of the New

York State Water Supply Commission was now invoked, in an effort to have the storage of water in the Genesee above Letchworth Park undertaken by the state itself. In 1908 the legislature directed the State Water Supply Commission to make the necessary surveys and maps and "to determine whether the flow of the river should be regulated under the river improvement act," which had been passed in 1904. Then, in September, 1908, the Board of Supervisors of the County of Monroe filed with the commission a petition for such a regulation of the flow of the Genesee.

New phase of water storage project

In anticipation of this new attack the Scenic and Historic Preservation Society, which the state, by contract with Mr. Letchworth, had invested with the custody and care of Letchworth Park, had already made haste to its defence. In January, 1908, it had addressed to the Water Supply Commission an ably prepared memorial, asking it to "disapprove of any plan for constructing a dam and storage reservoir on the Genesee River near Portage," setting forth the considerations that bear heavily against such plans,—such, in the main, as these: That any

Defence of the park by its custodians

impairment of the beauty of Letchworth Park, reclaimed, as it had been by Mr. Letchworth, from disfigurement and restored to its natural charm, during forty-eight years of labor and care and at a cost of about half a million dollars, would be a violation of the trust which the state has accepted; that the diversion of water from the Portage Falls would be no less a breach of faith; that the regulation of the stream for all purposes of public health and safety can be fully accomplished by the location of a dam as originally recommended, near Mount Morris; that Lord Kelvin, the highest authority on the subject, after examining the conditions on the Genesee, in 1902, with reference to the development of electric power, had condemned the plan of a dam at Portage, as dangerous and unnecessary, and declared the proper method to be by means of small dams at successive points; that geological investigation has shown the menace of a storage dam to be especially great at Portage, because of the existence of dangerous deposits of quicksand, underlying the site of the proposed dam; that Mr. Letchworth's experience with landslides in that vicinity gives warnings which it would be madness to disregard; that the large lake to be thus formed could not be of uniform level, but would be so drawn down in the summer season as to lay bare a number of square miles of the slime and drainage deposits which collect at the bottom of such bodies of still water, creating a culture-bed of noxious germs.

On the Monroe County petition there were hearings before the State Water Supply Commission, in Rochester, on the 2d, 3d, 15th and 16th of February and the 2d and 3d of March, 1911, at which many interested parties were present, personally or by representatives, and the questions involved were very fully discussed. Mr. Adelbert Moot, of Buffalo, appeared as counsel for the American Scenic and Historic Preservation Society, and for a number of persons joined with it in opposition to the granting of the petition. The argument submitted by Mr. Moot was principally a legal one, based on the contention that the state is placed under the obligations of a contract by its acceptance of Mr. Letchworth's gift of his estate, subject to the condition that the land thus conveyed "shall be forever dedicated to the purpose of a public park or reservation"; that the use of any part of it for another purpose, or a use which impairs its value as a public park, would be in violation of that clause of the Constitution of the United States which forbids to the states the enactment of laws impairing the obligations of contracts; that a dam for the storage of water above the Portage Falls can be built nowhere outside of lands covered, on both sides of the Genesee River, by Mr. Letchworth's deed of conveyance to the state; that the attempt to construct such a dam may be arrested by the injunction of a federal court, or, if permitted, may deprive the state of its title to Letchworth Park, and pass it to Mr. Letchworth's natural heirs. Mr. Moot, furthermore, drew attention to evidence of an existing monopoly in the control of electric power at Rochester, alike from sources on the Genesee and at Niagara Falls, so dominating the situation that further developments of power must inevitably pass under its control. He traced, in fact, the whole project of water storage on the Genesee to that origin of motive and aim.

The decision of the State Water Supply Commission was rendered on the 16th of June, 1911, by three of its members, against two, denying the application of the Board of Supervisors of Monroe County. In an extended review of the evidence and arguments

Success of the defence

submitted, the commissioners recognized the importance of the legal questions raised, but did not attempt to pass judgment on them, resting their decision on grounds more practical and more within their purview. This appears in the closing paragraph of their decision, which reads as follows: "On account of the impracticability of regulating the flow of the Genesee River and making the assessments for the cost thereof under the river improvement act, and the wider objection that an attempt to conserve the water powers of the state under such narrow limits will impede the greater movement in behalf of a general systematic development of such power for the general welfare, this application is denied."

So far as concerned any supposable survival of rights in the Genesee River Company which could still be a menace to Letchworth Park, they were extinguished five months later, on the 11th of November, 1911, when, on application of the attorney-general of the state, Justice Chester, of the supreme court, decreed the forfeiture and annulment of that company's charter.

Two years before his death, on the 10th of November, 1908, Mr. Letchworth addressed a letter to the American Scenic and Historic Preservation Society, setting forth the plans he had formed for the further improvement of the Letchworth Park estate, and which the Society had expressed a wish to follow. Since his death much has been done, generally on the lines indicated in his plans, to open the park in a larger way to public use by walks and drives, and in preparation, also, for more extensive plans. The chairman of the Letchworth Park Committee of the Board of Trustees of the American Scenic and Historic Preservation Society, the Honorable Charles M. Dow, of Jamestown, New York, who is also, by appointment of the society, the director of Letchworth Park, has organized and conducted this work, and gives much time and thought to the special duties accepted by him. Miss Caroline Bishop, formerly Mr. Letchworth's secretary, is the resident superintendent of the park.

Convenience in visiting the park has been improved greatly by a recent arrangement with the Erie Railway Company, which is to establish a station at the west end of the bridge where all trains will stop when flagged, and where suitable platforms and shelter will be provided.

A superb design for the future enrichment in interest and value of this rare tract of land devotes it mainly to the creation of a great arboretum, which will hardly be surpassed in the world. The project, fully adopted by the trustees of the custodial society and already entered upon, has been set forth interestingly by Mr. Dow, in an article contributed to the *American Review of Reviews* and published in its February issue, 1912. The following is quoted from the article by permission of Mr. Dow:—

The projected arboretum

The American Scenic and Historic Preservation Society has now under way and will soon establish a great forest arboretum at Letchworth Park. It will be a collection of the valuable timber trees of the world and will be the first of its kind, and its contribution to the cause of forest conservation in the United States will be of great economic and scientific value. Those who visit Letchworth Park after its arboretum has been established will see, planted singly and in groups, specimens of every important tree species with which experiment under local conditions of soil and climate is justified by a reasonable promise of success. Visitors thus will have ample opportunity to study the value of trees of many kinds for ornamental planting and for landscape purposes. But the object lesson of enormous economic significance, which will lie spread before their eyes, will be blocks of planted forest, in each of which will be set out one or more important commercial kinds of trees. In each of these blocks, irregular in form, each an acre or more in area, and set out with due regard for landscape and color effects, planting will be so close as rapidly to establish forest conditions, so that Letchworth Park will contain in miniature a forest of a richness and variety which can be witnessed nowhere else on the globe. When this experiment is completed the visitor can pass over winding forest paths, through forest growths in which will mingle the valuable commercial trees of the South, of the far West, of Europe, and from little known quarters of the world, which find at Letchworth Park the climate and soil suited to their needs. . . .

The principle upon which the Letchworth Arboretum is established is that it shall consist of a permanent collection of the various species of the world's timber trees likely to thrive in this northern climate, planted scientifically, to test their value and illustrate the processes of development, so supplying not only knowledge for knowledge's sake, but also knowledge for practical use.

It is intended that the value to the state and the nation of the arboretum will not consist merely in a demonstration, clear to every eye, of the results which may be expected from forest plantations of many different kinds of trees. The possibilities of the arboretum for extending exact knowledge of tree growth will also be fully developed. In each of these miniature forests systematic and skilled observations and records will be made. The growth of the trees will be measured periodically, their liability to disease will be noted, and their capacity for seed-bearing; their behavior in pure stands and in mixture, their influence upon the forest floor, and other practical considerations bearing upon their value for commercial tree-planting, will be carefully observed and recorded. By this means the Letchworth Park Arboretum will aid materially in laying an exact scientific basis for the successful extension of practical forestry in the United States. Every practical step will be taken, not only to insure results of the highest scientific value from forest work at Letchworth Park, but also to develop its usefulness as an object lesson to all park visitors. Circulars describing in plain and definite language the experiments in forestry being carried on will be made available for distribution, while labels and placards will facilitate the identification of trees in the arboretum.

The function of the arboretum, therefore, is obvious. In one sense it is a living museum; in another it is a laboratory; but it is both, out of doors, on a large scale, and the discovery or demonstration of a fact there, within a small area, is a benefit to the whole of mankind.

The part of the park which will be devoted to the

arboretum consists of about five hundred acres, formerly used for agricultural purposes, being well-drained, cultivated, open meadows and fields on various levels, bordered by either planted or natural regenerated forests. In the already existing forests demonstrations of economic planting in open spaces will be made, and varieties of wild flowers will be sown.

In addition to the topographical conditions, the atmospheric conditions at Letchworth Park are unusually favorable for an arboretum, and it is more favorably located in this respect than the gardens near large cities, which are affected by the city smoke and vapors. . . . The nearest large cities to Letchworth Park are Buffalo and Rochester, each about sixty miles away, and Hornell, twenty miles to the south, and the atmospheric conditions are ideal. The elevation above the sea level is about thirteen hundred feet.

Incident to the arboretum will be constructed a fireproof museum, library, and educational building, equipped with a practical working forest library and planned for a later and larger development. . . .

The Society has been fortunate in attracting the interest of Overton W. Price, of Washington, D.C., vice-president of the National Conservation Association, who has been entrusted with the establishment of the arboretum. Mr. Price is one of the best-known living foresters. He is a graduate of the Forest School at Munich, Bavaria, and his training in forestry was acquired both by study in this country and by nearly three years' work abroad, under the direction of the late Sir Dietrich Brandis, former Inspector-General of the Forests of India. Mr. Price was for ten years Associate Forester of the United States, and has been a great factor in the conservation movement. Mr. Gifford Pinchot, former Chief Forester, has expressed his deep interest in the Letchworth Park Arboretum and his willingness to aid in developing its fullest capacity for public usefulness.

The Committee of the American Scenic and Historic Preservation Society which has charge of the property and of the operations of the Society in connection with it, is composed of eleven gentlemen from various parts of the state, under the chairmanship of Honorable Charles M. Dow. It includes Professor L. H. Bailey, Dean of the Agricultural College of Cornell University. The president of the Society is George F. Kunz, Ph.D., Sc.D., New York City.

CHAPTER X

LETCHWORTH VILLAGE — LAST YEARS

In his weakened state Mr. Letchworth was much disturbed and distressed throughout the year 1906, by the menace to Glen Iris of the Portage Dam project and his anxious study of means for its protection and preservation. In March his secretary, Miss Bishop, wrote to Mr. Johnston: " Mr. Letchworth certainly has not gained in strength this winter, and in some ways he seems to me more feeble. He has not taken his rides as regularly this winter as last, and often it is an effort for him to rise from his chair or the couch without assistance. Still, he is as ambitious as ever." A little later she reported: " He seems to be improving some. He does good work yet, but it takes a long time to accomplish it. His correspondence has been large of late, and sometimes he says that the friends will have to excuse him from writing."

On the 11th of May, after the passage of the Genesee River Company Bill, he, himself, wrote to the same correspondent: "The scheme for destroying the beautiful scenery here was passed through the legislature with only three dissenting votes. It was done by what must be regarded as very dishonorable means. I am sure the members of the legislature did not know what they were doing. . . . How it was done matters not now. The deed is done and only awaits the governor's approval to become the law of the land. . . . If he signs the bill it will be my death-warrant, and I shall 'lay me down and die.' Glen Iris will only remain a

'Bright summer dream of white cascade,
Of lake and wood and river.'"

After his conferences with the American Scenic and Historic Preservation Society, and the determination of his purpose to offer the Glen Iris property to the state for use as a public park, subject to the condition that it should be under the control and jurisdiction of that society, his mind was greatly eased. The last weeks of the year were spent by him in Buffalo, for convenience in transacting the business incident to his conveyance of the property, and the deed of conveyance was signed on the last day of the year.

THE LOWER FALL OF THE GENESEE, LETCHWORTH PARK

LAST YEARS

The ensuing two years appear to have been quite uneventful at the Glen, except in the progress of the active work of improvement in the park which Mr. Letchworth had permission to continue to the end of his life. Some of this work, done in 1907, is thus described in the report of the American Scenic and Historic Preservation Society for that year: —

Mr. Letchworth's continued improvement of the park

The generous motives which inspired this gift to the people of the state have found continued expression during the past year in the making of the following improvements: The roads, woodland drives, paths, and stairways have been put in order. . . . Luncheon tables and benches have been provided in pleasant nooks for basket picnic parties. A stairway with frequent landings has been constructed on the left bank of the river by the Upper Fall. A bridge with masonry abutments has been built near the Cascade. A substantial gallery has been constructed along the face of the cliff opposite the Upper Fall. . . . A broad walk has been made along the high bank of the gorge between the Middle and the Lower Falls. . . . The picnic grounds at the Lower Falls have been improved by the erection of a substantial shelter or pavilion for refuge in case of storm. . . . The grove, picnic ground and playgrounds on the bluff overlooking the Glen Iris residence grounds have been developed, etc.

Mr. Letchworth was able to give more or less of personal supervision to this work, and he assisted the secretary of the American Scenic and Historic Preservation Society in preparing a new map of the park, laying out on it the lines of projected new drives and of certain areas designed for reforestation. He was still tasked much too heavily by an extensive correspondence and by the urgency of his desire to reduce an accumulated mass of letters and other papers to order. We may say, indeed, that he escaped from servitude to these tasks only by his death.

The last occasion on which a public audience had the privilege of listening to any words from him was that of the dedication of the new Home of the Children's Aid Society of Buffalo, February 10, 1908. He had been one of the founders of the society and one of the chief pillars of its support. It grieved him that he could not be present at the dedication, and he wrote to express his feeling.

In the work of that year on the park grounds a serious landslide had to be dealt with, on the left bank of the river west of the Upper Fall. "At this point," says the report of the American Scenic and Historic Preservation Society, "at right angles to the present course of the

Genesee River, geologists recognize a preglacial drift-filled gorge. Out of the soft and unstable material which fills this gorge the Degewanus Brook has excavated a ravine. . . . After a heavy rainfall the high sloping banks of this ravine began to settle. On one side the mass movement was so great as to destroy trees." And the movement of unstable soil went on through the year and into the next spring. As remarked in the Society's report, "This landslide has an important bearing on the safety of the proposed dam and storage reservoir at Portage, as the unstable soil involved in this slide is of the same character as the drift deposits on the right bank of the river, upon which the projectors of the Portage dam rely to hold back the waters of an enormous artificial lake."

A visit of Governor Hughes to the park in September was one of the incidents of 1908 which gave Mr. Letchworth much pleasure. A matter which gave him agreeable occupation of mind that year, and after, was the planning and preparation, with Mr. Johnston and Miss Bishop, of a new and enlarged edition of the collection of poems entitled "Voices of the Glen." This, as before stated, though made ready by Mr.

Letchworth in his lifetime, was not published until after his death. It seems an unjust omission in that little book that it does not contain the following lines which Mr. Letchworth received from Mr. Johnston on his eighty-sixth birthday, May 26, 1909: —

> "The higher thought his daily food;
> The evening sun still shining bright;
> The ancient promise still holds good, —
> 'At eventide it will be light.'"

At the time of his passing this eighty-sixth anniversary of his birth, the legislature of his state was preparing for him a very distinguished honor, connected with the founding of a great institution in the eastern part of the state. This institution was "for the custodial care of epileptics of unsound mind, exclusive of insane epileptics, and for the custodial care of other feeble-minded persons, including such as are in state charitable institutions or are supported at public expense and require custodial care." Two years previously, the establishment of such an institution had been decided to be necessary, and an act of the legislature created a commission to select a site. The commission, having the president of the State Board of Charities, the Honorable

"Letchworth Village"

William Rhinelander Stewart, at its head, found a noble tract of land in Rockland County, embracing "some 1354 acres of good farming and woodland for the main site and a mountain tract of 640 acres for the protection of the water supply." A further purchase in 1910 added several hundred acres to the tract. Every height on the ground chosen is said to command views of the Hudson, from High Tor to Stony Point. This property was acquired by the state for what was known in the first instance as "The Eastern New York State Custodial Asylum"; but when, May, 1909 (the constructive work on the ground being then well advanced), the legislature passed an act to provide for the management of the asylum, the first section of the act read as follows:—

The Eastern New York State Custodial Asylum, established by chapter three hundred and thirty-one of the laws of nineteen hundred and seven, as amended by chapter two hundred and ninety-two of the laws of nineteen hundred and eight, is hereby continued by the name and title of "Letchworth Village," in honor of William Pryor Letchworth of Portage, New York, whose efficient public services in behalf of the feeble-minded, epileptic, and other dependent unfortunates the state desires to commemorate.

On signing the bill which gave the name of Letchworth Village to so notable an institution of public beneficence, Governor Hughes wrote personally to Mr. Letchworth the following letter: —

I am very glad indeed that your name has been associated with the new State Custodial Asylum, and it gave me much pleasure to sign the Bill establishing "Letchworth Village." This will serve to aid in perpetuating the memory of your important relation to the charities of the state, and constitute a recognition, though only to a slight extent, of the obligation of our people for the services you have rendered. It must afford you the greatest gratification in these later years to realize the progress that has been made in the care of dependents, and to be assured of the high esteem in which your own share in the work of development is held by all those who are devoting themselves to our rapidly extending philanthropies.

A few days previously Mr. Stewart, chairman of the commission which chose the location of the village, had written to Mr. Letchworth : —

Would it not be possible for you to visit the site this month or in June? The trip will not be a very difficult one, and the commission could have no greater satisfaction and compensation — now that its work is practically completed — than the pleasure of showing

LAST YEARS

it to the man whose name the new institution will always bear. . . . On Friday of last week Mr. Kirkbride [of the commission and afterwards secretary of the board of managers of Letchworth Village] and I, with some friends, visited the site and revelled in its natural beauties.

Such a visit would have given pleasure beyond expression to the invalid at Glen Iris; but the journey was more than he could think of undertaking.

In an address before the National Association for the Study of Epilepsy and the Care and Treatment of Epileptics, at its meeting in Baltimore, May, 1910, Mr. Franklin B. Kirkbride, secretary of the Board of Managers of Letchworth Village, gave a comprehensive statement of the whole purpose and design of the institution, from which the following quotation will not be out of place in this connection: —

Notwithstanding the fact that there are already in New York four state institutions caring for the epileptic and feeble-minded, they are as yet inadequately provided for, and the village, first of all, will relieve the congestion of these institutions, which to-day are overcrowded and unable to meet the demands made upon them. Letchworth Village will admit both sexes of all ages, excluding the insane only. The ultimate capacity will be twenty-five hundred inmates. From Craig Colony will come patients who do not belong there, but who could be received nowhere else; from almshouses will come others; and from the long waiting-lists will come many more. . . . Letchworth Village, however, will be more than a custodial retreat. It will be a laboratory where the causes of abnormal and arrested development will be studied, with the advantage of abundant clinical material; and it will afford a unique opportunity for research and investigation in coöperation with the schools and colleges of New York City. In the schools at the village, the training of teachers for the backward and abnormal will go hand in hand with the instruction of the inmates. The village . . . is to be a community where, through segregation and classification, little groups of people will live separated from each other, but units in the larger settlement. . . . The groups to be established this autumn [1910] will closely resemble those at Templeton, Massachusetts, and the first patients will be feeble-minded cases fitted for farm life.

Letchworth Village received its first inmates — thirty-two in number — on the 11th of July, 1911. Two farm groups of buildings had then been constructed, with a dormitory capacity of one hundred beds. At the time of this writing (November, 1911), the inmate population is fifty-nine, as stated in a note from the secretary of the board of managers, Mr. Kirkbride, who adds the remark: " We expect [the beds] will all be filled within a very few weeks." This will fulfil the plans announced in the second annual report of the managers, made in January, 1911, which stated: " Provision will be made for one hundred feeble-minded men during 1911. No further admissions will be made until the buildings necessary for the administration of the village and the care of employés and patients are completed and equipped."

Speaking in this report of the death of Mr. Letchworth, the managers say : —

Mr. Letchworth took a keen interest in the village from its inception, and was kept constantly in touch with its progress by correspondence and visits to Glen Iris. His suggestions were invariably helpful and inspiring, and his love of beauty, his gentleness, and his delightful sense of humor, coupled with his indomitable faith in mankind, always sent one away from Glen Iris with renewed courage and an increased realization of the possibilities of achievement.

The same report makes the following announcement of the selection and appointment of the superintendent of the village : —

Dr. Charles S. Little, formerly superintendent of the New Hampshire School for Feeble-minded Children, was elected superintendent of Letchworth Village and entered upon the discharge of his new duties on July 1, 1910. He was selected, after a competitive examination, from the list of successful candidates submitted by the State Civil Service Commission. Dr. Little's name headed the list. The high standing of the New Hampshire school, of which he was the first and only superintendent, is sufficient demonstration of his fitness for the even more responsible post to which he has been called.

<small>The last two years of life</small>

Though confined to his home, with inability for much unassisted movement even there, Mr. Letchworth, in 1909, was still a busily occupied man, and continued to be so for another year. And he was kept in fresh remembrance by his younger and still active fellow workers in the fields of public charity and social reform. When the State Conference of Charities and Correction was assembled at Albany, November 18–20, 1909, it sent him this message : —

That the officers and members of the Tenth New York State Conference of Charities and Correction, assembled in the Senate Chamber in the Capitol at Albany, on Thursday, November 18, 1909, send affectionate greetings to Dr. William Pryor Letchworth, of Portage, the first president of the Conference.

LAST YEARS

They are not unmindful of the inspiration they early derived from the lifelong services to humanity rendered by Dr. Letchworth. In his venerable retirement he is not forgotten, and our earnest wishes for his future health and happiness we now convey to him.

A few days after receiving this affectionate and grateful message Mr. Letchworth suffered an accident which might easily have ended his life. He was being taken on his customary afternoon drive in the park, when something caused the horse to begin suddenly backing and turning. What happened then was described by Miss Bishop, in a letter written next day: "There is a steep but short bank on one side of the road, down which the carriage went, and Mr. Letchworth and Mrs. R—— were tipped out. Mr. Letchworth wore his thick, loose fur coat, and fell in the leaves; otherwise the result might have been very serious. . . . Mr. L.'s face was scratched a little by the bushes, but he seems to be suffering most from the jarring of his left shoulder." There must have been a quite dangerous shock sustained, which commonly would shorten life in a man of Mr. Letchworth's age and physical frailty; but it may not have done so in his case. He lived almost exactly a year after this occurred.

The present writer visited him in the following spring and found him feeble but comfortable, and manifesting quite perfect clearness of mind. His memory seemed little impaired, if at all, so far as concerned the distant past. Information that has been useful in this biography, on many matters, was obtained in conversations at that time.

It was never out of his thought, however, that the days left to him could not be many. In a letter written May 17, 1910, he said: "I am expecting my brother Josiah and his wife here on Saturday next to spend a day or two. It is a long time since I have seen them, and this may be the last time that we shall meet."

On the 19th of September the ceremony of the unveiling of the bronze statue of Mary Jemison, near her grave and monument, in the Old Indian Council House ground, was performed, as related in a previous chapter, and Mr. Letchworth was fortunately able to be present.

The state election of November 8, this year, was made especially interesting to him by the submission to the people of a constitutional amendment relating to the acceptance of Mrs. Harriman's proposed gift of lands in connection with a purchase of other lands for a public park on the Hudson River. "Although very lame," he wrote two days afterwards to Mr. Johnston, "I managed to go to the polls on Tuesday to cast my vote for the constitutional amendment anent the proposed Harriman Park. I trust that the Palisades are now safe and that the Harriman gift will go to the people."

His last letter to Mr. Johnston, dictated to his stenographer, but signed by him with a firm hand, was written on the 28th of November, showing perfect clearness of mind and the command of all its faculties. Three days later, at seven o'clock in the evening of Thursday, December 1, 1910, the call of death came to him and he passed through the curtained gate which opens and closes at that call.

The gentle stroke of death

On the morning of that day, as was told by Miss Bishop at a memorial meeting held soon after, at Castile, "he had pencilled on a slip of paper a few lines suggestive of a plan which he thought might be of assistance to boys and girls seeking employment. A matter had recently been brought to his attention showing the dangers to which young persons are sometimes exposed when they go out from their homes to make their way among strangers." Thus the child-saving thought — the anxious care for the young — was in his mind to the very last.

That night he partook of his usual light supper, and said, presently, that he would take a rest. His nurse assisted him to his bed in an adjoining room, and had left him but a few moments when she heard some sound which caused her to return. She found that in those moments his life had come to its end. He had left it as quietly as if passing into sleep.

Funeral services at Glen Iris were held on the following Sunday. The remains were then taken to the residence of his brother Josiah, in Buffalo, for burial in the Forest Lawn Cemetery, preceding which there were impressive services on Tuesday in the chapel of the First Presbyterian Church, conducted by the pastor, the Reverend Dr. Andrew V. V. Raymond, assisted by the Reverend Dr. S. S. Mitchell, former pastor of the church, and by the Reverend Richard W. Boynton, pastor of the First Unitarian Church.

In a letter to his brother Josiah, written on the 1st of July, 1910, Mr. Letchworth had expressed his wishes with regard to the disposition of his remains. "I would like my remains," he wrote, "to be placed in a rough-hewn stone sarcophagus, after the general design of that illustrated in the sixth edition of the life of Mary Jemison, page 274. The sarcophagus I desire to have taken from the Blue Stone Quarry on the Genesee River, a few miles above Portageville. I desire that on the ground above it there be laid a perfectly plain slab, after the style of that shown in the enclosed illustration taken from the April number of *Country Life in America*, page 731, upon which slab shall be inscribed my name and the date of my birth and decease, only. If practicable, I desire that the slab be taken from the hard rock of the upper strata of Table Rock at the Lower Falls, which, if I remember rightly, is from twelve to sixteen inches thick. I think this slab had best be placed directly upon the surface of the ground, without any masonry underneath it, the inclination to be the same as the ground surrounding it."

Excepting in the matter of taking a slab of stone from Table Rock, at the Lower Falls, which Mr. Letchworth had desired "it practicable," these wishes were carried precisely into effect during the summer which followed his death. The removal of such a mass of stone from the position of Table Rock in the gorge at the Lower Falls was decided to be impracticable, while a slab of equal quality was found in the bed of the river, a little above the Middle Falls, and more closely associated, therefore, with the life it would commemorate. The inscription on it is as follows: —

WILLIAM PRYOR LETCHWORTH

BORN, FIFTH MONTH, 26, 1823

DIED, TWELFTH MONTH, 1, 1910

The importance that had been given to the life now ended, by the large fruitfulness of its labors in social good, was recognized widely by the newspaper press of the country, in its announcements of the death, and even more widely in affectionate and reverent expressions which came in great numbers of letters and official communications from societies, to Glen Iris and to Mr. Josiah Letchworth, in Buffalo. "The dear, dear man is gone! my heart aches to think of it," said one. "I have never known such another man," exclaimed a second. "His death brings to me almost as much sorrow as the death of a parent," wrote a prominent journalist, who added: "He seemed to be a sort of patriarch among the people of Western New

LAST YEARS 423

York." In a private letter, the secretary of the Board of Managers of Letchworth Village wrote: "I feel that in our work at this end of the state the mere fact that Mr. Letchworth's name is associated with the Village will be a tremendous help in keeping us up to the standards and ideals for which Mr. Letchworth has stood during all his life."

The New York State Board of Charities, at its next stated meeting (January 11, 1911) after Mr. Letchworth's death, expressed its estimate of his long service as a Commissioner of the Board for nearly twenty-four years, and as its president for ten years, in an extended inscription on its minutes, partly in these words:—

He entered the Board early in its history, and during his long term of service exerted a controlling influence in the development of its policies and methods of procedure in the supervision of the charitable institutions of the State. As he was of a cautious and deliberative temperament he impressed upon the practical operations of the Board a conservative and paternal attitude towards the public charities, which had its expression in friendly and advisory conference with the officers and managers of these institutions.

His personal devotion to the service of the Board was of the most exemplary character. He gave his time, his thought and his means cheerfully, and at all times, often at great personal sacrifice, to the duties then imposed upon the individual commissioners. Many of these duties, such as close inspection of almshouses of that time, were extremely unpleasant; but he never shrank from the most exhaustive inspections of these and many similar public charities, and drew from them valuable lessons which resulted in the adoption of important remedial measures. In his zeal to improve the condition of dependent children he visited not only almshouses, but also all of the orphan asylums and children's homes in the State.

This appreciative tribute from the official body which had the fullest knowledge of his work goes on to review its " notable features," in the removal of children from poorhouses, and in labors for the better care and treatment of the insane, of epileptics, of the idiotic and the feeble-minded,— all of which has been set forth in this book.

CHAPTER XI

THE MAN

THE story of Mr. Letchworth's life, as told in the preceding pages, is almost wholly a story of noble labors; and inasmuch as he spent it A life of in labor, it could not be other than labor that. Many lives are so spent; but his differed from most of them in the motives and objects of his life-absorbing work. He toiled for the bettering of conditions among the unfortunates of his part of the world, as others toil for the rewards that come back to the laborer's self, in luxuries and gratifications that go with wealth, or in the honors of public life. To the extent that he had what might be called wealth, in a comparative sense, it can almost be said that he took to himself no luxuries from it and little of the gratifications that depend on wealth. He gave himself the great indulgence of One great Glen Iris; but he held that only as indulgence a life tenant, preparing it always for public possession and use. Meantime its atmosphere of beauty and peace and happiness, and the simple hospitalities it enriched, and the days of joy it brought into his friendships,—these seemed to fill the whole measure of self-seeking in his desires.

It is because he made so little of the personal side of his life, and took into it so much from the other life around him, that the account of it is meagre in biographical incident. What he did has no dramatic quality for a reader's entertainment; but its high purpose and its measureless worth offer much more than entertainment to a thoughtful mind. If these give an undertone of seriousness to the biography, they carry through it overtones of happiness, none the less. Mr. Letchworth was one of the happiest of men; in his benevolent serenity of temper; in the warmth of fellow-feeling which made mankind interesting to him; in his many friendships; in the assurance he could feel of holding a high place in public esteem; and, above all, in the satisfying fruits of his work. In much of the work itself we cannot suppose that he found enjoyment, full as it was of distressing scenes, painful experiences, revolting matters of investigation; but certainly there was joy to him of high quality in the great results of good

The overtones of happiness

that he could see to be coming from what he did.

No man enjoyed friendships more than he, and he accumulated them richly as his life went on, especially after he came into extensive relations with the charity workers of his own state and of the country at large. To find a spirit kindred to his own in earnestness and sincerity was to find a new friend; and he found so many! His correspondence with the colleagues and associates who came into really close and sympathetic participation with any part of his work gives many charming evidences of the warm feeling that grew between them. Especially in the later years, when the elder co-workers with him were being succeeded by a younger corps,—in state charity boards, in national and state conferences, in the heads of institutions and societies,—the affectionate deference and reverence with which these junior friends wrote to him is beautifully significant of the feeling he inspired.

Accumulated friendships

One who looks through his correspondence can see the sources of the great influence he came to exercise in the philanthropic field. While he specialized his own main undertakings in that field, he never specialized his interest in its subjects and objects. He could always enter with warm sympathy and understanding into the feelings of those who shared his benevolent spirit, but were moved by it on other special lines than his; and he was never so busy in his own burdensome tasks that he could not give attention to these collateral tasks, to acquaint himself with them and render help in them when it was sought. It was sought more and more, as the all-roundness of his study of the problems of philanthropy and the large helpfulness of his disposition became known. The people who struggled with difficulties and discouragements in various undertakings of good work, and who came to him for counsel or assistance, were very many; and very many were the grateful acknowledgments of wise advice and effectual help that he had in return. Quite often, too, there had been a purse as well as a pen in the helping hand.

Sources of great influence

Those, too, who worked for him, as well as those who worked with him, were invited, as we may say, always, to give friendship a place in the relations between employer and employed, and lasting ties were formed by whatever in their natures could re-

Affection of employés

spond to his. The writer of this has come upon many disclosures of feeling between him and his employés, either in business at Buffalo or in home and farm service at Glen Iris, and they testify alike to his interest in them and to their filial attitude of affection toward him. A very few weeks before he died he received a letter, which must have given him much happiness, from one who had served for many years, long before, in the establishment of Pratt & Letchworth; who had afterwards established himself prosperously in business, and who had been a useful, excellent citizen in all the relations of life. Among other things the writer said to him this:

You will never know the debt of gratitude I owe to you, and to our Heavenly Father for bringing me into touch with you many years ago. . . . My life has been different ever since I met you and came under your helpful influence. The fact that I have been able to pass the good things I received from you on to others, and they, in turn, to others, tends to make one feel that his life has not been lived in vain. Your influence over my life has been great, and I feel that I am a truer, better man, husband and father, for having been under your inspiration.

Since Mr. Letchworth's death, the writer of this high tribute to his influence has related a most interesting bit of antecedent story, in a letter addressed to Mr. Howland, the administrator of Mr. Letchworth's estate. Writing to express thanks for a copy of the new edition of "Voices of the Glen," and for the return to him from Glen Iris of a package of his letters, he adds:—

An incident that reveals the man

I do not know that you know the fact, but in the latter part of April, 1866, while I was a newsboy on the Erie Railroad, Mr. Letchworth was a passenger on the morning train, on his way to Glen Iris, and he happened to observe that I was courteous to some passengers on the opposite side of the car. When I came to him he bought some oranges from me; then made inquiry as to my school advantages, and took my father's name and inquired the nature of his business. I thought at first that he was a professor in some large school and interested to find out if my father was in a position to give me additional education. Then he inquired what I was to do in life; and the result was that I returned to Buffalo the following Monday morning, and, as you know, was with him for over thirteen years. For a number of years he kindly asked me to share a room with him in the Bank Building, and his helpful, watchful care of me, and the most excellent advice given at that time, were a great help to me in my early days. I cannot tell you how much I have thought, in the years which have passed, of this very pleasant association. He was indeed a "father unto me," and I am indebted to him for the start which I got in life.

We may be sure that the "helpful influence" and the "inspiration" which the writer quoted above was so conscious of having received from Mr. Letchworth came in the largest measure from the example of his employer's character and life. The sense of responsibility for that influence of example was singularly keen and held rare authority in Mr. Letchworth's mind, ruling his conduct with scrupulous care. This was finely illustrated in the circumstances under which he banished wine from his table. During his travels in Europe, in 1858, he had suffered much from drinking deleterious waters in many places, and was finally persuaded to resort to wine. Until that time he had followed the teaching and example of his father in total abstinence from alcoholic drinks of every nature whatsoever; but he found a comfort and benefit from the wines, in this experience of them, which led him to modify his views and the previous habits of his life. He brought home some varieties of choice quality and introduced

Why wine was banished from his table

their use at his table for a time. But presently there came to his knowledge what seemed to be a resulting influence which troubled his mind. Among the tenants of his land was a young mechanic who had been enslaved by the appetite for intoxicants, and who gave himself up to days of drunkenness from time to time. Mr. Letchworth had tried often to rouse resisting energies in him, but with no lasting effect; and now there came a report of his saying, in one of his outbreaks: "Mr. Letchworth talks to me about my drinking; but he drinks wine with his friends, and I do only about the same. I think as much of my friends as Mr. Letchworth does of his." After the latter had been told of this remark there was no more wine on his table or wine-drinking in his house. He went to the young man, told him that nothing intoxicating should be used by himself or offered to his guests thereafter, and asked him to follow that example,—far better, as it was, than the one he had accepted before. The impression made on the man was profound. He gave the promise that he would do as Mr. Letchworth had done, and the promise was kept. He married, reared a well-educated family, accumulated property and earned universal respect. In the old age of Mr. Letchworth there can hardly have been another reminiscence that brought him more happiness than this.

To illustrate another side of his careful thoughtfulness for those who formed his staff at Glen Iris, the following letter has interest. It was written by him, in October, 1876, to a father, in Germany, whose son, a young man, had been employed at the Glen for some years. It caught the attention of the biographer as he ran through a letter book of that period, and seemed to represent an impulse of kindliness which would not have moved many busy men.

Another characteristic incident

Your son, who has been in my employ for the past seven years, excepting a short period of two months, and who has been during a large portion of the time a member of my household, having signified to me his intention of visiting his parents, brothers, sisters, and friends in the Fatherland, it has seemed to me that it would afford you satisfaction if I should inform you of the good character he has established while living in this country. I do this unsolicited by him and with great pleasure, in view of his worth, the attachment to him I have formed, and the esteem in which he is held by all my friends who know him. I do it with greater cheerfulness, also, because I feel assured that

I am addressing a person of good sense and of principle; for none other could have instilled into the mind of youth the substantial elements of character which Martin possesses.... You may be assured that when you welcome him after this long absence you take to your embrace a son worthy of your love and of whom you may be proud, possessing as he does the attributes of true respectability and manhood.

As a response to the claims of human fellowship, the mere generosity of money-giving is so easy, compared with Mr. Letchworth's giving of himself, in his abiding altruism of action, interest, thought, sympathy, that it seems hardly worth while to speak of his liberalities from the purse. What has been shown of him otherwise could leave no doubt of his disposition on that side. There was no prodigality in his use of money, gift-wise or otherwise. He had acquired early a practical appreciation of its important function in life, and it ruled his personal economy. As a philanthropist he did not cease to be a business man, and the coalescence of the two characters had much to do with his success in the former. He spent money on benevolent objects as carefully, as judiciously, and as freely as on commercial objects, but no differently, as to the exercise of discriminating care.

Careful liberality in giving

His position and reputation drew upon him many solicitations, for help to public undertakings of charity and social reform and for relief to private distress. He contributed constantly to the support of great numbers of the former, and his annual subscriptions and dues of membership to institutions and societies, at home and abroad (for he was a patron or member of some in Great Britain and France), must have drawn heavily from his income each year. As for private appeals, he was no more likely to be victimized by the leeches who prey on careless benevolence than the most penurious of men would be. A need, self-proclaimed and self-pleaded for, would be suspicious to him, and he would give it rigid scrutiny; but his eyes and ears were always open and alert to make discovery of needs that were silently endured. From the grateful acknowledgments to be found among the letters he received (of which he seems never to have destroyed any) it is evident that such discoveries were frequent, and that he could act on them with so much delicacy and kindliness that no feeling of intrusion or wounded pride would be occasioned by what he did.

Delicacy in giving

The larger of Mr. Letchworth's givings,

however, were made to the public directly, not only in the final gift of his whole superb landed estate, but in the expense as well as the labor of his twenty-three years of official service to the state. During the time of his service as State Commissioner of Charities no pay was attached to the office; but he was entitled by law to a reimbursement of all travelling and other expenses incurred in the performance of its duties. He drew nothing from the state treasurer, however, under that provision of the law, though practically devoting his whole time to an activity of inspection, investigation, study of institutions and their methods, in his own state and out of it, which called for more constant and extensive travel than falls to the lot of most business men. To the expenses of travel, moreover, he added an almost constant employment of clerical assistance in his official work, and the accompaniment of a stenographer in most of his journeys of inquiry outside of the state. It has been said by some who had means of knowing, that the cost to him of his public service was some thousands of dollars per year.

Magnitude of gifts to the public

In 1896, the year of his resignation from the State Board of Charities, an amendment of the law relating to it provided that each commissioner should not only receive the reimbursement of his expenses, but should be paid a compensation of ten dollars " for each day's attendance at meetings of the Board, or of any of its committees, not exceeding in any one year five hundred dollars." Mr. Letchworth protested against this, and his reasons for doing so are set forth in a statement to which he never gave publication. It explains at the same time the motive which actuated him in declining even a reimbursement of the expenses of his public service. In this statement, after citing the fact that the enactment of 1867 which created the Board provided no compensation for their time or services, he remarks:— His reasons for assuming this cost

It is therefore evident that it was the original intention of the legislature to place the Board on a purely disinterested and philanthropic basis, and above all political and partisan influence.

Then, quoting the terms of the amendment of 1896, he says:—

Against this amendment I protested, believing that it set aside the benevolent principle in the original act, depriving the Board of its unselfish character, and endangering its usefulness. As far back as 1873 the appropriation made by the state for the office expenses, clerk hire, etc., exclusive of the salary of the secretary, was only about $3000. Some thought that even this small sum was greater than it should be, and that the Board was an unnecessary appendage to the state government. It was partly to meet this criticism, and to popularize the Board, that I exercised the self-denial I did. . . . I believed that more efficient and capable persons could be found to fill an uncompensated Board than a paid one, and that in this way the temptation to make the office serve political ends would not exist. It has seemed to me, moreover, that, as the work of the Board was mainly in the supervision of charities, in which large numbers of individuals were engaged who sacrificed, in many instances, not only all their time but much of their means in conducting the work, there should be found people to act as state supervisors of such work who would set a worthy example, by receiving no compensation for their time, and that such self-denial would encourage and stimulate all benevolent work.

All that has been noted thus far, in this summary of the character which expressed itself in the life and work of William Pryor Letchworth, is consonant with what would be the most natural expectation of one who met him at any period of his matured life. It goes natur-

Gentle appearance and demeanor

ally with the modest and gentle air, the quiet speech and manner, — the whole aspect of countenance and bearing, which betokened tranquillity of spirit, mild evenness of temper, geniality and kindliness of heart. No one can ever have heard his voice raised in anger, or seen the flush of passion in his eyes, or the hard lines of sternness in his face. In appearance and demeanor he realized always the ideal of a true representative of the Society of Friends, moulded outwardly by the inward moulding of Christian teaching as construed by George Fox. And this could raise no expectation of the resolution, the will, the energy which went with his benevolent quietude of spirit into all that he undertook to do.

Nothing that he undertook had been taken hastily in hand. He set his foot in no path until he knew fully the ground to be traversed in it, as well as the end to which it led, and saw clearly the right and the need or the good reason for going forward therein. Pending these determinations of his mind he showed often much hesitancy and seeming indecisiveness of will; but when the light he sought had been obtained, and the practicable way to a desirable and right object of endeavor could be seen distinctly, he became, in his quiet way, one of the most inflexibly determined of men, — undiscouraged by obstacles, undaunted by opposition. Some instances of the positively militant force he could bring into action, out of the quietude which masked it, when hostilities were encountered in his work, have been noticed heretofore. These surprises (if we may call them so) of force in Mr. Letchworth were described happily by Dr. Stephen Smith, his colleague of many years in the New York State Board of Charities and his warm friend, in an affectionate and admiring "appreciation" prepared for the meeting of the New York State Conference of Charities and Correction, at Watertown, in October, 1911.

Inflexible determination underneath

The personality of Mr. Letchworth [said Dr. Smith] was a self-revelation. He was of medium height and size, very unassuming in all his acts, diffident and hesitating in his speech, very deferential, especially to an opponent, face always expressive of kindliness and benevolence, even when most excited; but these conspicuous personal appearances of indecision did not conceal from his business associates an expression of his features indicative of a fixed determination to exercise his own judgment when called upon to act. He had an indomitable will; but in exercising it he was extremely careful not to do injustice to one of opposing views, or even to " wound his feelings." I have known him, after an exciting discussion in the State Board of Charities, in which he took a prominent part, to hasten to the railroad station and find the member or members whom he had opposed and beg their pardon if he had said anything offensive to them.

This peculiarity, so unusual in men of strong convictions and aggressive methods of enforcing them, might be attributed to a want of mental capacity to form positive opinions; but such a conclusion would be altogether unjust. On the contrary, it only emphasizes the suggestion as to his inherent nervous sensibility. His conclusions were never formed on any subject without the most painstaking inquiry, and he always maintained an open mind while discussion was in progress; but when the testimony was all in, his judgment was as unerring as human capacity would permit. His extreme sensitiveness lest he should give pain, or do an injustice to another, dominated his private and public acts, and forms an exquisite setting of a true portraiture of his entire life.

While the more pronounced traits of character were so visibly stamped upon Mr. Letchworth's personality that an ordinary observer who met him socially would recognize his large intelligence, refined manners, and benevolent disposition, it was only to his more intimate friends that he revealed his keen sense of humor, his acute observation of nature, his appreciation of the due proportion and arrangement of living things, and, withal, a poetic or imaginative temperament.

Another of the long-time associates of Mr. Letchworth in the New York State Board of Charities, the president of the Board during many recent years, Mr. William Rhinelander Stewart, has described his character similarly, in a memorial presented to the National Conference of Charities and Correction, at Boston, in June, 1911. "Modesty, purity, patience, thoroughness, and gentleness," he wrote, "were among Mr. Letchworth's most noticeable characteristics. He disliked and avoided strife, and chose rather to yield than to take precedence; but his opinions, carefully formed, were tenaciously held. Happily endowed with a lively sense of humor, his laughter was hearty and contagious, and to his intimate friends he was a genial companion. He carried to his grave the heart of a child. The honorable positions he filled with so much dignity came unsought, and while valued as proofs of esteem, were most prized for the increased opportunities of useful service which they afforded. Throughout his life he was sustained by profound religious convictions, and no one who knew him well could doubt that, had he lived in mediæval times, he would, if called upon, have gone to the stake unflinchingly for his creed."

Mr. Adelbert Moot, of Buffalo, who was Mr. Letchworth's legal adviser in the later years, and who, as he says in a note to the writer of this biography, "had numerous consultations with him that revealed his thoughts and feelings as only such consultations do reveal the very soul of a man to his lawyer," received the same impression of a force unlooked for in so sweetly tempered a man. " I had a chance," writes Mr. Moot, " to see how free he was from the ordinary small failings of mankind, and how broadly courageous he was in any fight involving the best interests of mankind." " His portrait is that of a typical philanthropist, and his character was absolutely in keeping with his portrait."

Only those who came into both working and social intimacy with Mr. Letchworth could learn how distinctly his nature united two temperaments which are very seldom balanced so evenly in the same individual. To know him in the relations that exhibited but one of these was to think of

The two temperaments

him, most probably, as a sentimentalist,—a man of too much emotionality for successful dealing with the hardness and aggressiveness of the ruder conditions of life. This, it could easily be thought, would not only explain his philanthropy, but throw doubt on the judgment and efficiency with which its promptings would be directed. And he did have an emotional susceptibility and a delicacy of mind which in most makings of character would warrant that conclusion. His enjoyments were of the sweeter and gentler sort. The lovelier sides of nature, the finer things of art, the generous exhibitions of humanity, appealed to him most. He was exceptionally fond of poetry, and with a catholic taste; delighted in reading it and having it read to him, and carried in memory a large store of it, which he had begun to accumulate in his youth.

To know him in this character, and to have acquaintance, at the same time, with the strenuous business man that he was for thirty years and the strong state official that he was for twenty-three more,—vigilant, decisive, resolute, practically sagacious, successful beyond the common, in both exhibitions,—was to have a revelation of character that is exceedingly rare in its combination of qualities, and exceedingly fine. This book is an attempt to carry the interesting revelation, in some imperfect measure, beyond the circle which was privileged to receive it from the nobly charming man himself.

THE END

APPENDIX

CHRONOLOGICAL LIST OF THE WRITINGS AND PUBLICATIONS OF WILLIAM PRYOR LETCHWORTH, LL.D.

1874. (1) Sketch of the Life of Samuel F. Pratt; with some Account of the Early History of the Pratt Family. A Paper read before the Buffalo Historical Society, March 10, 1873. By William P. Letchworth. Buffalo: Press of Warren, Johnson & Co. 1874. 211 pp.

1875. (2) Report relating to Pauper and Destitute Children.
> (In Report of New York State Board of Charities, 1875.)

1875. (3) Supplementary Report, relating to Pauper Children in New York County [Randall's Island].
> (In Report of State Board of Charities for 1875; also in pamphlet.)

1876. (4) Pauper Children in Michigan. (An appeal on behalf of pauper children in the poorhouses of Michigan, in a letter addressed to the Secretary of the Michigan State Board of Charities, Charles M. Croswell.)
> (In manuscript.)

1875. (5) Argument relating to Pauper Labor, made before the State Convention of Superintendents of the Poor, 1875.
> (In pamphlet.)

1877. (6) Report on Dependent and Delinquent Children.

(In Proceedings of National Conference of Charities and Correction, 1877; also in pamphlet.)

1877. (7) Report of an Examination of Institutions for the Education of the Blind in Massachusetts, Pennsylvania, Ohio, and Indiana. Appended to a Committee Report on the Management of Affairs of the New York State Institution for the Blind at Batavia.

(In Report of N. Y. State Board of Charities for 1877; also in pamphlet.)

Also later committee reports on the same institution.

1877–78. (8) Reports on the Charities of the Eighth Judicial District of the State of New York.

(In Reports of the N. Y. State Board of Charities for the years stated; also in pamphlet.)

1878. (9) Report on Disasters by Fire in the Steuben County [New York] Poorhouse.

(In report of State Board of Charities for 1878; also in pamphlet.)

1878. (10) An Account of the Cottage Plan of Caring for the Harmless Insane, about to be tried in Cattaraugus County.

(Given in the course of a Debate on Insanity at the National Conference of Charities and Correction, 1878, and published in its Report.)

1878. (11) Plans for Poorhouses.

(In Report of New York State Board of Charities for 1878; also in pamphlet.)

APPENDIX 449

1879. (12) Report on the Management and Affairs of the Insane Asylum of the Onondaga County Poorhouse, by Joint Committees of the State Board of Charities and of the Board of Supervisors (Commissioner Letchworth, Chairman).

    (In Report of the State Board, 1879; also in pamphlet.)

1879. (13) Address in response to Major-General Henry W. Slocum, President of the Board of Trustees of the Soldiers' and Sailors' Home at Bath, New York, on the occasion of the Dedication of the Home, January 23, 1879.

    (In pamphlet.)

1880. (14) Report to New York State Board of Charities of the Committee (Commissioner Letchworth, Chairman) appointed to Investigate Charges against the Society for the Reformation of Juvenile Delinquents, Randall's Island, New York.

    (In Report of State Board for 1880; also in pamphlet.)

1880. (15) The Pauper Children of Ohio. (An appeal to county poor officials.)

    (In manuscript.)

1881. (16) Report by Commissioners Letchworth and Carpenter on the Chronic Insane in certain Counties [of New York] exempted by the State Board of Charities from the operation of the Willard Asylum Act.

    (In report of the State Board, 1881; also in pamphlet.)

1882. (17) Labor of Children in Reform Schools. Argument before Senate Committee on Miscellaneous Corporations, March 22, 1882, on the Bill introduced by Senator Titus, entitled An Act relating to the employment of Children by Contract in Houses of Refuge, Reformatories, Correctional, and other Institutions.
(In pamphlet.)

1882. (18) Classification of Children needing Care, Training, or Reformation. Argument before the Committee on State Charitable Institutions, made April 12, 1882, against Assembly Bill No. 390, in relation to the Western House of Refuge.
(In pamphlet.)

1882, '94, '95, '96. (19) Reports on Thomas Asylum for Orphan and Destitute Indian Children.
(In Reports of New York State Board of Charities; for the years stated; also in pamphlet.)

1883. (20) A Paper on Classification and Training of Children, Innocent and Incorrigible.
(In Proceedings of the National Conference of Charities and Correction, 1883; also in pamphlet.)

1883. (21) A Paper on Dependent and Delinquent Children of the State of New York. Prepared upon the invitation of the Société Générale de Protection pour l'Enfance Abandonnée ou Coupable, for the Congrès International de la Protection de l'Enfance, held at Paris, June, 1883.
(In pamphlet.)

APPENDIX 451

1883. (22) Report on the Orphan Asylums and Homes for Destitute Children in the Sixth Judicial District of New York.
(In Report of the New York State Board of Charities for 1883; also in pamphlet.)

1883. (23) Expression of Views on the Industrial Training of Children in Houses of Refuge and other Reformatory Schools; addressed to the Hon. Robert C. Titus, State Senator.
(In pamphlet.)

1883. (24) Letter to the Chairman of the Judiciary Committee of the Assembly, on Public Official Care of Orphan and Destitute Children versus Private Benevolence. [The same printed under the title of " Reasons against the passage of the Bill entitled An Act to Incorporate the Home for Destitute Children of Suffolk County."]
(In pamphlet.)

1884. (25) Address as President at the opening of the National Conference of Charities and Correction, at St. Louis, October 13, 1884.
(In Proceedings of the Conference; also in pamphlet, under the title of " Relief and Reform.")

1884. (26) Technologic Training in Reform Schools. An Address before the Board of Managers of the Western House of Refuge, at Rochester, N. Y.
(In pamphlet.)

1884. (27) On Legislation forbidding Employment of Children under the Contract System; be-

ing an Answer to Objections urged by the Managers of the New York House of Refuge.
(In pamphlet.)

1885. (28) Report of Committee on Preventive Work among Children.
(In Proceedings of the National Conference of Charities and Correction, 1885.)

1885. (29) Address on Poorhouse Administration, at the New York State Convention of Superintendents of the Poor.
(In Report of the New York State Board of Charities for 1885; also in pamphlet.)

1886. (30) Address on Children of the State.
(In Proceedings of the National Conference of Charities and Correction, 1886; also in pamphlet.)

1886. (31) Report of Commissioners [William P. Letchworth, Chairman] appointed to Locate an Asylum for the Insane in Northern New York.
(As Assembly Document 11, Session of 1886; also separately, in pamphlet.)

1887. (32) A Tribute to the Memory of Miss Dorothea Dix.
(In Proceedings of the National Conference of Charities and Correction, 1887.)

1887. (33) Reasons for establishing a Separate Girls' Reformatory, instead of Rebuilding on the old site the Edifice recently Destroyed by Fire, at the State Industrial School, for-

APPENDIX 453

merly the Western House of Refuge, Rochester, N. Y.; embodied in a Letter addressed to the Hon. James W. Husted, Speaker of the Assembly.

(In pamphlet.)

1887. (34) Communication of Commissioner Letchworth and Secretary Hoyt, of the New York State Board of Charities, to the Chairman of the Committee on Poorhouse and Insane of the Erie County Board of Supervisors, regarding the purchase of additional lands in the country for the Insane of the County.

(In Report of the State Board for 1887.)

1888. (35) Memorial Resolutions and Personal Tribute to the late T. Barwick Lloyd Baker, Esq., of Hardwick Court, Gloucester, England.

(In Proceedings of the National Conference of Charities and Correction, 1888.)

1889. (36) The Insane in Foreign Countries. Illustrated. New York and London: G. P. Putnam's Sons, 1889, 374 pp.

(Large page octavo volume.)

1889. (37) Miss Mary Carpenter. (A biographical tribute.)

(In manuscript.)

1890. (38) A Paper on Poorhouse Construction, read at the New York State Convention of Superintendents of the Poor.

(In Report of the State Board of Charities for 1890; also in pamphlet.)

1890. (39) Reports on the Mikanari Home, of Jamestown.
(In Report of the New York State Board of Charities, 1891; also in pamphlet.)

1891. (40) Report on the Poorhouses of the Eighth Judicial District of New York.
(In Report of the New York State Board of Charities for 1891; also separately, in pamphlet.)

1892. (41) A Paper on the Origin, Powers and Duties of State Boards of Charities.
(In Proceedings of National Conference of Charities and Correction for 1892; also in Report of New York State Board; also in pamphlet.)

1892. (42) Memorial embodying Reasons why the Asylum for Insane Criminals at Auburn should not be made a receptacle for the Non-Criminal Insane.
(In pamphlet.)

1892. (43) Report on the New York State Institution for the Blind [at Batavia].
(In Report of the New York State Board of Charities for 1892.)

1893. (44) History of Child-saving Work in the State of New York, embodied in the Report of the Committee of the National Conference of Charities and Correction on the History of Child-saving Work, 1893.
(In Proceedings of the Conference; also in pamphlet.)

1893. (45) Report on Institutions Conducting Charitable and Reform Work in the Eighth

APPENDIX 455

Judicial District of the State of New York. Also, Report on the Poorhouses in the Eighth Judicial District.

(In Report of the New York State Board of Charities, 1893; also in pamphlet.)

1894. (46) A Paper on Provision for Epileptics.

(In Proceedings of National Conference of Charities and Correction, 1894; also in Report of New York State Board of Charities, 1894, and in pamphlet.)

1894. (47) A Paper on the Removal of Children from Almshouses in the State of New York.

(In Proceedings of National Conference of Charities and Correction, 1894.)

1894. (48) Report of Committee (Commissioners Letchworth and Smith) on the Construction of Buildings for Charitable and Correctional Institutions, on the Plans and Estimates for Improvements at the Craig Colony for Epileptics.

(In Report of the New York State Board of Charities, 1894; also in pamphlet.)

1894. (49) Report of Committee (Commissioners Letchworth and Smith) on the Construction of Charitable and Correctional Institutions, on the Plans of the Eastern New York Reformatory.

(In the Report of the New York State Board of Charities for 1894; also in pamphlet.)

1894. (50) Report on Thomas Asylum for Orphan and Destitute Indian Children.

APPENDIX

(In Report of the New York State Board of Charities for 1894; also in pamphlet.)

1894. (51) Remarks in opening Discussion on the Care of the Insane.

(In Proceedings of the National Conference of Charities and Correction, 1894.)

1895. (52) Report on the Thomas Asylum for Orphan and Destitute Indian Children.

(In pamphlet.)

1896. (53) A Paper on the Care of Epileptics.

(In Proceedings of the National Conference of Charities and Correction, 1896.)

1896. (54) Report on the Erie County System of Placing Dependent Children in Families.

(In Report of New York State Board of Charities for 1896; also in pamphlet.)

1896. (55) Report on the Poorhouses of the Eighth Judicial District of New York.

(In Report of the New York State Board of Charities for 1896; also separately in pamphlet.)

1896. (56) Report on Observance of the Rules of the State Board of Charities in the Eighth Judicial District.

(In Report of the State Board for 1896.)

1897. (57) A Paper on Dependent Children and Family Homes.

(In Proceedings of National Conference of Charities and Correction, 1897; also in pamphlet.)

APPENDIX

1897. (58) Historical Address at the New York State Convention of Superintendents of the Poor.
(In pamphlet.)

1899. (59) Care and Treatment of Epileptics. Illustrated. New York and London: G. P. Putnam's Sons, 246 pp.
(Large page octavo volume.)

1900. (60) Address, as President, at the opening or the First New York State Conference of Charities and Correction, 1900.
(In Proceedings of the Conference; also in pamphlet.)

1901. (61) Transactions of the National Association for the Study of Epilepsy and the Care and Treatment of Epileptics, at the First Annual Meeting, held in Washington, D. C., May 14–15, 1901. Edited by William Pryor Letchworth, LL.D. Buffalo: C. E. Brinkworth, 1901, 221 pp.
(Cost of publication paid by Mr. L.)

1903. (62) Homes for Homeless Children: a Report on Orphan Asylums and other Institutions for the Care of Children. [To which is appended a Report on Pauper and Destitute Children, and a Report on Pauper Children in New York County, the three brought together in one volume, and all appearing likewise as separate publications in the list above.]

1905. (63) Notes and Correspondence relating to the Founding of the First State Colony for Epileptics [Craig Colony] in the State of New York. Compiled by William Pryor Letchworth.
(In manuscript, 70 pp., unpublished.)

1910. (64) Care of the Insane in New York State. Compiled from Notes made by William Pryor Letchworth.
(In manuscript, 94 pp., unpublished. Brought down, under Mr. Letchworth's direction, to 1910.)

1910. (65) A Narrative of the Life of Mary Jemison, De-he-wa-mis, the White Woman of the Genesee. By James E. Seaver. Seventh Edition, with Geographical and Explanatory Notes. This edition also includes numerous illustrations, further particulars of the history of De-he-wa-mis, and other interesting matter collected and arranged by Wm. Pryor Letchworth. New York and London: G. P. Putnam's Sons, 305 pp.
(Mr. Letchworth had edited and published two previous editions of this book, in 1877 and 1898.)

COLLECTIONS OF PAMPHLETS IN BOUND VOLUMES

In 1908 Mr. Letchworth made up four collections of his pamphlet publications, bound together in that number of volumes, with title-pages and tables of contents. Three of the volumes were in one series, as shown below. The contents are indicated in this place by numbers which refer to the numbered titles in the list above: —

Miscellaneous Papers relating to Charity and Correction. By William Pryor Letchworth, LL.D., 3 volumes.

Vol. 1. Containing 25, 26, 33, 29, 30 and 21, of the papers numbered above, in the order shown here.

Vol. 2. Containing 6, 14, 18, 17, 23, 27, 20, 22, 44, 57, 13, 41, 49, 60.

APPENDIX 459

Vol. 3. Containing 11, 38, 9, 12, 16, 31, 34, 42, 46, 48, 58.

Charities in Western New York, Eighth Judicial District. A Record of Examinations and Official Inspections of Charitable Institutions in the Counties of Allegany, Cattaraugus, Chautauqua, Erie, Genesee, Niagara, Orleans, and Wyoming, in the State of New York.

Containing 7, 8, 19, 39, 40, 45, 55, 54 of the papers numbered in the above list, in the order of the numbering here.

MINOR MANUSCRIPTS

The following writings, preserved in manuscript at the Glen Iris homestead, include some finished papers that have not gone into print, but are, for the most part, the first drafts of addresses and essays, or notes and memoranda on subjects discussed finally in the printed writings of the list above.

The Saving of Homeless and Destitute Children.

Care and Reformation of Homeless and Dependent Children.

Removal of Homeless Children from the Erie County Poorhouse.

Removal of Children from Almshouses. (Several papers and letters, some of which are in print elsewhere.)

Origin of the New York State Board of Charities.

The State Board of Charities. (Historical memoranda.)

Notes and References relating to Reformatory Work, including Notes while visiting Reformatory Institutions for the Young in Europe.

Child-saving Work Abroad. (Memoranda of observations in 1880.)

The Buffalo Children's Aid Society. (A sketch of the circumstances in which it originated.)

Women Managers on Boards of State Charitable Institutions.

Rain Baths. A paper on the sanitary importance of the shower or rain bath, as a substitute in poorhouses and similar institutions for the bathtub, accompanied by eight descriptions of the arrangement and construction of these baths and of the mode of using them in several institutions.

Some Reminiscences of Childhood.

A Spelling-Match. [Describing the old-time country school spelling contests as he knew them in his boyhood.]

Example Stronger than Precept.

A Description of Mount Vernon as it appeared in 1861. Read at the Anniversary of Washington's Birthday, 1862, at the Baptist Church in Castile.

Notes relating to Colonel Williams [who was one of his early neighbors at Glen Iris, and an interesting character].

The Hospice of Saint Bernard.

INDEX

Allen, Orlando, 86.
Almshouses, children in, 110, 161, 204–05.
Almshouses. *See, also*, Poorhouses.
Alt-Scherbitz Insane Asylum, 176–80, 190, 279, 289, 300, 301.
American Scenic and Historic Preservation Society, 50, 55, 65, 97–98, 381, 389, 392, 394, 404, 407–09.
Anderson, President Martin B., 66, 108, 119, 262.
Annan, Annie R., 59–60.
Appenzeller institutions, 183–84.
Arboretum, Letchworth Park, 400–04.
Arey, Mrs. H. E. G., 34–35.
Auburn, asylum for insane criminals, 303–04.
Auburn, N. Y., 6–8, 15–21.
Auchmuty, Mr., 233, 246.

Bailey, Prof. L. H., 98, 382, 404.
Baker, T. Barwick Lloyd, 202, 225.
Bâle, Institutions at, 183.
Barrows, Samuel J., 161.
Barton, Clara, 316.
Batavia, N. Y., State Institution for the Blind at, 254–55, 315.

Bath, Soldiers' and Sailors' Home at, 256–58.
Belgian benevolent institutions, 189–93.
Bell, Dr. Clark, 300.
Bennett, Carlenia, 98–99.
Berlin, Institutions in, 180.
Berne, Institutions in, 184.
Bethel Colony for epileptics, 337.
Bicêtre, 185.
Big Tree Council and Treaty, 92, 102.
Bishop, Miss Caroline, 69–70, 99–100, 297, 342, 357, 363, 405, 409, 417, 419–20.
Blacksnake, William and Jesse, 78.
Blind, N. Y. State Institution for the, 254–55, 315.
Boyd, Lieutenant Thomas, 352.
Brandt, Captain, 67, 77.
Bridge, Portage, 49, 61–63.
Bristol, Miss Carpenter's reformatory schools at, 199–201.
Brown, David E., 307.
Bryant, William C., 37, 73, 95, 103.
Buffalo, N. Y., Mr. Letchworth's life in, 25–41, 68.
Buffalo Creek Reservation, 93.
Buffalo Fine Arts Academy, 39–41.

INDEX

Buffalo Historical Society, 78, 102–03.
Buffalo State Hospital for Insane, 282, 291–94.
Burnham, Frederick J., Burnham Industrial Farm, 239–40.
Bush-Brown, Henry K., 97.
Byron, Lady Noel, 200.

Campbell, Mrs. Helen Thornton, 307.
Caneadea Council House, 67, 73–89, 95–100, 418.
Care of the Insane in N. Y. State; historical account, 295.
Carpenter, Miss Mary, 139, 156, 199–201.
Carpenter, Miss Sarah M., Commissioner, 273.
Central Islip Farm for the Insane, 279.
Children, homes for the homeless, 123–30, 147–49, 205–06.
Children, innocent and incorrigible, classification for, 201, 222–26.
Children in jails and penitentiaries, 212–16.
Children in poorhouses, 110–61, 204–05.
Children, Mr. L.'s interest in, 68–71.
"Children of the State," 229–33.
Children's Act, The (New York), 122–24, 150, 155.
Children's Aid Society, Buffalo, 305–07.
Child-saving propositions, seventeen, 236–39.
Child-saving work abroad, 164–208.

Child-saving work in New York; history of, 315.
Child-saving work: prevenient, 106–63.
Child-saving work: reformative, 210–50.
Christiania, institutions in, 171.
Clarke, Dr. John M., 391.
Classification of children in institutions, 201, 222–26, 236.
Clermont-en-Oise, colonies of the insane, 185–87.
Clinton, Judge George W., 63, 66.
Cole, Thomas, painting of the Genesee Falls, 54.
Conference of Charities and Correction. *See* National Conference, and State Conference.
Congrès International de la Protection de l'Enfance, Paris, 236, 308.
Conolly, Dr., 196.
Contract labor in reformatories, 241–45.
Copenhagen, institutions in, 172–73.
Cornplanter (John O. Bail), 78, 83.
Cornplanter Medal, The, 104.
Cottage system for residential institutions, 173, 178–79, 193–95, 205.
Council House, the Old Indian, 67, 73–89, 95–100, 418.
Craig, Oscar, 314, 317, 319, 333.
Craig Colony, 317, 319, 321, 333–39, 359.
Crozer, Mrs. Mary A., 9, 23–24, 253, 318–19.

INDEX 463

De-ge-wa-nus, 51, 409.
Denmark, Mr. L.'s inspections in, 172–73.
Dix, Miss Dorothea L., 263, 267, 292.
Dow, Hon. Charles M., 98, 382, 399, 400, 404.
Dublin, institutions at, 165.
Dymphna, St., 190.

Edinburgh, institutions at, 168–69.
Eighth Judicial District, N. Y., 107, 254, 256, 315.
Engelken, Dr. H., 301.
England, benevolent institutions of, 195–208.
England: Local-government Board, gift from, 208–09.
Epileptics, care and treatment of, 319, 321, 327–50, 354, 410–16.
Erie County insane asylum, 265–67, 285–91, 303.
Erie County "placing out" system, for children, 126–28, 321.
Erie County poorhouse, children in, 112–16.

Fairchild, Prof. H. L., 392.
Falls of the Genesee, 34, 42, 48–50, 52–53.
Fillmore, Millard, 67, 79, 86.
First N. Y. Dragoons, rendezvous camp, 105.
Fish, E. E., 64–65.
Fitz-James Colony of Insane, 186.
"Friends Retreat," The, 197–98.
Friends, Society of, 2, 3–4, 5, 30.

Ganson, Senator John, 144.
Gardeau or Gardow Tract, 54, 93, 96.
Genesee Falls, The, 34, 42, 48–50, 52–53, 372–80, 393–98.
Genesee River Company, 376–79, 393–98.
Genesee Valley: its beauty, 34, 48; memorials of its history, 72–104, 351–52, 418.
Genesee Valley Museum, 100–02.
Germany, Mr. L.'s inspections in, 173–82.
Gheel Colony of Insane, 190–93.
Gibbons, Mrs. Abby Hopper, 280–81.
Gildersleeve, Mrs. C. H., 34–35.
Glasgow, Institutions at, 168–70.
Glen Iris: First seen by Mr. L., 34; acquisition and development, 42–68; topographic features, 48–50; described by David Gray, 51–54; represented in poetry — the "Voices of the Glen," 55–61; the railway bridge, 61–63; flora and fauna, 63–66; memorial trees, 66–67; local historical memorials, 72–105; Portage Dam project, a menace to the falls and the glen, 352, 362–63, 370–80, 393–98; Mr. L.'s early plans for the future of the glen: the Wyoming Benevolent Institute, 364–70, 380–81, 389; gift of the estate to the state, which names it Letchworth Park, 380–404; continued improvements by

Mr. L., 407; plans of the Scenic and Historic Preservation Society, for the development of the park, 400–04.
Glenny, Mrs. William H., 59–60.
Gothenburg, institutions in, 170–71.
Gowanda State Homœopathic Hospital for Insane, 290.
Grabau, Dr. A. W., 391.
Gray, David, 36–37, 51–54, 57–58, 67, 87–89, 313.
Greene (Cordelia A.) Memorial Library, 389.
Grout, Comptroller Edward M., 152–55.

Hai-wa-ye-is-tah, 89.
Hall, Edward Hagaman, 98, 382, 392.
Hall, Prof. James A., 391.
Halsey, Francis Whiting, 382.
Hamburg, the Rauhe Haus at, 173–75.
Hance, Ann. *See* Letchworth, Mrs. Ann Hance.
Hanwell Asylum, 196.
Hardwicke Court Reformatory, 202.
Harris, Dr. Elisha, 130, 131, 145, 146, 211–16.
Hayden and Holmes, 15–21.
Hill, Governor David B., 308–09.
Historical memorials, Genesee Valley, 72–104, 351–52, 418.
Ho-dé-no-sáu-nee, The, 80, 86.
Holland, benevolent institutions of, 193–95.
Home Monthly, The, 35.

Homes for homeless children, 123–30, 147–49, 205–06.
Howland, Henry R., 2, 38, 58–59, 67, 73, 78–89, 100–02, 364, 430.
Howland, Mrs. William, 9, 357.
Hoxie, Mrs. Eliza, 9.
Hoyt, Dr. Charles S., 108, 117, 146, 285, 339, 352–53.
Hughes, Gov. Charles E., 383, 386, 387, 409, 412.

Immigration, pauper, 259–62.
Indian Council, the last, 67, 76–89.
Indian Council House, 67, 73–89, 95–100, 418.
Indian Mission burial ground, Buffalo, 96.
Industrial training in reformatories, 245–50.
Insane, the: Mr. L.'s interest in their treatment, 162; his study of institutions in Europe, 164–98; his work at home, 263–304; his book on "The Insane in Foreign Countries," 164, 167, 172, 177, 190, 197, 296–302, 312.
Insane in New York State, the, 263–94.
International Prison Association, 157.
Ireland, Dr. W. W., 300.
Ireland, Mr. L.'s inspections in, 164–66.
Iroquois history, 72–104.

Jacket, John, 67.
Jails, county, 212–16, 355–57.
Jemison, Mary, 67, 75, 78, 89–100, 418.

INDEX 465

Jemison, Thomas, 67, 78, 82.
Jenisheu, 82.
Johnston, James Nicoll, 37, 38, 56–57, 67, 136–38, 141, 297, 313, 327–28, 342, 360–61, 405, 409, 410, 419.
Jones, Amanda T., 60–61.
Jones, Capt. Horatio, 102.

Kennedy, Mrs. Thomas, 98–100.
Kerr, Col. Simcoe, 77, 80, 85.
King George canon, 79.
King's County almshouses, children in, 111–12, 140, 150, 152–55.
Kingsford, Hon. Thos. F., 382.
Kingswood Reformatory, 200.
Kirkbride, Franklin B., 413.
Koeppe, John Maurice, 177.
Kunz, George Frederick, 98, 381, 392, 404.

Lalor, Dr. Joseph, 164–65.
Larkin, Mr. and Mrs. John D., 96.
"Last Indian Council on the Genesee," 87–89.
Leipziger, Dr. Henry M., 382.
Letchworth, Ann Hance (mother of W. P. L.), 6, 14, 18, 28, 46, 252.
Letchworth, Charlotte (Mrs. Byron C. Smith), 9, 28, 29, 31.
Letchworth, Edward Hance, 9, 28, 364.
Letchworth, Eliza (Mrs. Hoxie), 9.
Letchworth, George Jediah, 9, 28, 312, 364.
Letchworth, Hannah (Mrs. William Howland), 9, 357.

Letchworth, John, Jr., 5.
Letchworth, John, Sr., 4–5.
Letchworth, Josiah, Jr., 9, 32, 33, 365, 418, 420, 422.
Letchworth, Josiah, Sr., 5–8, 12–17, 22, 27, 28, 32.
Letchworth, Mary Ann (Mrs. Crozer), 9, 23–24, 253, 318–19.
Letchworth, Ogden P., 380.
Letchworth, Robert, 3–4.
Letchworth, Thomas, 3–4.
Letchworth, William, 5.
Letchworth, William Pryor: Characteristics of his life, 1; English Quaker ancestry, 2–5; parentage, 5–8; brothers and sisters, 9; boyhood, 10–15; leaving home, 15–18; clerkship at Auburn, 18–21; at New York, 21–25; in business at Buffalo, 25–27; the Pratt & Letchworth establishment, 26–30; life in Buffalo, 28–31; vacation in the South, 31–32; a year in Europe, 32; establishment of malleable iron manufacture, 33; widening social relations, 33–38; first seeing of Glen Iris, 34; writing for *The Home Monthly*, 34–35; entering The Nameless Club, 36–37; President of The Buffalo Fine Arts Academy, 39–41; acquisition and development of Glen Iris, 42–68; hospitality at Glen Iris, 54–55; description of burning of railway bridge, 61–62; planting memorial trees, 66–68; interest in schools, and the young, 68–70; preserving

memorials of Genesee Valley history, 72–104; honors to memory of Mary Jemison, 89–100; adopted into the Seneca Nation and named, 89; president of the Buffalo Historical Society, 102–03; recipient of Cornplanter Medal, 104; retirement from business, 106; appointed (1873) Commissioner on N. Y. State Board of Charities, 107; child-saving work: prevenient, 109–61; removal of children from poorhouses, 110–52; vice-president of the State Board (1874), 111, 147; special report on children in poorhouses (1874), 119–21; securing mandatory legislation, 121–23; on family homes for homeless children, 123–29; Randall's Island investigation, 136–42; successes against Tammany and Albany politicians, 140–46; Mr. L.'s strength of will, 142–47; investigation of orphan asylums, etc., 147–49; official praise of work from New York City, 152–55; missionary work in other states, 156–61; tour of investigation in Europe (1880), 161, 164–209; his book on "The Insane in Foreign Countries," 164, 167, 172, 177, 190, 197, 272, 296–302; on classification of children in institutions, 201, 222–36; child-saving work: reformative, 210–50; connection with Prison Association, 217–18; plan for dealing with juvenile delinquency, 229, 234; his effectual study of problems, 234–35; his seventeen child-saving propositions, 236–39; campaign against contract labor in reformatories, 241–45; work for improved industrial training in reformatories, 245–50; impressive incident at Rochester, 249–50; reappointment (1877) on State Board, 253; president of the Board, 253; labors for the insane, 263–304; advocacy of women on boards of managers, 279–82; on commission to locate state hospital for insane in northern N. Y., 282–85; second reappointment on State Board, 308–11; resignation of the presidency of the Board, 314; establishment of Craig Colony, 317, 319, 333–39; fourth consecutive appointment on the State Board, 317; received honorary degree of LL. D., 317–18; resignation from State Board, 321–26; work for the Epileptic, 327–50; president of national association concerning epilepsy, 346; the menace of the Portage Dam project, 352, 362–63, 370–80, 393–98; president of first State Conference of C. and C., 354; stricken with partial paralysis, 357–58; early plans for the future of the glen: the Wyoming Benevolent Institute, 364–70, 380–81, 389; gift

INDEX

of Letchworth Park to the State, 380-404; continued improvements by Mr. L., 407; Letchworth Village named in his honor, 410-16; his last year, death and burial, 417-24; characteristics of the man, 425-45.
  Chronological list of Mr. L.'s writings and publications, 447-60.
Letchworth parish and village, Eng., 2, 3.
Letchworth Park, 364-404.
Letchworth Village, N. Y., 410-16.
Little, Dr. Charles S., 415-16.
Livingston County Historical Society, 351.
Lowell, Mrs. Josephine Shaw, 214-16, 253, 278.
Lunacy, State Commission in, 289, 294-96.

McCloud, Miss, 357, 362.
McPherson, Mrs. Robert, 115-16, 127.
Marshall, Orsamus H., 73, 103.
Massachusetts, Conference about immigrant paupers with, 260-61.
Massachusetts juvenile reformative system, 219, 226-30.
Mettray, Netherland, 193-95, 242.
Mettray reformatory colony (French), 185, 187-89, 242.
Michigan State Industrial Home for Girls, 248.
Mohawk Nation, the, 77, 79, 85.
Moot, Adelbert, 396-97, 443.
Morgan, Lewis H., 95.

Mount Morris, 50, 334, 372-74.

Nameless Club, The, 36-37, 55.
Nash, George V., 65-66.
National Conference of Charities and Correction, 125, 156, 201, 221, 225, 227, 228, 236, 241, 261, 270, 282, 319, 341, 350, 442.
National Prison Association, 211, 216.
Netherlands Mettray, 193-95, 242.
New York City almshouses, children in, 111-12, 131, 135-42, 150, 152-55, 220, 258-59.
New York State Board of Charities, Mr. L.'s service in, 107-63, 210-326, 423.
New York State Conference of C. and C., 354-57, 361, 416, 440.
New York State Water Supply Commission, 394-98.
Norway, Mr. L.'s inspections in, 171.

O'Bail, John (Cornplanter), 78, 83.
O'Bail, Solomon, 83-85.
Ogdensburg State Hospital for Insane, location of, 282-85.
Ohio Hospital for Epileptics, 331.
Onondaga County institutions, 268-69.
Ordronaux, Dr. John, 331-32.
Orphan Asylums, 115, 121-30, 134, 147-49.
Osborn, Mrs. Kate, 67, 78.
Osler, Prof. William, 346.

INDEX

Paetz, Dr. Albrecht, 179, 300–01.
Pandy, Dr. Kálman, 300–01.
Paris, benevolent institutions of, 185.
Parker, Prof. Arthur C., 98–100.
Parker, Sergeant Michael, 351.
Parker, Nicholas H., 78, 80–82.
Pauper immigration, 259–62.
Paupers, employment for, 132–34.
Peterson, Dr. Frederick, 300, 332–33, 338, 346.
Phillips, Hon. N. Taylor, 382.
Poorhouse, Erie Co., 112–16, 265–67.
Poorhouse asylum, Onondaga Co., 258, 268–69.
Poorhouses, children in, 110–61, 204–05.
Poorhouses, plans for, 255.
Poorhouses. *See, also,* Almshouses.
Portage. — Portage Bridge, 34, 41, 46, 49, 61–63.
Portage Dam water-storage project, 372–80, 393–98.
Pratt, Pascal P., 26.
Pratt, Samuel F., 26.
Pratt & Letchworth, 26–33, 106.
Price, Overton W., 403.
Prison Association of N. Y., 130, 211–18.
Prison Commission, N. Y. State, 218.
Prospect Home, 371.
Prussian reformatories for boys, 182.
Pruyn, John V. L., 108, 144, 253.

Putnam, Harvey W., 326.
Putnam, James O., 66, 107.
Quaker ancestry, 2–5.
Rafter, George W., 375–76.
Rain baths in poorhouses, etc., 320.
Randall's Island institutions, 131, 135–42, 150, 154, 220, 258–59.
Rauhe Haus, Hamburg, 173–75, 180, 187, 193, 205, 210, 242.
Rayner, Dr., 196.
Red Jacket, 67, 78, 103.
Red Lodge Reformatory, 200–01.
Reformative child-saving work, 210–50.
Reformatories, juvenile, 147–49, 164–208, 241–45, 245–50.
Reformatory institutions abroad, Mr. L.'s studies of, 165–208.
Runkle, John D., 245.
Rutter, Dr. H. C., 346.

Sackett, Colonel Henry W., 382.
St. Hans Hospital for Insane, 172–73.
St. John, Evangelical Foundation of, 180.
Salpêtrière, La, 185.
Sanborn, F. B., 66.
Sargent, Prof. Charles S., 68.
"Saxa Hilda," 35.
Schools, Mr. L.'s interest in, 68–70.
Schuyler, Miss Louise Lee, 131.
Scotland, Mr. L.'s inspections in, 166–70.

INDEX 469

Seaver, James E., 94–95.
Selkirk, George H., 37.
Seneca Nation, the, 72–104.
Seventeen child-saving propositions, 236–39.
Seward, William H., 7–8, 54.
Shaker Settlement of Sonyea, 334–36.
Sherwood, N. Y., Mr. Letchworth's boyhood in, 6, 10–18.
Shongo, George, 93.
Shongo, James, 78.
Shower baths in poorhouses, etc., 320.
Sibbald, Dr. John, 300.
Skinner, John B., 364.
Smith, Mrs. Byron C., 9, 28–29, 31.
Smith, Dr. Samuel Wesley, 300.
Smith, Dr. Stephen, 295–96, 300, 315, 319, 324–25, 338, 358, 440.
Society for Reformation of Juvenile Delinquents, 258–59.
Sonyea, 334–36.
Spratling, Dr. William P., 337, 339, 346, 360.
State Board of Charities. See New York State Board.
State care (N. Y.) for all insane, 288–91.
State Charities Aid Association, 124, 131, 253, 288, 333.
State hospitals (N. Y.) for the insane, 282–85.
State Industrial School (N. Y.), 247–50.
Stewart, William Rhinelander, 278, 319, 411–12, 442.
Stillson, Jerome B., 37.
Stockholm, institutions in, 171–72.

Superintendents of the Poor, state conventions of, 118, 222, 315, 350.
Sweden, Mr. L.'s inspections in, 170–71.
Switzerland, Mr. L.'s inspections in, 183–84.

Thay-en-dan-ega-ga-onh, 85.
Thomas Orphan Asylum, 103–04, 308, 315.
Titus, Senator Robert C., 244–45.
Truancy, treatment of, 230–31.
Tuke, William, 197.
Turner, Dr. Wm. Aldren, 343.

University of the State of New York, 318.

Vail, Charles Delamater, 98.
Van Campen, Major Moses, 74–75, 101.
Villers Colony of Insane, 186.
"Voices of the Glen," 55–61, 409–10.

Warren, Joseph, 39, 143.
Warsaw, N. Y.: soldiers' and sailors' monument, 252, 361.
Western House of Refuge, 224–25, 246–50.
"White Woman of the Genesee." See Jemison, Mary.
Whitney, Elias J., 297.
Wichern, Immanuel, 173–75, 180, 193, 205, 210, 242.
Wilber, Dr. H. P., 114–15.
Wildermuth, Dr., 345, 349.
Willard Asylum for the Insane, 263, 264, 276, 282, 287, 303.

Wine banished from Mr. L.'s table, 431-33.
Wines, Dr. E. C., 157, 211, 216-17.
Wise, Dr. F. N., 283-85, 300.
Women on boards of managers, 279-82.
Women's Educational and Industrial Union, Buffalo, 282, 319.
Wright, Mrs. Asher, 94, 95, 100, 104.
Wyoming Benevolent Institute, 364-70, 380-81, 389.
Zurich, institutions at, 183.

PATTERSON SMITH SERIES IN
CRIMINOLOGY, LAW ENFORCEMENT, AND SOCIAL PROBLEMS

1. *Lewis: *The Development of American Prisons and Prison Customs, 1776-1845*
2. Carpenter: *Reformatory Prison Discipline*
3. Brace: *The Dangerous Classes of New York*
4. *Dix: *Remarks on Prisons and Prison Discipline in the United States*
5. Bruce et al.: *The Workings of the Indeterminate-Sentence Law and the Parole System in Illinois*
6. *Wickersham Commission: *Complete Reports, Including the Mooney-Billings Report.* 14 vols.
7. Livingston: *Complete Works on Criminal Jurisprudence.* 2 vols.
8. Cleveland Foundation: *Criminal Justice in Cleveland*
9. Illinois Association for Criminal Justice: *The Illinois Crime Survey*
10. Missouri Association for Criminal Justice: *The Missouri Crime Survey*
11. Aschaffenburg: *Crime and Its Repression*
12. Garofalo: *Criminology*
13. Gross: *Criminal Psychology*
14. Lombroso: *Crime, Its Causes and Remedies*
15. Saleilles: *The Individualization of Punishment*
16. Tarde: *Penal Philosophy*
17. McKelvey: *American Prisons*
18. Sanders: *Negro Child Welfare in North Carolina*
19. Pike: *A History of Crime in England.* 2 vols.
20. Herring: *Welfare Work in Mill Villages*
21. Barnes: *The Evolution of Penology in Pennsylvania*
22. Puckett: *Folk Beliefs of the Southern Negro*
23. Fernald et al.: *A Study of Women Delinquents in New York State*
24. Wines: *The State of Prisons and of Child-Saving Institutions*
25. *Raper: *The Tragedy of Lynching*
26. Thomas: *The Unadjusted Girl*
27. Jorns: *The Quakers as Pioneers in Social Work*
28. Owings: *Women Police*
29. Woolston: *Prostitution in the United States*
30. Flexner: *Prostitution in Europe*
31. Kelso: *The History of Public Poor Relief in Massachusetts, 1820-1920*
32. Spivak: *Georgia Nigger*
33. Earle: *Curious Punishments of Bygone Days*
34. Bonger: *Race and Crime*
35. Fishman: *Crucibles of Crime*
36. Brearley: *Homicide in the United States*
37. *Graper: *American Police Administration*
38. Hichborn: *"The System"*
39. Steiner & Brown: *The North Carolina Chain Gang*
40. Cherrington: *The Evolution of Prohibition in the United States of America*
41. Colquhoun: *A Treatise on the Commerce and Police of the River Thames*
42. Colquhoun: *A Treatise on the Police of the Metropolis*
43. Abrahamsen: *Crime and the Human Mind*
44. Schneider: *The History of Public Welfare in New York State, 1609-1866*
45. Schneider & Deutsch: *The History of Public Welfare in New York State, 1867-1940*
46. Crapsey: *The Nether Side of New York*
47. Young: *Social Treatment in Probation and Delinquency*
48. Quinn: *Gambling and Gambling Devices*
49. McCord & McCord: *Origins of Crime*
50. Worthington & Topping: *Specialized Courts Dealing with Sex Delinquency*
51. Asbury: *Sucker's Progress*
52. Kneeland: *Commercialized Prostitution in New York City*

* new material added

PATTERSON SMITH SERIES IN
CRIMINOLOGY, LAW ENFORCEMENT, AND SOCIAL PROBLEMS

53. *Fosdick: *American Police Systems*
54. *Fosdick: *European Police Systems*
55. *Shay: *Judge Lynch: His First Hundred Years*
56. Barnes: *The Repression of Crime*
57. †Cable: *The Silent South*
58. Kammerer: *The Unmarried Mother*
59. Doshay: *The Boy Sex Offender and His Later Career*
60. Spaulding: *An Experimental Study of Psychopathic Delinquent Women*
61. Brockway: *Fifty Years of Prison Service*
62. Lawes: *Man's Judgment of Death*
63. Healy & Healy: *Pathological Lying, Accusation, and Swindling*
64. Smith: *The State Police*
65. Adams: *Interracial Marriage in Hawaii*
66. *Halpern: *A Decade of Probation*
67. Tappan: *Delinquent Girls in Court*
68. Alexander & Healy: *Roots of Crime*
69. *Healy & Bronner: *Delinquents and Criminals*
70. Cutler: *Lynch-Law*
71. Gillin: *Taming the Criminal*
72. Osborne: *Within Prison Walls*
73. Ashton: *The History of Gambling in England*
74. Whitlock: *On the Enforcement of Law in Cities*
75. Goldberg: *Child Offenders*
76. *Cressey: *The Taxi-Dance Hall*
77. Riis: *The Battle with the Slum*
78. Larson: *Lying and Its Detection*
79. Comstock: *Frauds Exposed*
80. Carpenter: *Our Convicts*. 2 vols. in one
81. †Horn: *Invisible Empire: The Story of the Ku Klux Klan, 1866–1871*
82. Faris et al.: *Intelligent Philanthropy*
83. Robinson: *History and Organization of Criminal Statistics in the U. S.*
84. Reckless: *Vice in Chicago*
85. Healy: *The Individual Delinquent*
86. *Bogen: *Jewish Philanthropy*
87. *Clinard: *The Black Market: A Study of White Collar Crime*
88. Healy: *Mental Conflicts and Misconduct*
89. Citizens' Police Committee: *Chicago Police Problems*
90. *Clay: *The Prison Chaplain*
91. *Peirce: *A Half Century with Juvenile Delinquents*
92. *Richmond: *Friendly Visiting Among the Poor*
93. Brasol: *Elements of Crime*
94. Strong: *Public Welfare Administration in Canada*
95. Beard: *Juvenile Probation*
96. Steinmetz: *The Gaming Table*. 2 vols.
97. *Crawford: *Report on the Penitentiaries of the United States*
98. *Kuhlman: *A Guide to Material on Crime and Criminal Justice*
99. Culver: *Bibliography of Crime and Criminal Justice, 1927–1931*
100. Culver: *Bibliography of Crime and Criminal Justice, 1932–1937*
101. Tompkins: *Administration of Criminal Justice, 1938–1948*
102. Tompkins: *Administration of Criminal Justice, 1949–1956*
103. Cumming: *Bibliography Dealing with Crime and Cognate Subjects*
104. *Addams et al.: *Philanthropy and Social Progress*
105. *Powell: *The American Siberia*
106. *Carpenter: *Reformatory Schools*
107. *Carpenter: *Juvenile Delinquents*
108. *Montague: *Sixty Years in Waifdom*

* new material added   † new edition, revised or enlarged

PATTERSON SMITH SERIES IN CRIMINOLOGY, LAW ENFORCEMENT, AND SOCIAL PROBLEMS

109. *Mannheim: *Juvenile Delinquency in an English Middletown*
110. Semmes: *Crime and Punishment in Early Maryland*
111. *National Conference of Charities & Correction: *History of Child Saving in the United States*
112. ‡Barnes: *The Story of Punishment*
113. Phillipson: *Three Criminal Law Reformers*
114. *Drähms: *The Criminal*
115. *Terry & Pellens: *The Opium Problem*
116. *Ewing: *The Morality of Punishment*
117. ‡Mannheim: *Group Problems in Crime and Punishment*
118. *Michael & Adler: *Crime, Law and Social Science*
119. *Lee: *A History of Police in England*
120. ‡Schafer: *Compensation and Restitution to Victims of Crime*
121. †Mannheim: *Pioneers in Criminology*
122. Goebel & Naughton: *Law Enforcement in Colonial New York*
123. *Savage: *Police Records and Recollections*
124. Ives: *A History of Penal Methods*
125. *Bernard (ed.): *Americanization Studies.* 10 vols.:
    Thompson: *Schooling of the Immigrant*
    Daniels: *America via the Neighborhood*
    Thomas: *Old World Traits Transplanted*
    Speek: *A Stake in the Land*
    Davis: *Immigrant Health and the Community*
    Breckinridge: *New Homes for Old*
    Park: *The Immigrant Press and Its Control*
    Gavit: *Americans by Choice*
    Claghorn: *The Immigrant's Day in Court*
    Leiserson: *Adjusting Immigrant and Industry*
126. *Dai: *Opium Addiction in Chicago*
127. *Costello: *Our Police Protectors*
128. *Wade: *A Treatise on the Police and Crimes of the Metropolis*
129. *Robison: *Can Delinquency Be Measured?*
130. *Augustus: *John Augustus, First Probation Officer*
131. *Vollmer: *The Police and Modern Society*
132. Jessel & Horr: *Bibliographies of Works on Playing Cards and Gaming*
133. *Walling: *Recollections of a New York Chief of Police;* & Kaufmann: *Supplement on the Denver Police*
134. *Lombroso-Ferrero: *Criminal Man*
135. *Howard: *Prisons and Lazarettos.* 2 vols.:
    The State of the Prisons in England and Wales
    An Account of the Principal Lazarettos in Europe
136. *Fitzgerald: *Chronicles of Bow Street Police-Office.* 2 vols. in one
137. *Goring: *The English Convict*
138. Ribton-Turner: *A History of Vagrants and Vagrancy*
139. *Smith: *Justice and the Poor*
140. *Willard: *Tramping with Tramps*
141. *Fuld: *Police Administration*
142. *Booth: *In Darkest England and the Way Out*
143. *Darrow: *Crime, Its Cause and Treatment*
144. *Henderson (ed.): *Correction and Prevention.* 4 vols.:
    Henderson (ed.): *Prison Reform;* & Smith: *Criminal Law in the U. S.*
    Henderson (ed.): *Penal and Reformatory Institutions*
    Henderson: *Preventive Agencies and Methods*
    Hart: *Preventive Treatment of Neglected Children*
145. *Carpenter: *The Life and Work of Mary Carpenter*
146. *Proal: *Political Crime*

* new material added † new edition, revised or enlarged

PATTERSON SMITH SERIES IN CRIMINOLOGY, LAW ENFORCEMENT, AND SOCIAL PROBLEMS

147. *von Hentig: *Punishment*
148. *Darrow: *Resist Not Evil*
149. Grünhut: *Penal Reform*
150. *Guthrie: *Seed-Time and Harvest of Ragged Schools*
151. *Sprogle: *The Philadelphia Police*
152. †Blumer & Hauser: *Movies, Delinquency, and Crime*
153. *Calvert: *Capital Punishment in the Twentieth Century* & *The Death Penalty Enquiry*
154. *Pinkerton: *Thirty Years a Detective*
155. *Prison Discipline Society [Boston] Reports 1826-1854.* 6 vols.
156. *Woods (ed.): *The City Wilderness*
157. *Woods (ed.): *Americans in Process*
158. *Woods: *The Neighborhood in Nation-Building*
159. Powers & Witmer: *An Experiment in the Prevention of Delinquency*
160. *Andrews: *Bygone Punishments*
161. *Debs: *Walls and Bars*
162. *Hill: *Children of the State*
163. Stewart: *The Philanthropic Work of Josephine Shaw Lowell*
164. *Flinn: *History of the Chicago Police*
165. *Constabulary Force Commissioners: *First Report*
166. *Eldridge & Watts: *Our Rival the Rascal*
167. *Oppenheimer: *The Rationale of Punishment*
168. *Fenner: *Raising the Veil*
169. *Hill: *Suggestions for the Repression of Crime*
170. *Bleackley: *The Hangmen of England*
171. *Altgeld: *Complete Works*
172. *Watson: *The Charity Organization Movement in the United States*
173. *Woods et al.: *The Poor in Great Cities*
174. *Sampson: *Rationale of Crime*
175. *Folsom: *Our Police [Baltimore]*
176. Schmidt: *A Hangman's Diary*
177. *Osborne: *Society and Prisons*
178. *Sutton: *The New York Tombs*
179. *Morrison: *Juvenile Offenders*
180. *Parry: *The History of Torture in England*
181. Henderson: *Modern Methods of Charity*
182. Larned: *The Life and Work of William Pryor Letchworth*
183. *Coleman: *Humane Society Leaders in America*
184. *Duke: *Celebrated Criminal Cases of America*
185. *George: *The Junior Republic*
186. *Hackwood: *The Good Old Times*
187. *Fry & Cresswell: *Memoir of the Life of Elizabeth Fry.* 2 vols. in one
188. *McAdoo: *Guarding a Great City*
189. *Gray: *Prison Discipline in America*
190. *Robinson: *Should Prisoners Work?*
191. *Mayo: *Justice to All*
192. *Winter: *The New York State Reformatory in Elmira*
193. *Green: *Gambling Exposed*
194. *Woods: *Policeman and Public*
195. *Johnson: *Adventures in Social Welfare*
196. *Wines & Dwight: *Report on the Prisons and Reformatories of the United States and Canada*
197. *Salt: *The Flogging Craze*
198. *MacDonald: *Abnormal Man*
199. *Shalloo: *Private Police*
200. *Ellis: *The Criminal*

* new material added   † new edition, revised or enlarged